The Jesus of Asian Women

WOMEN FROM THE MARGINS

An Orbis Series Highlighting Women's Theological Voices

Women from the Margins introduces a series of books that present women's theological voices from around the world. As has long been recognized, women have shaped and continue to shape theology in distinctive ways that recognize both the particular challenges and the particular gifts that women bring to the world of theology and to ministry within the church. Their theological voices reflect the culture in which they live and the religious practices that permeate their lives.

Also in the Series:

Grant Me Justice! HIV/AIDS & Gender Readings of the Bible, Musa W. Dube and Musimbi Kanyoro, editors

Korean Women and God, Choi Hee An

Ecofeminist Theology from Latin America, Judith Ress

African Women, Religion, and Health: Essays in Honor of Mercy Amba Ewudziwa Oduyoye, Isabel Apawo Phiri and Sarojini Nadar, editors

The Jesus of Asian Women

Muriel Orevillo-Montenegro

Maryknoll, New York 10545

Founded in 1970, Orbis Books endeavors to publish works that enlighten the mind, nourish the spirit, and challenge the conscience. The publishing arm of the Maryknoll Fathers and Brothers, Orbis seeks to explore the global dimensions of the Christian faith and mission, to invite dialogue with diverse cultures and religious traditions, and to serve the cause of reconciliation and peace. The books published reflect the views of their authors and do not represent the official position of the Maryknoll Society. To learn more about Maryknoll and Orbis Books, please visit our website at www.maryknoll.org.

Published by Orbis Books, Maryknoll, New York 10545–0308.
Manufactured in the United States of America.
Manuscript editing and typesetting by Joan Weber Laflamme.

Library of Congress Cataloging-in-Publication Data

Orevillo-Montenegro, Muriel.
The Jesus of Asian women / Muriel Orevillo-Montenegro.
p. cm. — (Women from the margins series)
Includes bibliographical references and index.
ISBN-13: 978-1-57075-533-0 (pbk.)
ISBN-10: 1-57075-533-7
1. Christianity—Asia. 2. Jesus Christ—Person and offices. 3. Christian women—Religious life—Asia. I. Title. II. Series.
BR1065.O74 2006
232.082'095—dc22

2006017205

To
Lemuel, Nabi, and Dev,

and to
my sisters in Asia who struggle to claim their voices,

Mabuhay!

Contents

Acknowledgments

This book is a product of my life journey and my search to make sense of the faith tradition I inherited in a world full of suffering and pain. Somehow, the traditional package of male-constructed, ready-made answers—dogma—that the seminary offered left me in a quandary. My work with the poor fisherfolk and farmers and, later, my immersion in the life of the poor in the slums and depressed areas led me to more questions about God and the function of Christ in this suffering world. Providentially, the Association of Women in Theology helped me wrestle with my questions and pressed me to probe the meaning and relevance of the Christian faith by asking me to lead bible studies and reflections on many occasions.

At that time Renate Rose introduced me to feminist writings. Then I realized that theology, after all, is not about grounded faith unable to respond to the challenges of the times, especially to the struggles of women. Theology became an exciting task. I decided to plunge deeper into the theological waters. In my sojourn a host of women and a few good men came along my way. They inspired, guided, and supported me in many ways. Elizabeth Tapia and Corazon Tabing-Reyes gave clues that led me to a new world. The team of Barbara Maubach and John Backer insisted that I test the waters at Union Theological Seminary in New York and worked on my papers for admission to Union. With a small suitcase and a few dollars in my pocket, I flew to the "city that doesn't sleep" and knocked at the doors of Union. There, I felt that I had just come out of the deep, dark pit to bask in the horizon of vast scholarship that unfolded before me. For opening its doors to me and for teaching me where and how to find a good dipper with which I can draw water from the spring of life to quench my thirst, I am greatly indebted to Union.

My sojourn became challenging and meaningful because of people who affirmed my capacity to do doctoral work. My main mentor and tough critic, James H. Cone, challenged and encouraged me to pursue doctoral studies in theology. His passion to articulate a theology from the underside inspired me to find my voice. For believing in my potential and for reminding me "to love God not only with your heart, but also with your mind," I am deeply thankful and indebted to him. Chung Hyun Kyung's radical openness and boldness to transgress the boundaries of traditions encouraged me to probe deeper into Asian religiosity and ecofeminist spiritualities. With his "dogmatics of disbelief" Christopher L. Morse gave me new lenses through which to see Christian tradition. He has inspired me to celebrate humor and laughter in the midst of serious theological work. Beverly W. Harrison has affirmed my anger in the work of love for what is right and just. Emilie M. Townes's presence on my dissertation committee reminds me to continue to participate in the struggle to "break the fine rain of death," and she challenged me to push the boundaries of Christology further. Delores Williams consoled me when I expressed regret for coming late into the theological field. Larry Rasmussen has been supportive from the time he endorsed my application for admission into the doctoral program until I received the degree. Renate Rose was there for me all those years.

Although his endorsement was for me to pursue studies in the field of Christian education, I thank Bishop Erme R. Camba just the same. The liturgies at James Chapel created with Troy Messenger's guidance, along with James Forbes's sermons at Riverside Church, recharged my spirit. I am also grateful to Riverside's Space for Grace, which challenged me every Wednesday to sing, "I feel like going on," when things were getting rough.

On the practical side, I cannot imagine writing without the help of the Burke Library staff, with whom I worked as a student assistant. Claire McCurdy and Seth Kasten especially helped me find the materials in the archive section. Betty "Caroline" Bolden and Lee Eun-Ja Lee not only helped me get books from libraries outside New York, but they also introduced me to soul food and Korean cuisine. To all of them I am profoundly grateful.

For helping me find funds to buy books, for sustenance, and for supplementary scholarships needed especially during the summers, I am also indebted to Jenny Pia-Chapman, Karen Prudente, Gary Hoff, David Maxwell, John Derby, Tara Tautari, and John Backer. I thank Sr. Mary John Mananzan, Jane Ellen Montenegro, and Angeling

Esquierdo for helping me to access materials in the Philippines. Kwok Pui-lan sent me the manuscript of her book review at a time when I needed it most. I am also thankful to Pacific, Asian, and North American Women in Theology and Ministry, along with Kwok Pui-lan and Rita Nakashima Brock, for the much-needed practical tips and advice on writing and surviving as an Asian feminist theologian. I am thankful to my colleagues at Union: Sylvester A. Johnson for giving me an orientation about the exams I had to go through; to Gabriella Lettini, Sarah Anderson-Rajarigam, Adam Clark, and Hector LaPorta for reading some chapters of my dissertation; to Stamenka Antonova, Yuki Yamamoto, Moatemsu Imchen, Rachel Starr, Chang Yoon-Jae, and Lee Jae-Won for their willingness to listen to my theological ramblings, and to Johannes and Ulrike Wittich for their support and concern that I should spend Christmas with my family. I am indebted to Eileen Crowley for helping me clarify and express my thoughts in English. For moments of respite outside the academic setting and for providing venues to recharge my body and spirit, I am grateful to Josephine "Joy" Abat, Sylvester "Jun" and Jean Almiron, Vicky Furio, Becky Asedillo, and Ramon Castañeda. I must also thank the Native American shaman who, during our brief meeting, reminded me to meditate in silence in order to have a clear mind.

When I came to the stage of publishing this book, I must say I have been lucky to have Susan Perry, with her great patience and thoroughness, as my main editor. Likewise, Catherine Costello, Orbis production manager, and Joan Laflamme, edisetter, also painstakingly worked on the details of the manuscript to correct my inconsistencies. I must also thank reader-critics who read my manuscripts at the early stage and gave their comments and suggestions. To Silliman University's FADECO, I am thankful for allowing me to go on study leave. To friends in the United Church of Christ in the Philippines and in the National Council of Churches, I am grateful for their encouragement. For inquiring when my book is coming out, I say "thank you for asking" to my friends and my colleagues at Silliman University Divinity School.

Finally, I thank my late father, Benjamin H. Orevillo, Sr., who instilled in me the value of speaking out and the faith to find strength in God in the midst of adversities and to work with communities. To my mother, Concepcion, for birthing me, and for the encouragement and moral support of my brothers, Ben Jr. and Roy, and sisters, Ann, Ellen,

Ella, and Estrellita. Most of all, I am grateful to my supportive and loving husband, Lemuel P. Montenegro, and to my wonderful sons, Nabi Karl Bayani and Dev Luke Kalayaan, who prodded me to take time to finish this book project.

Prologue

"And There Was No Room in the Inn" (Luke 2:7b)

"You cannot have that room. Your children may disturb the students who are living in that house." This was the dean's response to my request. Theoretically, though I was a new member of the faculty at the Divinity School of Silliman University in the Philippines, I should have had priority in regard to the seminary's housing facility. Besides, I had only requested one room of a faculty house. Yet, the dean gave it to a single, white woman who was not even connected to the university or to the seminary. I realized there was no room for me and my small children in the inn at the foot of Mt. Talinis. I discerned, however, that the dean's "no room in the inn" attitude was only a symptom of the maladies such as racism that compound the colonial mentality, classism, and patriarchy that have deeply permeated Filipino society. This experience swung open not only the floodgates of memories of abuse, rejection, and discrimination, but also of anger and protest. I saw myself in the lives of women who struggled to survive in a macho society. As Filipino women, our stories may be different, yet in some ways, our stories are also similar.

I had lived like a single mother for five years in Negros Island when my husband decided to go back to Mindanao[1] in an attempt to reclaim his family's farm. His family had abandoned the farm when the dictatorship of Fernando Marcos declared the area a "no man's land" at the height of the martial-law years,[2] and the area continued to be so even long after the dictator was deposed. At the dawn of the third millennium, Negros continues to be an "island of tears."[3] The yawning gap between the landowners and the tenants has turned Negros into a social volcano. The wrinkled, emaciated, and stunted bodies of severely malnourished children give an ugly face to the poverty of Negros. Poverty is only one of the symptoms of the social cancer that beleaguers the country.

THE HISTORICAL ROOTS OF THE SOCIAL CANCER

The social cancer has historical roots in the Philippine experience of colonization and Christianization. Christianity first came with the sword of the Spanish colonizers and with the cross in the sixteenth century. On March 16, 1521, barely three years after Luther nailed his 95 theses to the doors of the Wittenberg castle, the Spanish *conquistadores*, led by a Portuguese mercenary, landed on the Philippine shores. Contrary to the claims of some writers,[4] the main objective of the colonizers was to pursue mercantilist interests.[5] Thus, the conquistadores named the islands after their king, Philip II, and claimed both land and people as Spanish property. The subjugation was ritualized by "branding" people with Spanish names and by baptizing them into Iberian Christianity. Religion was used to pacify and weaken the native people's resistance. The spread of Christianity was subsumed under the primary objective.

Closer to the twentieth century a different strand of Christianity came, this time with rifles and bibles. Like the Spaniards, the second wave of invaders also used religion to justify its interest in gaining economic and political power. The invaders masked their motive with discourse on their "destiny" to "liberate" the natives from paganism and ignorance.

In 1898, when the revolutionaries were about to defeat the Spaniards, the Americans came and maneuvered to gain control. The *ilustrados* (elite, upper-class Chinese and Spanish *mestizos*) viewed them as heroes, and the Americans used the *ilustrados* to quell the revolution of the peasant and working classes. Then, the Americans bought the Philippines from Spain for $20 million and staged a mock battle with the Spaniards.[6] When the *ilustrados* proceeded to set up an independent Filipino government, the Americans fired the first shot, starting the Filipino-American War. Tainted with racism, soldiers turned the islands into a "howling wilderness."[7] Eventually, the Americans ensnared even the unvanquished Moro and indigenous people as they consolidated their control over the Philippine islands. An article in a

San Francisco–based newsletter in 1902 tersely expressed the American interest in the Philippines:

> Let us be frank—all our troubles in this annexation matter have been caused by the presence of the Filipinos in the Philippine Islands. Were it not for them, the Treaty of Paris would have been an excellent thing. The purchase of the archipelago for $20 million would have been cheap. . . . But unfortunately, they are infested with Filipinos. There are millions of them there, and it is to be feared that their extinction will be slow. . . . Therefore, the more of them killed the better. . . . We don't want the Filipinos, we want the Philippines.[8]

Eusebius's interpretation of the cross in Emperor Constantine's dream as a mandate to conquer in the name of Christ the Victor justified colonization.[9] Christians in North America hailed themselves "liberators" of the Filipinos[10] and believed the invasion was God's work to spread the gospel in "the Orient."[11] Some thought the occupation was preparatory to the conquest for Christ.[12] Others held the Americans' first shot was a "revelation and a prophecy," and the takeover was "baptized by the divine Spirit."[13]

Colonization used education effectively to control the minds of the natives. Scholars sent from the United States, called Thomasites,[14] served as multipliers of colonial mentality and sensibility among the people, especially the middle class. They wrote books that hid, even erased, the atrocities done by the colonizers[15] from the nation's memory. Protest voices among the natives—and even among their own kind, such as that of Mark Twain—were stifled.[16] Toward the end of the twentieth century some missionaries criticized their content and method. Others continued to propagate the "save the soul" theology that renders the people incapable of seeing social realities clearly.

Today, many ordinary Filipinos have no room in the inn. In recent years foreign individuals and companies have acquired vast areas of land for agribusiness, real estates, and resorts. In the village where I live, Europeans, Americans, Chinese, and Japanese nationals are acquiring land and building beautiful homes while pushing the natives to the congested squatter areas. More and more Filipinos are becoming squatters in their own land. This system generates a vicious cycle of poverty—material and spiritual—a form of violence that strips Filipinos of dignity. Moreover, the neoliberal globalization that government officials promote fails to improve the lot of ordinary Filipinos.

Spiritual poverty is glaring, especially in the Philippine government system. Deception, wanton graft, and corruption even in the highest ranks of leadership have dragged the country into the quagmire of poverty. External debts have become huge.[17] Ten percent of the 85 million Filipinos—professionals, skilled, and semi-skilled workers—have left to seek jobs abroad and are scattered among 181 countries[18] as overseas contract workers (OCWs). Thousands of medical doctors and other professionals are now studying to become nurses abroad, mostly in the United States.[19] Eighty percent of the OCWs are women who work mostly as nannies, domestic helpers, maids, mail-order brides, and entertainers.[20] Many of them do other low-paying jobs that drag them into prostitution.[21] Many find themselves in life-threatening conditions; some are raped, murdered, and come home in their coffins.[22] Others come home with HIV or AIDS. As more foreign nationals came as tourists, the incidence of HIV or AIDS in the country has rapidly increased. Meanwhile, human rights violations and summary executions of dissenting persons continue to happen. These are but a few symptoms indicating the extent of the social cancer that spreads and drags the country to the brink of death. All of these have brought indescribable pain and hardship to the Filipino people, and their condition begs for radical treatment.

SURVIVING IN THE MIDST OF POVERTY AND DISCRIMINATION

Poverty has always been my shadow. Life has always been a struggle for survival—food, shelter, education, the opportunity simply to live. Being the eldest of eight children, I had to stop schooling for some time to take care of my younger siblings. I always had questions, but in my teenage years I began to search for real answers to my questions. I began to question the relevance of the faith I had inherited in the midst of hunger and poverty. The memory is still vivid. It was lunchtime, some months after my father had died. We sat around the table—my younger siblings, my mother, and me. All we had were two pieces of boiled *koló* or breadfruit and some *unâ* (salted fish sauce) for dipping. Somebody said the prayer for the meal. The last sentence struck me: "For all these we pray in the name of our Lord and Savior,

Jesus Christ. Amen." My chest was bursting. I stared at the mud floor; my eyes burned with tears. Savior? Jesus Christ? What does it mean? Why are we poor? Why can't Jesus Christ save us from poverty and hunger? Why are some people so rich?

With their meager wages as government employees my parents could hardly make ends meet. Poverty brought malnutrition, poor health care, and infections that resulted in some hearing problems for my siblings and me. The experience of humiliation and being scorned for my physical disability left a scar inside me. I moved to Negros, worked through college, and tried to learn to navigate around regional cultures. I have seen the evil of inherited racism and of regionalism, and I have experienced social-class discrimination.

I realized, however, that my own experiences of poverty paled in comparison to the experiences of thousands of children who labor in the sugarcane plantations of Negros and in the slum areas of the cities. Other women carried heavier loads compared to mine. It dawned on me that all the causes of suffering are interlocking: poverty, ethnocentrism, racism, classism, sexism, and patriarchy. These can destroy human beings—both the oppressed and the oppressors. These are not only social problems, but also theological problems.

The redeeming grace in my life came in the form of an image of a woman who began to appear in my dreams after an abusive experience in my early childhood. As if in a cameo, she would appear with a smile tinged with sadness. No words ever came from her mouth. She would slowly fade away with ripples that would spread out around her. She continued to appear in my dreams until the time I prepared to go to New York for my postgraduate studies. I did not know who she was, but her image sustained me. Her image strengthened me and helped me keep my sanity. Eventually, her image led me to work among the marginalized and the poor. That work helped me to understand better the struggles of ordinary people to survive and their struggles against hopelessness. Among the enlightened poor there are no pretensions. I found my experiences in these poor communities to be healing and affirming.

In difficult moments of my life, the church seemed too far away. It did not impress me as the body of the liberating Christ. It seemed to be just another social club, one that maintains the ethos of classism and perpetuates patriarchy. The fellowship of the politically progressive Christians did not impress me as an alternative to the institutional church and did not seem to make a big difference at all. My earlier seminary studies did not help me find the answers to my life-long questions. However, I was drawn to the beauty of Mt. Talinis. I would sit and watch this mountain, which provides a backdrop for the school campus. The mountain evokes a sense of steadfastness as she towers silently, usually behind a veil of clouds. Somehow I sensed a connection between the mountain and the woman who comes to me in my dreams with her sad smile. Looking back, I decided the image was a theophany, the grace of the sacred who came to rescue me from meaninglessness. The spirit of that mountain gave me inspiration. Talinis (the Cebuano word for "pointed") to me symbolizes a woman's disfigured breast. For many years the mountain served as a life-support system for the natives. Today, Talinis is losing her flora and fauna, her forests, and the rest of the wildlife that she nurtures in her bosom. She is ravaged and desecrated; her "milk" has been squeezed almost to the last drop. Her language may be different, but I sensed that she, too, wants to tell the story of her pain.

Fighting depression was always a challenge. I struggled to rise above my troubles and reclaim myself. I had to lick my wounds and untangle the messy threads of my life by telling bits and pieces of my story, one at a time. It was, and still is, a difficult process, but storytelling is cathartic, healing, and empowering. It has become a starting point for resistance. Storytelling allows me to name and confront the evils that shackled my life; it also makes me see my own demons, wrestle with them, make peace with them, and let them go. It has not always been easy, as freedom almost always comes with a twin—fear.

For many centuries, the patriarchal system has suppressed women's voices and their stories of oppression, abuse, questioning faith, and other experiences. Rather than protecting the abused, patriarchy protects the honor of the family, even of the abuser, and instills shame and fear in women. In becoming detached from their stories, women become "alienated from those deeper experiences of self and world that have been called spiritual or religious."[23] Yet, some brave women have blazed a trail of defiance against oppressive traditions. They inspire other women to tell their stories and to define their own lives as they negotiate the complex path and discursive webs of power, symbols, and meaning.[24] My story is not unique. It is just one of the myriad stories of Filipino women woven into the historical realities of the Philippines. Our stories, however, have provided the impetus for my search to make sense of the Christian faith and the meaning of Jesus as the Christ.

To sum up, the story of the Christianization of the Philippines can never be extricated from the story of colonization and from the people's resistance to subjugation. Any attempt to set Christianity free from the memory of its entanglement with colonialism runs the risk of making theology go blind in the face of the rising empire in the twenty-first century. It will fail to see the complex reality of domination that intricately weaves the fibers of patriarchy, classism, ethnocentrism, and racism into the suffocating veil that makes people suffer. This web of domination continues to find an ally in theologies that distort the image of Jesus of Nazareth and delete from memory the meaning of Christ. Therefore, in making sense of the Christian faith, a reinterpretation of Christology is crucial.

MEETING JESUS IN THE LAND OF SPIRITS, GODS, GODDESSES, AND TEARS

This book surveys Asian Christian women's thoughts and understanding of Jesus the Christ as shown in their writings. Asian women have shaped their reflections on Jesus in response to Asia's realities of poverty and religious plurality. These realities intersect with the racism, ethnocentrism, class oppression, and patriarchy that are explicitly or subtly embedded in Asian cultures and religions. This work puts forward the thesis that when Asian women struggle to free themselves from patriarchy and from the blinders of traditional male Western theologies, they see new visions of liberating Christologies. How do Asian Christian women theologians understand the meaning of Jesus as the Christ? In what ways do they appropriate the symbol of Jesus the Christ in response to Asian women's experiences at the intersection of poverty and religiosity, racism and ethnocentrism, classism and casteism, patriarchy and sexism?

Considering Asian women's contextual differences, I explore the themes central to women's Christologies and evaluate their various approaches. Chapter 1 discusses the Christologies from Asian male theologians' perspectives. These Christologies emerged as a critique of the inadequacies of Western Christology that spread in Asia. Chapter 2 discusses and interprets the Christologies of Indian women theologians. Indian women's Christologies criticize Christianity's use of Jesus' maleness as a norm. These Christologies reveal these women's view of the cross in light of Indian women's experience of complex suffering at the intersection of caste, ethnicity, religion, gender, race, and poverty. Indian women also explore the meaning of Jesus the Christ in connection with the degradation of women and the exploitation of nature. Chapter 3 explores the Christologies of South Korean Christian women who draw resources from Korean women's experiences and Korean indigenous religions in their search for a creation-centered or life-centered Christology. Chapter 4 describes the Christologies of Filipino women that emerged from their involvement with the Filipino people's continuing historical struggle for freedom. In the face of environmental problems, Filipino women have also begun to look at indigenous traditions as a source for constructing their theologies. In Chapter 5 I examine the Hong Kong feminist theologians' use of postcolonial theory in constructing their Christologies. Hong Kong women speak of the "hybridized" Jesus, Jesus-in-trial, a subject-in-process, a Christ with multiple identities.

The Epilogue provides a summary of Asian women's Jesus, the Asian Christ. It also attempts to articulate my preliminary christological reflections. Christology is interwoven with the work of God the Creator and of the Holy Spirit. From the gospels I understand that the human Jesus shows us the way of Christhood defined by his liberating acts. Jesus of Nazareth calls us to embody this christic gift and to carry on this christic task on earth. This task demands the praxis of compassion and risk taking. Asian women's Christologies do not glorify the cross. Even so, these Christologies do not negate the cross's reality because the cross is very real in the everyday life of most Asian people. Ultimately, the meaning of Jesus the Christ is experienced in communities of genuine caring and solidarity. The task of articulating Christology is a continuing journey with communities that seek to embody the Christ, even as they discern the signs of God's revelation in other traditions and communities. It is a journey toward the fullness of life for all.

Chapter 1

Looking at Jesus through Asian Eyes

Why should not Asians draw on their own hermeneutical reservoir to fashion Jesus for their own time and place?

—R. S. Sugirtharajah, *Asian Faces of Jesus*

ASIA–LAND OF THE SPIRITS, GODS, AND GODDESSES

The largest of the earth's seven continents, Asia is home to 58 percent of the world's population.[1] It is diverse in culture, language, race, and political governance. Asia has seven major linguistic groups and hundreds of dialects within each group.[2] It gave birth to some of the oldest civilizations in the world. Asia has a colorful mosaic of rich cultures, traditions, and religions; it is the birthplace and "cradle of all the spiritual religions of the world."[3]

Religion is a system of symbols that rouses strong emotions and motives in humans as they create concepts to explain the existence of things and beings. Thus, religion has powerful effects on one's behavior and relationships with the world. This is true of Asian religions. Except for the three monotheistic religions—Judaism, Christianity, and Islam—Asian religions are cosmic in that they revere gods and goddesses, nature spirits, cosmic deities that dwell in the universe, and the spirits of the ancestors. Nature is commonly regarded as a living entity that has a spirit, and disruptions of nature's cycle and rhythm affect people's lives—both their production and their reproductive capacities.[4]

Other religions are metacosmic in the sense that they assume and worship the reality of the divinity as an immeasurable presence of the mystery believed to be "salvifically encountered by humans, through liberating knowledge and redemptive love."[5] Metacosmic religions such as Buddhism that migrated to other parts of Asia found ways of merging with the indigenous cosmic religions, those that Christians pejoratively call animism.[6] Indigenous religions, and to some degree Shintoism and Shamanism, regard nature as a living entity that has a spirit. Disorder in nature's cycle and rhythm affects all dimensions of people's lives.[7] This view of the universe shapes the Asian ecological anthropology interwoven into the indigenous cosmic religions.

Most host communities received these new religions as they were. Some appropriated and transformed these religions into ones more suited to the natives' existing religious views.[8] Thus, we find metacosmic Hinduism and Buddhism in some parts of Southeast Asia in their original forms. Yet, strands of popular Buddhism are also found in South China. In some cases the gods metamorphosed. For instance, when Hinduism and Buddhism reached China, the Hindu god Avalokitesvara crossed over and became the Buddhist goddess Kuan-yin. Another Hindu god, Maitreya, transformed into the Buddhist goddess Mi-lo.[9] Confucianism was able to weave itself into religions like Taoism, which found a home in China and its ancient tributary, Korea.[10] Metacosmic in character, Christianity seemed to have trouble connecting with native and cosmic religions of Asia. Its core teachings, particularly Christology, hindered it from harmonizing with the indigenous religions, whereas other Asian metacosmic religions were able to insert into them and create an even "higher level of intellectual sophistication."[11] The concern for salvation and liberation is central to most Asian religions, but their enslaving dimensions tarnish them.[12] Christianity is not an exception. These religions' concerns for salvation and liberation, as well as their weaknesses, have affected cultures in many ways.

THE COLONIAL JESUS: A STRANGER TO ASIAN CULTURE

Jesus was born in Asia. The memory of his ministry and his teachings became the impetus that gave birth to the Christian faith that believers take on their life journeys. Christianity as a religion left Asia in its youth. It reached the continent of Europe, where it flourished, but Christians began to use it to gain power for their interests and colonial ventures.[13] It came back to Asia fifteen centuries later as a

Western religion and as a partner of the Western colonialist enterprise. It attempted many times to overthrow the religions of Asia. Yet, despite its feverish missionary campaigns to convert the "pagan" Asians, Christianity today can claim less than 4 percent of the Asian population.[14] Except in the Philippines, Christianity did not attract many followers.

Why did Christianity fail to attract followers? Some observers say Christianity, being the religion of the colonizers and empire builders, had a negative impact on Asians, even though Asians were eager to gain knowledge from Western education that they could appropriate into their contexts.[15] Moreover, Aloysius Pieris, Jesuit theologian and scholar of Buddhism from Sri Lanka, theorizes that religions that hold on to the reality of an immanent but transcendent power such as Christianity had difficulty becoming established in regions already occupied by another metacosmic religion such as Hinduism or Buddhism. While metacosmic religions found cosmic indigenous religions to be natural landing pads, the "first come, first served" basis of accommodation[16] deterred Christianity from advantageous positioning. Thus, Pieris predicts that Asia "will remain a non-Christian continent."[17]

The Western strand of Christianity that came back to Asia constructed its central figure, Jesus the Christ, in the image of the male, white Western European conqueror. This Jesus had a superiority complex and became a stumbling block to the kinship of Asian religions. This Jesus came back to Asia not as a *balikbayan*, who comes home to reclaim Asian roots.[18] Rather, this Western Jesus was a total stranger to Asia who despised the spirits, gods, and goddesses of Asia. This Jesus was the colonial Christ who judges the adherents and practitioners of Asia's cosmic indigenous religions and its great living religions as sinners and idolaters who must be saved from the darkness of evil.[19] Redemption is possible only if Asia's heathen souls adopt Western culture and abandon Asian religions and ways of life. This kind of Christology has blurred the visions of many Christians in Asia and continues to do so. Most Asians, however, closed their doors and refused to let the colonial Christ come into their homes.

Adaptation–Early Attempts to Make Christianity at Home in Asia

Adaptation, a low-level interaction between religions and cultures, is generally associated with the manipulation of culture.[20] The relation has usually been understood as external in that there was no mutual assimilation of culture and religion. It is about the adjustment that theology had to make in order to fit into a new situation and survive and multiply there. In the context of liturgical discussion in the Roman Catholic Church, *adaptation* was understood as synonymous with *accommodation*, meaning "temporary change or modification of the rite made by the minister to accommodate the special interest or needs of various groups."[21] In the spirit of Vatican II some liturgical writers refer to adaptation as "incarnation," based on the understanding that Christ incarnated and lived among people. Indeed, the term is culturally neutral. However, theologians were uneasy with it because cultural adaptation has been linked with the "colonizers' manipulation of culture in the past."[22]

Some missionaries recognized that Asians have grasped the light of God through their cultures and have "put to shame many Christians for their upright life."[23] Some were creative in their desire to communicate and spread Christianity. Among the better-known cases is that of the seventeenth-century Jesuit missionaries, namely, Matteo Ricci (1552–1610) and Roberto de Nobili (1577–1656), who went to China and South India, respectively.

The Italian Matteo Ricci originally went to India as a volunteer, but his superiors assigned him to China in 1583. There he learned and Romanized Chinese, translated the works of Chinese scholars of his day, and published books for catechumens. He became a scholar of Confucianism and of the Mandarin language. Aside from his acceptance of ancestor veneration, Ricci presented Jesus as a wise man, similar to Confucius, and "the Christian's God as the Lord of Heaven."[24] This position led to the Rites Controversy, which was settled only in 1742, but it also gained him favor among the Chinese elite, including the emperor.[25]

Born to a well-off family in Rome, Roberto de Nobili went to India in 1605. He found that Indians thought becoming Christian meant abandoning their culture and traditions. De Nobili thought one could be a Christian *and* remain Indian. To prove his position, he decided to become not just an Indian but to wear saffron robes and become a Brahmin *sannyasi*, an ascetic who is in the fourth and final stage of a Brahmin's life.[26] He learned several Indian languages, studied the Hindu scriptures, and accepted the Hindu culture, including its rigid caste system.[27] De Nobili's "policy of accommodation" drew converts from different Indian castes but also dragged him into the Malabar Rites Controversy, which was stirred by those who accused him of syncretism.[28]

In effect, Ricci and De Nobili metaphorically dressed Jesus in Asian garb and gave him an Asian tongue. They attracted converts to Christ, particularly from high-caste Hindus and elite Chinese audiences. Although their Christologies may be considered exclusivist and true to orthodox Catholicism, their method of adaptation helped these missionaries gain converts to Christianity. Nevertheless, one may say that their Christ, although accommodated to a particular setting, retained the bias of the colonial Christ who looked down on Asian religions, though secretively. Their use of some aspects of Asian cultures may be considered mere ploys to hide their Western Christ behind Asian robes in order to attract converts. A Buddhist compared this approach to a chameleon waiting to gobble its deceived prey.[29] One cannot, however, discount the invaluable contributions of Ricci and De Nobili to Christian missionary work in Asia.

The Impact of Jesus on Asians of Other Faiths

In India the figure of Jesus stirred the nationalist Hindus to think of national and religious reforms as early as the nineteenth century. In doing so, Hindu thinkers also inspired Christian theologians to reimage Jesus in light of religious diversity.[30] Stanley Samartha (1920–2001) of the Church of South India and an advocate of interreligious dialogue was correct when he wrote that Christ cannot be imprisoned in one tradition.[31]

The "unbound Christ," to use Samartha's term, has drawn different responses from people. One response was a nationalist movement called Arya Samaj (*samaj* means "community"), which sought to reform the local religious tradition to keep Christianity at bay. Arya Samaj was centered on the Vedas, sacred Hindu texts, and "sought militant revival of Hinduism in its Vedic purity in defense against Christianity."[32] Founded by Dayananda Sarasvati (1824–83) of Gujarat, Arya Samaj affirmed Sarasvati's criticism of some idolatrous elements of Hinduism. The movement encouraged people to serve human beings in society in order to live a full life.[33]

Another type of response to the "unbound Christ" was the founding of Brahmo Samaj in 1815 by Ram Mohan Roy (1772–1833). Roy was considered a prophet of Indian nationalism and a pioneer of liberal Hindu reforms.[34] In *The Precepts of Jesus* he portrayed Jesus as a compassionate human being, a *guru* whose ethical teachings could help reform Hinduism.[35] Unlike Arya Samaj, Brahmo Samaj adopted

Christian principles and values to change Hinduism. Following the steps of Roy and a member of Brahmo Samaj, conservative Hindu Keshub Chandra Sen (1838–84) behaved and thought like a Christian but was never one. He understood Jesus in light of the parallel he drew between the Brahman as Satchitananda (*sat*, "being, true"; *chit*, "intelligence, awareness"; *ananda*, "bliss, joy") and the Christian notion of the Trinity. Sen understood Jesus as the Mediator and the Logos who was, and is, involved in the process of creation and the perfection of the world. The universal Jesus the Christ is the devout yogi and loving *bhakta* (person of devotion), the norm for Hindu pantheism.[36]

Individual Hindu thinkers responded to the "unbound Christ" in their writings. Prominent were Swami Vivekananda (1862–1902), known as the symbol of religious awakening of India, and Sarvepalli Radhakrishnan (1888–1975), a philosopher and former president of India. They reaffirmed *advaita*, the Hindu philosophy and belief based on the principle of "not-twoism or non-duality."[37] *Advaita* is a kind of Hindu theism that believes in the inseparable nature of God and the created world. This notion provided Vivekananda and Radhakrishnan the lens to see Jesus as the Master Yogi,[38] one who is in eternal union with God. Jesus is one incarnation of God among others, just like Buddha and Krishna. They also considered Jesus as one manifestation of the eternal principle of Vedanta, the Hindu scriptures. At the Parliament of World Religions in Chicago in 1893, Vivekananda reinterpreted the Vedanta as a universal religion, integrating into it the Christian idea of social service. Moreover, Vivekananda interpreted Jesus in light of the Vedantic impersonal principles, such as Christ and Buddha, and not on the basis of the historicity of a person, as in Jesus and Gautama.[39] For Radhakrishnan, Jesus is the "mystic Christ who believes in the inner light" and who rejects ritual and legalistic piety.[40]

Mohandas Karamchand Gandhi, more commonly known as Mahatma Gandhi (1869–1948), was fascinated with the Beatitudes. He held that God is the *satya* (truth), and when one seeks truth, beauty and goodness follow. To Gandhi, this is what Christ and Jesus was—a "supreme artist because he saw and expressed Truth."[41] Jesus embodied his teachings through his ethic of love, which Gandhi appropriated as *ahimsa* or nonviolence. Thus, Gandhi saw Jesus as the Supreme *Satyagrahi*,[42] one who holds on to truth and practices nonviolent resistance to evil.[43]

THE OPPRESSIVE ELEMENTS OF CULTURE AND RELIGION

Culture and religion have enslaving aspects. In India the two are intertwined in the caste system, which assigns people to a particular level of a ladder that transcends social and economic class. Those who are outside the caste are regarded as non-persons, as pollutants, as outcastes. In the same way the *burakumins* in Japan are discriminated against and deprived of social services and employment. This discrimination is rooted in the Shinto and Buddhist notion that those who slaughter animals and those who dispose of human and animal corpses are polluted. As such, they are not allowed to take part in religious rites. They are considered as "filth *(eta)* and as non-people *(hinin)* and settled in ghettos *(buraku)*."[44]

In India, the dalits are treated the same way the *burakumins* are treated in Japan. While the missionaries' strategy of accommodation attracted converts to Christianity, Ricci and De Nobili ignored the oppressive elements of culture and religion. This was acutely felt among the outcastes, whom Indian society traditionally called untouchables. The outcastes called themselves dalits. The term comes from the word *dal*, which means "crushed" or "broken."[45] Statistically, the dalits compose the majority, but sociologically, they are a minority. Most of them are economically impoverished and deprived of the right to participate fully in the sociopolitical aspects of society.[46] The caste system has imposed on the dalit psyche a sense of low self-esteem within a culture of fear, despair, and hopelessness. The dalits insist that the Indian Christologies speak only to Brahmins and upper-caste intellectuals, not to them. They need a Jesus who not only speaks to them about their economic oppression, but one who addresses the core of their "dalitness." Thus, dalit theology emerged in 1981 to identify Jesus as one among them: a dalit. Arvind P. Nirmal, a Protestant, first articulated dalit theology and asserted that dalitness makes dalit theology a Christian theology.[47] Nirmal is a professor of systematic theology at Gurukul Theological College and Research Institute in Madras, and heads the department of dalit theology. He insists that dalit theology must assume a kind of exclusivism to guard itself from incursions by dominant traditions.[48] The cross was the fullest manifestation of the dalitness of Jesus. There, Jesus went through the experience of abandonment, of being God-forsaken. That experience is at the core of dalit experience and consciousness.[49] This pathos makes dalits especially sensitive in grasping the humanity and divinity of the dalit person of Jesus.[50] Nirmal contends that even if the struggle is not yet over, dalit theology is "doxological in character," because such struggle is strengthened by dalit experiences of exodus and hope for liberation.[51]

Dalit theologians affirm dalit theology as one that is truly Indian and liberationist,[52] because it expresses dalit pathos, hopes, and visions. Like other peoples' theologies, dalit theology takes history seriously.[53] In the New Testament, Jesus is very much a dalit, one who did not even have a place to lay his head (Mt 8:20). Indeed, he is the prototype of all dalits, one who declared the manifesto for dalits:

> "The Spirit of the Lord is upon me,
> because he has anointed me to bring good news to
> the poor.
> He has sent me to proclaim release to the captives,
> and recovery of sight to the blind.
> to let the oppressed go free,
> to proclaim the year of the Lord's favor." (Lk 4:18–19)

Jesus went through all the dalit experiences of rejection, mockery, contempt, suffering, torture, and death under the dominant political and religious powers.[54]

Nirmal was worried about foreign concepts filtering into dalit theological articulations. Yet, traces of Euro-American patriarchal notions certainly converge with Asian cultures' own brand of patriarchy. This is evident in some dalit theological constructions and sacralizes the sufferings of the dalits, especially the women.[55] Dalit women have complained that male dalit theologians seldom address the issues affecting the women. They think the dalit Christology of the suffering servant is not liberating to dalit women. If dalit theology's task is to humanize dalits, then it must stop being anthropocentric, patriarchal, and androcentric. It must take seriously women's bodily experience of oppression.[56] Some dalit theologians contest the highlighting of obedience as a virtue in christological formulations. In the context of dalits, the concept of disobedience to an oppressive religio-cultural tradition is liberating.[57] This idea is novel in Christology, but it is not new in the praxis of resistance movements. On the one hand, as a theological theme, the liberating element of disobedience is worth exploring in order to depart from the universalizing view that disobedience is sin. On the other hand, disobedience viewed as freedom from the "bonds of nature" must be clarified and explored critically so that it will not lead us back into the notions that endorse the exploitation of the earth and vulnerable beings.

THE LIBERATING DIMENSIONS OF RELIGION AND CULTURE

One must also recognize that religion and culture have emancipatory elements. Culture is a way of life, and religion and art are parts of it. Culture plays an important part in the formation of beliefs and in the construction of a religion's articles of faith. In some parts of Asia, culture is an important resource in doing theology. An example of this is the mask dance of Korea. The mask dance is a social, political, and religious event. It is people's art and therefore non-elitist. In Asia people's art, theater especially, is a powerful tool to arouse people's visions for struggle and protests against injustice. Historically, the oppressive governments in Korea have forbidden the performance of mask dances in the villages, because these dances inspire political resistance. The mask dance is embedded in Korean culture as one of the vehicles for expressing and releasing *han*. Taking a cue from the works of the Korean poet-activist Kim Chi-Ha, Korean *minjung* theologian Suh Nam-Dong defined *han* as the "accumulation of suppressed and condensed experiences of oppression."[58]

Korean theologian Suh David Kwang-sun, who now heads the Asian Christian Higher Education Institute based in Hong Kong, cited the Maltugi mask dance in his writings. In the Maltugi mask dance the protagonist releases his *han* at the hands of the *yangban* (ruling class) through crude language and satirical humor as an idiom of protest. As Maltugi fights to stop the cycle of oppression toward the end of the play, the audience joins the masked performers as critical, integral participants of the dance. The play ends with a dance of freedom.[59] The mask dance demonstrates that embedded in culture is its inherent revelatory and emancipating potential. Affirming the idea found in Aloysius Pieris's work, Suh David Kwang-sun urged Asian theologians to discern God's revelation and the presence of God in our cultures, as well as in the prophetic and revolutionary energy in them. In the mask dance Christ does not transform culture that is liberating;

rather, culture redefines Christ. Thus, Suh Kwang-sun insists, "Christ becomes Christ-of-culture."[60] Conscious of not falling into the narrow concepts of indigenization, he calls for a "liberational indigenization" that puts the *minjung* Jesus at its center.[61] As Suh David Kwang-sun points out, "Jesus Christ with our Maltugi mask liberates us and liberates the suffering *minjung* of Asia and in the world."[62] However, his hesitance to identify Jesus as the Christ behind the mask dance confuses his statement. His description of the mask dance's ending is baffling. He notes that the "clear voice of Maltugi," who had a cross on his forehead, shouts, "Prepare the way of the Lord, make his path straight" [Mt 3:3; see Is 40:3–5]." This is definitely the voice of John the Baptist calling out from behind the mask, not the voice of Jesus. Does Suh Kwang-sun equate the voice of John the Baptist with Jesus' voice? I resonate with his "Christ-of-culture." His understanding that Christ does not transform culture but that culture transforms Christ is thought provoking. Nevertheless, I am wary about making this understanding absolute. In the present age there are people who have actually transformed Christ into one who endorses their death-peddling and Mammon-worshiping culture. In this case there is a need for the Christ to transform such cultures into ones that are life affirming and life sustaining. I would rather say that the Christ interacts with culture as believers attempt to make sense of the Christ from their cultural location.

US-based Taiwanese theologian C. S. Song affirms the entertaining value of the mask dance, but he points out that its significance lies more in the comfort, hope, and empowerment it bestows upon people who see themselves and their struggles articulated in the dance.[63] Song is straightforward in his reflection that behind the mask dance, the people grasp Jesus as the Christ. The Lord of the dance, Jesus, dances the pain of the suffering people and the love of God that sustains the miracle of life in this world. To Song, Jesus is not just the mask of God; Jesus is the mask dance of God.[64] Jesus dances God's love expressed in pain to meet people in despair. Thus, in Jesus, God and people "reach for each other to bring about a new world."[65] This dance culminates in the cross, where Jesus and the people become one in suffering, humiliation, rejection, and death.[66] Jesus becomes the story of the people who grasp the Christ, and the Christ behind the mask dance grasps them.[67] One may only wonder what the mask dance can say about the *han* and struggle of women in the patriarchal, Confucianist society of Korea.

To sum up, the pioneers of indigenization and inculturation have done much to move away from the colonial Christ that condemned Asian religions as pagan, barbaric, and sinful. Yet, we see that the colonial Christ continues to hold many churches, pastors, and theologians captive to the metaphysical, speculative realm of Western dogma. Ironically, these Christians enjoy their captivity. Consequently, the inculturated Christ seems to remain buried "in the writings and inscriptions in the past."[68] The Gnostic, unknown Christ of the Hindu renaissance is "entombed in the archive of historical studies and remained to be unknown to the Hindu masses."[69] However, indigenization and inculturation have made an impact in some Christian communities. There are theologians who have taken up the challenge to do Christology using their own cultural resources. External changes have been visible in terms of training a native clergy, portraying an Asian Jesus in visual arts and iconography, and using indigenous elements in liturgies. Inculturation has also sown the seeds of interreligious dialogue. Christology, however, must take another step. It must face the challenge of exposing the oppressive elements of religion and the dehumanizing structures of society. Christology should not endorse the oppressive structures in culture, religion, and society by being silent and by hiding behind metaphysical concepts while the broad masses of Asian peoples, mostly adherents of Asian religions, suffer poverty, exploitation, and marginalization under the imperial powers of this world. Women and children in particular continue to suffer under patriarchy and sexism in church and society.

THE LEGACY OF COLONIALISM IN ASIA

The peoples of Asia always have had a deep sense of identity; their cultures and religious practices give witness to this consciousness. The pre-colonial Asian peoples may not have been conscious of forging a collective identity,[70] but trade has certainly connected peoples, religions, and cultures.[71] The sense of being "one Asia" may have arisen in resistance to Western colonization.

Typhoons, earthquakes, and tsunamis often visit Asia. But the arrival of the Portuguese, led by Vasco da Gama, in Calicut (now India) in 1498[72] and their conquest of Malacca in 1511[73] signaled the beginning of more devastating storms of foreign domination. In Europe, conflicts between church and state ended with the agreement that territorial extension of kingdoms also meant the expansion of Christendom.[74] Thus, geographical explorers had to secure from the Holy See in Rome the *Patronato Real* or *Padroado* that gave them exclusive rights over particular territories in Asia, so long as they established missions in the area.[75] The Protestant Dutch and the Anglican British also were catching up in the race to found colonies in Asia.

The Industrial Revolution in the latter half of the eighteenth century gave rise to new desires. The craving to control capital, production, and distribution of goods transformed European economies. Land was reduced to a capital good, and people became mere tools of production. Nature, once sacred, was stripped of its mystery and became an object of scrutiny, manipulation, and exploitation.[76] Reason and theology supplied justifications for the colonialist projects of Europe.[77] Christianity became a tool of colonization, and, to use K. M. Panikkar's phrase, the "Vasco da Gama epoch of Asian history," a storm of enslavement and defilement of people and nature, of genocide and ecocide, swept over Asia. The land of the spirits, gods, and goddesses became a land of tears.

For a time, the use of the adaptation or accommodation approach in mission was useful. The employment of native clergy and the adaptation of some aspects of local culture began.[78] Despite the positive results of this approach, the International Missionary Council[79] of the Protestant group was still wary about adaptations in the non-Western world. In 1938, in Tambaram (Madras, India),[80] the IMC's position was given voice by Hendrik Kraemer, who advocated reinstalling the Western hegemony over the church in Asia:

> The conference was the first act of united and co-ordinated reconnoitring [*sic*] of the non-Christian world . . . by . . . the Protestant missions. It seemed as if the non-Christian world was spread out before the eye as a world to be conquered. It was not only the eye of faith, but also the eye of the Westerner, who subconsciously lived in the conviction that he could dispose of the destiny of the world, because the absorption of the Eastern by the Western world appeared to come inevitably.[81]

A Dutch Reformed lay theologian, missiologist, and expert in Indonesian Islam, Kraemer (1888–1965) wrote a book commissioned by the IMC in preparation for the Tambaram meeting. This book echoes the thoughts particularly of Karl Barth[82] and insists that there is no continuity between nature and revelation, that is, Jesus the Christ. Asserting the uniqueness of Jesus Christ and of Christianity, Kraemer regarded Asian religions as merely a culture of group solidarity.[83] He chided scholars—both European and Asians—who held on to the idea that the primitive and tribal religions are preparation for the fulfillment of the gospel through the church.[84] Kraemer argued that "paganism and the prophetic revelation of biblical realism are not continuous with each other."[85] Biblical realism holds that scripture, particularly the New Testament, contains the fundamental core of Christian doctrines; therefore, it contains all the doctrines needed for salvation. Kraemer concluded that the aim of mission work is to "persuade the non-Christian world to surrender to Christ as the sole Lord of Life."[86]

Kraemer's position has drawn strong criticism from some theologians.[87] The criticism indicates that some Asians saw the irrelevance of the colonizers' Jesus to Asia's multicultural setting. What happened in Tambaram stoked the fire of their desire to make sense of Jesus the Christ in the midst of the non-Christian world. Consequently, their Christologies seek to remember Jesus and to reconnect him to the Asian life and milieu.

INDIGENIZATION/INCULTURATION: RESPONSES TO THE CHALLENGES OF RISING NATIONALISM

The colonization of the Asian mind was inherent in the scheme of Western education. Missionaries believed that "Western culture was a real preparation for the gospel of Christ."[88] In practical terms this meant training intellectuals to embody a colonial mentality and grooming them for leadership in their own countries, thus ensuring a smooth transition to neocolonialism. The scheme proved successful. Yet, paradoxically, the impact of the Western ethos awakened the people to a sense of nationalism. In the Philippines, intellectuals became involved in the peasant-led nationalist resistance to colonialism, the goals of which included the indigenization of the clergy, religious rituals, and church properties.[89] The founding of the Iglesia Filipina Independiente (Philippine Independent Church), also called the Philippine Catholic Church, indicated the success of the revolutionary effort to promote indigenization. The emergence of an icon of a woman garbed with the Philippine flag leading a small boy along a path strewn with images of colonial violence demonstrates the shift of the theological paradigm. It is a variation of the Pieta, of course, but the woman is also the Motherland leading the nation to freedom.

In India the impact of the nationalist awakening, led by the Western educated intellectuals in the Christian church, led to the exploration of the theology of nationalism.[90] The rise in the nineteenth century of nationalist movements to reform Hinduism brought about the Indian Renaissance, a blossoming of intellectual work and flourishing of literature that addressed politics, culture, society, and religion. This movement gave rise to the non-Western, inculturated images of Jesus Christ that Christian and Hindu leaders conceived to institute reforms in their nation and respective religions.

The term *inculturation*, which appeared in the 1970s, refers to a missiological approach that introduces the gospel into a new culture without losing or distorting the gospel's essential nature. In 1977 the Catholic Synod of Bishops used it to stress the reciprocity between a particular people in a specific culture and the gospel that makes both flourish.[91] Inculturation points to the transformation of the "authentic cultural values through their integration into Christianity and the rooting of Christianity in various human cultures."[92]

Among Roman Catholics the term *incarnation* was used interchangeably with *inculturation*, while Protestants preferred the term *indigenization.* Some assert that *indigenization* has even deeper meaning, as it seeks to set free the community of faith from colonized consciousness, the "most damaging legacy of colonialism" that churches continue to perpetuate.[93] In liturgy, *indigenization* was understood not only as "Indianization" or "Filipinization" or conferring on liturgy a cultural form native to the community; it also meant reading the Rig Vedas "as part of the Liturgy of the Word."[94]

The earliest experiment with inculturation and indigenization in Asia goes back to the seventh century, when Asians searched for a meaningful image of Jesus the Christ in their lives. Sri Lankan theologian Aloysius Pieris calls this early attempt at inculturation "interreligionization," a process whereby a religion that holds on to the reality of an immanent-and-transcendent God, such as Christianity, cultivated "a new Asian identity within the idiom and ethos of another metacosmic religion,"[95] such as Buddhism.

Thriving between 635 to 845 CE, the Nestorian community in China experimented with interreligionization.[96] Though labeled Nestorian, this community had nothing to do with the Nestorianism of the fifth century.[97] The community emerged with the concept of the Christ that was shaped according to the Buddhist world view. This "Buddhist Christ" emerged from the Chinese community, following the model of the transformation of the Hindu god Avalokitesvara into the Buddhist goddess Kuan-yin. In this case Jesus Christ is one who manifests the character of Kuan-yin. The Nestorian community not only came up with a Buddhist Christ, but it also developed a religious text called the Jesus-Messiah *sutra*, which is full of ideas from the Gospels. Christian historians of China found that the section on salvation in the *sutra* contains borrowings from Chinese religions, though the predominant concepts and images are from Buddhism. Jesus is the "boat of mercy," which obviously points to the goddess of compassion, Kuan-yin, who is the "boat of mercy" to Buddhists.[98]

It is unfortunate that this religious experiment did not survive. In 845 the moody Taoist emperor Wu-tsung, who hated foreign religions, issued a decree that suppressed the Nestorian community, along with the Buddhists.[99] Some scholars believed that the Nestorians in China were simply heretics, that "there was nothing Christian" in these Nestorian communities, as shown by their writings, which are littered with concepts from Chinese religions. This is the reason, they believed, that these communities failed to survive.[100] One should not forget, however, the strong impact of political factors on its disappearance. It would have been fascinating to see how the Nestorian christological model that incorporated the transcultural and transgendered images of Avalokitesvara/Kuan-yin would have impacted later Christologies. Had it survived, this Nestorian Christology could have served as an antidote to the patriarchal model that became dominant for so long in the Christian world.

INDIAN EXPERIENCES OF INDIGENIZATION/ INCULTURATION

Among the Indian Christian pioneers of indigenization was Bhawani Charan Banerji, a Brahmo Samaj member. He took the name Brahmobandhav (Theophilus) Upadhyaya (1861–1907) when he became a Christian because he was drawn to Jesus' faultless life. He was baptized an Anglican but became a Catholic within the same year. Upadhyaya lived a life of a *sannyasi* and called himself a Hindu Catholic. He held that God the Brahman's name in Sanskrit, Satchitananda, corresponds to the Christian concept of the Trinity. Thus, he constructed a Christology from a trinitarian perspective, using a Thomistic framework. God the Father is the Absolute Sat; the Son, the Logos, and the second Person in the Trinity is Chit, the intelligence, thought, and awareness; and the third Person, the Holy Spirit, is Ananda, the bringer of joy. He argued that the teachings of *advaita* Vedanta were very much part of natural theology and as good as the philosophy of Plato and Aristotle.[101] They teach that among everything that exists, God's existence is the only essential; all the rest have conditional existence.

Upadhyaya's way of translating the Christian faith to the Indian people earned him Rome's rejection, in spite of his view that Christianity is the fulfillment of religions and the purifier of Hinduism.[102] The earlier Upadhyaya seemed to have simply translated the traditional Christian doctrine into Hindu philosophical categories and maintained that Christ is the unique incarnation of God. Yet, he later integrated into his Christian practice the "worship of some Hindu gods and goddesses as 'attributes of God.'"[103] Upadhyaya's use of the Thomistic paradigm made his version of inculturation problematic. He did not explore the liberating dimension of the Hindu culture in relation to the realities of Indian life. For Upadhyaya, revelation is beyond the natural. Consequently, salvation and revelation remain, for him, at the metaphysical level. Whether Upadhyaya forced Indian thought into the Thomist mold, as some Indian theologians thought,[104] or whether he forced traditional Christian doctrine into the Hindu philosophy, the result is the same: he failed to see revelation as the encounter of Christ with the totality of human life.[105] His metaphysical Christ made him unable to see the evils of the caste system that he integrated into the Indian Christian life.[106] His rejection of the historical Jesus, of Jesus the Avatar (God who came down to earth as human) and his upper-caste background as a Bengali Brahmin caused his failure to address the social realities of India.

Jesus the Most Ego-less Person

Another prominent voice in the era of nationalism in Asia was that of Vengal Chakkarai (1880–1958), who came from a wealthy Hindu family and was a member of the Chetty caste in Madras. He converted to Christianity and was associated with the Danish Lutheran mission but left later to join Gandhi's movement for independence. A lawyer by profession, he became involved with labor unions, and later he became a mayor in Madras. As a lay theologian, he took Upadhayaya's christological approach of drawing a correspondence between the Sanskrit name of Brahma, Satchitananda, and the Christian doctrine of the Trinity. Chakkarai was coming close to Keshub Chandra Sen's interpretation of Satchitananda (*sat* as being, truth: *chit* as awareness and intelligence; and *ananda* as bliss or joy). However, he reinterpreted Satchitananda as the unity of the universal spirit of beauty *(sat)*, love *(chit)*, and truth *(ananda)*. Jesus embodies the immortal unity of Satchitananda. Unlike Upadhyaya, Chakkarai held that Jesus is the Avatar. Keshub Chandra Sen, a Hindu devotee of Jesus Christ and leader of Brahmo Samaj, influenced Chakkarai's understanding of Jesus. Jesus the Avatar is the "most ego-less person," and this essence makes Jesus the "most universal of all."[107] Jesus' ministry was a manifestation of his "ego-lessness." The ego is the seat of pride and self-consciousness of the "I." It is the location of the original sin of human beings. Chakkarai connects Christology with the ethical demands of the Christian life. Involved with rethinking Christianity and envisioning a reformed Indian society, he urged people to seek union with Christ and to lose their ego and rationality in the "ocean of His life."[108] Like Albert Schweitzer, Chakkarai laments that modern theology's over-reliance on reason has reduced the historical Jesus to a "mere dialectician, a reformer, and an asserter of messianic claims."[109] Schweitzer observed that the Jesus of the historical quest was simply a figure made in the image of the theologians who relegated the Christ of faith to the margins.[110]

Chakkarai equated the ego with egotism, arrogance, narcissism, and bigotry, characteristics of a sick ego. A healthy ego, as a "principle of unity," is important because it secures autonomy for the self and propels the will to be "responsible for making choices and becoming ethically involved."[111] Jesus of Nazareth lived with a robust ego that made him envision a just society. Such a healthy ego enabled him to wage peace and resist evil in a radical way—even to love his enemy (Mt 5:36–44). Chakkarai's "ego-less Jesus" may pose some danger to women. It could be used to reinforce the passivity and subservience that patriarchy has already instilled in women. It may promote internalization of oppression that makes women lose their sense of self-worth and personhood. The concept of an "ego-less Jesus" glosses over the suffering of women, children, and the vulnerable and may encourage them to sacrifice their bodies at the altar of male-constructed structures in the name of Christ. It may trap people in the abyss of resignation and fear.

Though a pioneer of the trade-union movement in Madras, Chakkarai's Christology does not reflect his engagement with labor issues and classism. Chakkarai may have had the best of intentions, but his upper-caste background, though non-Brahmin, did not allow him to see casteism. Like Upadhyaya, he was not able to connect the universal spirit of Satchitananda with the ugly social realities that encompass caste, class, ethnocentrism, gender, culture, and ecology. Jesus the Avatar, as an embodiment of Satchitananda, remains laudable only in the realm of theoretical discourse.

Jesus Christ as *Bhakti Marga*

Born into a Christian family, Aiyarudai Jesudasan Appasamy (1891–1975) was a former bishop of the Church of South India and an advocate of indigenous Indian Christian theology.[112] He used Ramanuja's *visisthadvaita*, the notion of devotional tradition, to approach Christology. Appasamy contends that Christ fulfills the goal of all religious quests to be in communion with God. The union, however, is not metaphysical as the Chalcedonian formula puts it. Jesus was able to do his earthly tasks because he was of the same reality with God. To support this argument, Appasamy connected Jesus' prayerful life and his "I and my Father are one" discourse to the Hindu concept of *bhakti marga*, a path of devotion espoused by Ramanuja. *Advaita* teaches that the goal of religion is for the believer to be absorbed into the divine, or attain a mystical union of non-duality. On the contrary, Appasamy thought that the union is both moral and functional but, more than that, a believer as *bhakti* follows the path of devotion to God in loving and personal union with Christ. Unlike Upadhyaya, Appasamy's inculturation was selective; he rejected aspects of Indian religion and culture that he considered evil, such as the concept of transmigration, the fatalistic interpretation of karma, idolatry, and the caste system.[113]

Jesus Giver of Creative Energy

A lawyer and Protestant lay theologian, Pandipeddi Chenchiah (1886–1959) belonged to a Telugu clan in Madras that converted to Christianity. He aimed to articulate an Indian theology that takes Christ as the point from which Christians can "swing" into the new world of understanding and practice.[114] To Chenchiah, no religion has a monopoly on, or contains the full revelation of God. However, he considered Christ as unique in terms of being the "new creative factor" that emerged in cosmic history.[115] Christ is "the central point of all religions" in the sense that Jesus the Christ, the reality of the new being and giver of creative energy, is the key to the transformation of humanity, nature, and the whole universe.[116] This is where the universality of Christ lies. Chenchiah's thought is close to Vengal Chakkarai's understanding of Jesus' humanity. However, Chakkarai's Jesus is the Avatar, the human manifestation of God, while Chenchiah's Jesus is the historic figure, the raw "cosmic fact" that reveals the full meaning of Christ in a cosmic context.[117]

Chenchiah implied that religions are the "pre-Christian revelation" that serve as the platform on which one could perch to "catch the dawn of the new day."[118] This approach makes Chenchiah's Christology sound inclusivist, a posture that displays different levels of openness to religions but ultimately claims that the salvific principle, such as Christ, is located only in Christianity. Inclusivism holds that religions may have some sparks of God's revelation only because the Christ of Christianity operates secretly in them. However, one needs also to understand that Chenchiah considered Hinduism his "spiritual mother." Thus, he blended his theology with the Hindu concept of the integral yoga that aims to attain the transformed human being as its goal. *Yoga* means "union." It is a discipline and a way of attaining unity with God. The term also refers to a school of philosophy and to techniques of spiritual discipline and prayer.[119] Hinduism had nurtured Chenchiah to discern spiritual greatness and had led him to grasp the meaning of Christ. Consequently, he did not discount the possibility of syncretism. In fact, he even challenged the Indian church to take a brave "plunge into the depths" of intimate relationship with Hinduism and Islam and to emerge with an "enlarged and renovated Life."[120] Those who knew him note that Chenchiah was able to synthesize Western naturalist philosophy and Indian spirituality—two streams enriched by Christian cosmology, that is, Jesus' teachings of the kingdom of God.[121]

Chenchiah's notion of Christ as "creative energy" could be a refreshing starting point for dialogue with Asian religions. However, this view shows some strains of anthropocentrism. For him, one may attain a new life when "in man as in Jesus, a new creative factor has entered" and, therefore, "man" becomes the "centre and the creator of a new order."[122] Although this view may have some positive value, in the male-dominated societies in Asia the anthropocentric view has done much violence to women and the earth. Anthropocentrism has provided a theological justification for male domination over women, the earth, and everything therein. It is surprising that while Chenchiah encouraged different revelations to "flow into each other," he did not make a connection between Christ as the "creative energy" and Shakti, the "creative energy" and the feminine principle in the goddess tradition of Hinduism, his "spiritual mother." While one should not underestimate the contribution of Chenchiah to the effort of forging relationships with other religions in India, Chenchiah's Christology was silent about the reality of the caste system in India.

REINSCRIBING ADAPTATION AS AN APPROACH TO RELIGIO-CULTURAL PLURALITY

Paul David Devanandan (1901–62), born in Madras and an ordained presbyter of the Church of South India, basked in the light of the great minds that pioneered dialogue among the religions of Asia. However, a closer look at the writings of the Yale-educated Devanandan shows that, at the core, his Christology hardly moved beyond adaptation, if adaptation is understood as a low-level interaction between religions and cultures. He strongly objected to Chenchiah's position regarding the possibility of syncretism, and he also had reservations about the Indian church's forging a close relationship with Hinduism and Islam. He recognized that the Holy Spirit works in religions, but he insisted that there is nothing in Hindu doctrine that is compatible with Christian thought. His interest in using the philosophical and religious discourse of the non-Christian faith was functional, he admitted. These frameworks are mere "instruments" through which the gospel could be translated and interpreted into Indian idioms. Dialogue is useful to edify Christian life only in terms of practical matters such as the adaptation of some Hindu religious practices to enrich approaches in religious education.[123]

Rather than placing stress on Jesus of Nazareth, Devanandan was drawn closer to the metaphysical notion of the Christ. He disagreed with Chakkarai's view that human beings can mold themselves into "Christ-likeness." This is not possible, he argued, because people cannot duplicate Jesus' "perfect manhood," which was a "minor incident in the eternal fact of Christ."[124] To Chenchiah's view that Jesus is the "new man" and "raw cosmic fact," Devanandan countered that the Hindu avatar simply teaches ethics, while Jesus Christ in fact "stands for the Divine power" and for the "central doctrine" of the Christian creed.[125] Christianity is not a mere ethical culture or a moral endeavor. The ethics of Jesus were ideal, not practical. The resurrected Jesus offers spiritual salvation, in the sense that "the symbol of triumphant Christendom is not the cross; it is the Open Tomb."[126]

Devanandan appropriated and Christianized Hindu terms. He used the term *avatara* for the "fact of Christ," that Christ the Avatar's absolute purpose is redemption. Christ's historical fact must be substantiated by the eternal fact.[127] What is crucial is believers' abiding faith in the Avatar's redemptive fact, not their being a *bhakti* or devotee of Christ. Jesus as the Avatar opens the channel of grace for the forgiveness, healing, and perfection of those who discern the mystery of God.[128] Although he spoke very briefly of Christ as Shakti, the Eternal Life, and as the content of the Christian *dharma* that animates one to do good works,[129] the bottom line for Devanandan was this: in Jesus of Nazareth, the Word of God has been manifest unequivocally and finally. Devanandan does not give in to Chenchiah's plea for Christianity to find a common ground with Hinduism, to consider religious experience, and to rethink its claim on the "finality" in salvation. Instead, Devanandan adamantly argues that it has "been decided once and for all," that "in Christ God Himself has spoken," and that "in the Gospel there can be no element of falsehood."[130] Jesus Christ is the event. God entered into history in Jesus Christ, became human, "unique, final and completely adequate."[131]

Devanandan would repeatedly argue that syncretism is impossible because fundamentally, the "Gospel and Hindu *dharma* are more than oil and water";[132] they never mix. Furthermore, he dismissed Chenchiah's notion of Jesus as the universal teacher and of Christ as the creative agency of a new cosmic order. To Devanandan, this notion "will not get the Christians anywhere."[133] Some Indian theologians follow Devanandan and argue that, unlike the Christian faith that values the right relationship of God with human beings, Hinduism "lacks emphasis on the sinful nature of human person and the purposive will of a personal God."[134]

THE TRAGEDY OF POVERTY: A CONTINUING LEGACY OF NEOCOLONIALISM

Poverty continues to be a stark reality in Asia. It is a continuing legacy of neocolonialism. The Asian countries succeeded in gaining independence from their colonizers, but before long they fell into a new form of domination. Strong nations, such as the United States and the dominant European countries, exercised political, economic, and social hegemony over them. Once the sole colony of the United States in Asia, the Philippines served as a launching pad for US political and economic maneuvers in Asia. Thus, the United States established control over not only the Philippines[135] but South Korea, Taiwan, and even to some extent Japan.[136]

After its defeat in Vietnam the United States launched a more aggressive policy of political and economic control[137] through the Bretton-Woods[138] international financial system, the rules of which became instruments of "colonization without an occupation force."[139] Through infusion of funds in the form of loans and aid, the Bretton-Woods financial system sought to promote "economic growth" in Asia[140] without paying attention to the issues of justice, equal distribution of wealth, and ecological balance. Through the IMF and the World Bank powerful countries are able to manipulate the finances, economic reconstructions, and trade systems of the "beneficiary" countries.[141] This neocolonial scheme traps developing countries in enormous debt and uneven economic growth, while the powerful nations subjugate their priorities and interests.

South Korea, Taiwan, Singapore, and Hong Kong emerged as dragons and tigers, newly industrializing countries (NICs) aiming to catch up with Japan even at the expense of their people and of nature.[142] As these tiger economies became a threat to their interests, the powerful nations sought to drive the tigers to extinction.[143] The tigers collapsed by the end of the 1990s, ending the Asian "miracle." The tigers recovered after some time, but the collapse exposed the cause of the Asian crisis.

Asian countries like the Philippines literally mortgaged their future when they took the bait of the international financial institutions. Poverty is harder on women and children. Sex tours and sex trafficking also contributed to the rise of HIV and AIDS, as "more than half of all infections have been contracted during paid sex."[144] There is also an increase in child labor and migration of workers. Such a system leaves an increasing number of people with feelings of powerlessness, vulnerability, despair, and meaninglessness.

CONTEXTUALIZATION: TOWARD A RELEVANT CHRISTOLOGY

Asian theologians realized the critical role of people's experience of oppression and poverty in doing Christology. Inculturation did not pay attention to the social context of believers. The term *contextualization*, introduced by the World Council of Churches, takes seriously the contexts of contemporary struggles for economic progress, social justice, and political freedom. It challenges the church to be relevant.[145]

The early development of contextualization theologies goes back to movements in reaction to the authoritarianism of the Roman Catholic Church. Churches supportive of the anti-capitalist and anti-neocolonialist struggles of oppressed peoples, such as those in Russia, China, and Vietnam, reflected their engagement with the people in socialist settings. They also needed, however, to give voice to prophetic theologies that criticized the weaknesses of their own societies.[146] Outside Asia, contextualization theologies found expression in a variety of liberation theologies in the Third World. The first was James H. Cone's *Black Theology of Liberation* (1970), followed closely by Peruvian Gustavo Gutiérrez's *Teología de la liberacíon: Perspectivas* (1971).[147] These works have had strong influence on some Asian theologians, although the Asian contexts caused the Asian theologies to emerge. Asian contextualized theologies usually locate Jesus the Christ in the faces of the poor, deprived, and oppressed—the dalits, the *minjung*, and other Asians—struggling for justice, freedom, and full humanity. Owing to Asia's contextual diversity, one finds different faces of Jesus in Asia.

Jesus the Secular Christ

A militant image of Jesus is prevalent in Asian contexts where people struggle for freedom from neocolonization and autocratic governments. One sees this image in the work of M. M. Thomas (1916–96), an Indian theologian who became a world figure in the ecumenical movement. His life and ministry reflected his rootedness in the tradition of Mar Thoma Syrian Church. Thomas held that Jesus is the secular Christ. Trained in sociology and economics, Thomas found it important to reflect on the significance of Jesus the Christ not only in the realm of religions but also in the secular, political world.[148] Thus, Thomas consistently connected Christology with his understanding of humanity and salvation in the historical realm. He derived his theological anthropology from secular humanism, a system that affirms human creativity and humanization of nature, the basic need of freedom from the bondage of social evils, and the realization of love in human relationships. To believe that God in Christ works for human salvation is to see Jesus as the ultimate pattern for human existence and the epitome of mutual self-giving love.[149]

In some ways, M. M. Thomas reflects the Christian, especially Protestant, aversion to the powers of nature, cosmos, spirits, gods, and goddesses. He thinks these divinized powers have enslaved humanity, and that Christ came to liberate humanity from this enslavement. Certainly, he valued the Enlightenment-inspired secularization of nature. Yet, he also saw that in the process of secularizing nature, human beings had divinized science and technology and thus become slaves of their own tools. Now, Christ must liberate human beings from the divinized power of science and technology that has turned human beings and the organic bases of human life into sacrifices—fodder to be fed into the machines of imperialism and war.[150] For M. M. Thomas, the metaphysical Christ of the traditional theologies—Indian and Western alike—is powerless in the face of this condition.

The notions of the unknown Christ and the anonymous Christian may seem to validate the universal Christ. However, to Thomas, the historical cross of Jesus is still the decisive criterion for discerning the stirrings of positive responses of faiths to the universal cross, upon which hangs the world's suffering.[151] The crucifixion of Jesus exposed the adversaries of God and the misdirection of humanity. Jesus Christ crucified is the "prototype of true manhood" in the historical realm and becomes a source of humanization for *homo sapiens*.[152] The cross provides the answer to the problem of justification of human existence. When humanity responds to the cross, the crucified Christ offers divine forgiveness that releases us from our obsession for selfish security. Jesus Christ moves others toward the mutual self-giving love of God that ultimately measures individual and collective maturity. Thomas also recognized that Christ is at work even in secular and non-Christian movements, in their creative struggle for freedom and for an independent home for the Asian spirit. The church, therefore, must discern Christ in the aspirations and events of the times.[153]

M. M. Thomas obviously stirred up neo-orthodox nervousness when he asserted that the revolutionary ferments in Asia have within them "the promise of Christ for a fuller and richer life for man and society."[154] He recognized the role of human structures and ideologies in creating conditions of political freedom and social justice. He suggested that these conditions could pave the way for human beings to respond to Christ in faith and love. Yet, he was also cautious of the way some ideologies and politics of justice turned themselves into new monsters of oppression, of "liberators-turning-oppressors" who become "self-idolatrous, . . . devouring their children."[155] He made it clear that the secular messiahs have their place, but they cannot replace the crucified Messiah. The gospel is about what God has done in the incarnation, life, and death of Jesus of Nazareth in one particular historical moment. This Christ-event gives all history a spiritual relevance and affirms God's act "through, in, and for Jesus Christ."[156] According to Thomas, we can only speak of the new humanity in terms of being in Christ, and it must transcend and transform Christianity, religions, and ideologies from within. Then we can envision a unity in Christ that accommodates diversity in fellowship.[157] Some Indian theologians note that M. M. Thomas's theological anthropology laid the foundation for a more active theological engagement in India.[158]

Jesus the Crucified People

The suffering brought about by historical evils has destroyed the beauty and humanity of Mother Asia's children.[159] Being conscious of Taiwan's religions and cultures, C. S. Song, a Protestant theologian, took indigenization as the central theme of his theological work. However, his awareness of the suffering of the poor not only of Taiwan but also of Asia challenged his theological vocation. This led to his personal participation in the political struggles over his homeland's future in relation to mainland China.[160] Song argues for a theology that balances the intellectual articulation with compassion. He takes Christology as a story of a Jesus who arises from the ashes of people killed in the battlefields and destroyed in the slums. The historical Jesus, not the domesticated Jesus of traditional historicism that propounds a posture of superiority over other religions, is significant in this Christology. God has been active in Asian people's cultures and histories, and Jesus the Christ deepens our understanding of God's "ways with *all* people." In Jesus, God meets humanity. Jesus' death on the cross is a judgment not only upon the sins of the world, but also upon a religion that "hides God from the people" and "misrepresents God to them."[161] We cannot locate Jesus in marble statues or in the ancient creeds and formulas. In Asia, the "who" cannot be severed from the question of the "where" when we speak of Jesus. Song demonstrates this for us. He connects the identity and location of Jesus with that of the suffering people—not just any people. Jesus is God made known in the midst of the suffering people.[162]

The phrase "crucified people" was used by El Salvadoran Jesuit Ignacio Ellacuría to refer to the suffering people of Latin America. In the same way, C. S. Song used the phrase to describe Jesus as embodied by the crucified people of Asia. He grounds this interpretation in his understanding of a phrase in Mark 14:22 (cf. Mt 26:28), the Greek *huper pollon*, "for many" or "in behalf of many." Rather than sticking to the translation that suggests Jesus as superior and not like ordinary human beings, Song preferred the translation of *huper pollon* as "to be on someone's side." Thus, Jesus is not only a representative of human beings; Jesus himself is one with the suffering people. Jesus becomes the people, not just a Passover lamb. Thus the historical Jesus, who is alive in the life stories of the oppressed people, becomes the historical Christ, who crosses geographical, time, and metaphorical barriers. The historical Jesus, who went through "christological conversion," therefore, can be any oppressed people in Asia.[163]

Although he does not go deeply into gender analysis, Song, who is now based in the United States, is one of the few male theologians in Asia who are sensitive to gender issues in their reflections. In his reflection on Edwina Sandy's sculpture of a woman crucified, *Christa*, Song notes that *Christa* reveals the basic inadequacies of traditional androcentric or male-centered theology. Christa is "the female Christ, the story of suffering women."[164] Song sees the divine compassion for the suffering actualized in human power to endure and to bear the burden for others.[165]

Song does not, however, comfort my uneasiness with the notion of Jesus' death as an act of obedience to God.[166] Patriarchy could easily twist and use this notion to perpetuate injustices done to women and to powerless people. Song's assertion that Jesus' death was not passive obedience to a wrathful God but that Jesus embodied a childlike obedience to a loving parent God also sparks some reservations because the analogy brings, to some women and even to some men, memories of child abuse by parents and trusted adults. One must note, however, that Song helps us remember that while Jesus was "obedient to the point of death" (Phil 2:8), Jesus was not submissive. Jesus painfully wrestled with the possibility of death (Mk 14:34) and prayed to God, "Remove this cup from me" (Mk 14:36). Taking the clue from Song, I am able to see Jesus as one who exercised moral agency. This made him bold in facing death. Jesus knew he could end up on the cross if he did not give up the life-giving, christic vision he shared with God, the essence of being anointed or set apart for the realization of God's kingdom on earth. Jesus extracted this understanding from the prophet Isaiah (Is 61:1–2) and articulated it, according to Luke (Lk 4:1–13). Jesus followed his own conviction and vision in light of his love for the world. This understanding challenges contemporary persons, Christian or not, to listen critically and courageously to the christic voice inside them. I recognize the tragic reality that human life is imperfect and sad because human beings are inevitably involved with corruption and evil. Thus, human constructions, including religion and theology, are always imperfect. Yet, this reality makes it urgent for Christians to consider Jesus seriously, for he gives us hope for redemption, shows us the way to humility, and models how to struggle against corruption.

Jesus the Counter-Culture Prophet

Following M. M. Thomas, Jesuit priest Sebastian Kappen of India paid attention to the revolutionary message of Jesus in the face of the social realities and human life in Asia.[167] Kappen's consciousness of the Indian context and his association with Indian activists impassioned him to construct an Indian theology of liberation that incorporates ecological issues. He takes the experiences of ordinary Indian people as his starting point. His work reveals the insights he gathered from the "radical elements" of Indian religions and "positive insights" from Marxist thought and practice.

Moving away from Indian and traditional speculative Christologies, Kappen focused his attention on the historical, secular Jesus who addresses the social problems of Indian society. He sees Jesus as the "unique, intense, unparalleled manifestation of the transcendent in the flow of history."[168] In this sense Jesus is a prophet of new humanity, one who manifests the Divine whom we encounter in beauty, love, friendship, and community. This encounter demands a "theandric practice," that is, the human being's embodied response to the Divine. As the divine appearance in history is a divine "gift-call,"[169] theandric practice is an expression of joy for the blessing received and an exercise of one's potentials to meet the challenge of the Divine's beckoning. Theandric practice is expressed in the interplay of "contemplation-action, celebration-creation, safeguarding-subverting, memory-hope, and self-transformation-world-transformation."[170] In practical terms the gift-call beckons one to practice discipleship, rather than just being a worshiper, and to follow Jesus in the journey to confront the cultures of oppression. Kappen's creation of a phrase to capture the meaning of Jesus' appearance in history to show that we have the gift to transform a decadent world into a better place is novel. Although Kappen does not explain the root of the term *theandric*, we gather that it is a combination of two Greek words, namely, *theos*, "god," and *andros (aner)*, "male person." One may note, however, that his choice of the Greek word *andros* over *anthropos*, which is more inclusive of male and female persons, makes the term *theandric* itself androcentric or male centered.

For Kappen, Jesus is the counter-culture prophet, one who creates a liberating culture and whose allies are the social and political forces that fight the oppressive castes and capitalism.[171] This secular Jesus has impact beyond the boundaries of Christianity because he lived what he taught, made history with God the center of his life, and met God in the heart of the world. Jesus' death is a consequence of his work for existential liberation.[172] Jesus transforms cultures from complacency to resistance, from the "pie in the sky" piety to ethical religiosity, from individualism to communitarian salvation, and from fear to freedom.[173] Kappen retrieves the goals of Indian religion, namely, union of the self with the divine and non-attachment, and reinterprets them in terms of people moving toward a spirituality of commitment through a process called integrated yogic concentration.[174]

Kappen addressed the issues of class, race, and caste extensively in his earlier writings, and in his later works he discussed the issues of gender and ecology briefly but profoundly. The Jesus of history, unlike the Jesus of dogma, initiated a humanizing praxis and proclaimed equality of all women and men of whatever race, color, caste, or class. Kappen holds that Jesus' teachings resonate with Asian sensibilities, that God reveals "himself not only in, but also as nature and history," and even beyond it. Jesus, therefore, urged the people to trust the motherhood of the earth to provide for our daily needs. However, a few pages earlier, Kappen seems to view history only from the scientific angle and tends to disconnect the indigenous or cosmic reality from Jesus of history.[175] Consequently, like many other contextual theologians, he tends to downplay any ethical and liberating dimension of cosmic religiosity.

Jesus and the *Minjung*

Earlier, we discussed C. S. Song's view of Jesus as the crucified people. The idea of connecting the suffering people with the crucified Jesus finds continuity in the Korean concept of *minjung*. Korean poet Kim Chi Ha's play "The Gold-Crowned Jesus" gives us a picture of people suffering poverty, discrimination, and oppression, such as jobless people, beggars, and prostitutes. The church venerates a Jesus imprisoned in a concrete statue crowned with gold. Jesus urges the beggars to set him free from the concrete prison and from the burden of the gold crown. Once freed, Jesus tells the beggars, "You have helped give me life again. You removed the gold crown from my head and so freed my lips to speak. People like you will be my liberators."[176] The police, of course, catch the beggars, put them in jail, and place the crown back on Jesus' head. The poet thus suggests that the church has reduced Jesus once again into a frozen statue, a decoration. As Jesus longed for liberation from classical notions formulated by Western churches, the poor people became the liberators of the colonial Christologies.

Taking the alienated and oppressed people referred to as *minjung*, Korean Protestant biblical scholar Ahn Byung Mu developed *minjung* theology. Ahn, born in 1922, spent part of his childhood in North Korea before it gained independence from the control of Japan. Ahn's passion for the *minjung*—not only the poor but also people who suffer from discrimination—led him to political activism and imprisonment as a political detainee. His experience of solidarity with the *minjung* in their struggle for democracy and for the removal of military dictatorship had a strong impact on his Christology.[177]

Ahn lamented over the tendency of some scholars to reinforce the Pauline disinterest in the historical Jesus and over their emphasis on making the Christ of the *kerygma* an object of worship.[178] The phrase Christ of the *kerygma*, that is, the Christ of faith who is being preached, has been distinguished from the Jesus of history. This distinction emerged from the debate over the liberal quests for the historical Jesus. To Ahn, the *kerygma* paradigm not only de-historicized the Jesus-event, but it also propped up the authority of the church.[179] He criticized the paradigm because, in his view, "the Christology in this Kerygma has greatly served as an ideology to preserve the Church, but at the cost of silencing Jesus."[180] The *kerygma* paradigm blurred the picture of the historical Jesus, spiritualized the events surrounding the murder of Jesus, and distorted the meaning of people in the Gospels.

In the Gospel according to Mark, Ahn discovered that the writer used the Greek word *ochlos* more than *laos*. This gave him a better understanding of the deeper connection between Jesus and the people. Rather than using the word *laos*, which means "the people of God,"[181] the Gospel writer used *ochlos*, which includes the crowd of sick people, tax collectors, sinners, the materially poor, and the women.[182] *Laos* also refers to those whom the Pharisees define within the frame of national and religious boundaries. We can only understand the *ochlos* in a relational way. Although potentially powerful, these followers were unorganized. Jesus had compassion for them, and he described them as being like sheep without a shepherd.[183] The *ochlos* is the *minjung*. Jesus did not operate within the framework of the drama of obedience and fulfillment of God's will according to Ahn. It was the will of the *ochlos* to be healed that drew out Jesus' potential power to heal. Jesus' posture of standing with the *minjung*, facing God from their side, defines his Christhood. Thus, for Ahn, this makes Jesus *minjung*, noting also that the Jesus in the Gospels is a "collective being," for "where there is Jesus, there is the *minjung*; and where there is the *minjung*, there is Jesus."[184]

Another Korean *minjung* theologian, Kim Yong-Bock, sees Jesus in a different way. Like most of the first-generation *minjung* theologians, Kim Yong-Bock, a Protestant, was also involved with the *minjung* struggles against the military dictatorship in Korea. He preferred to identify Jesus as the Messiah of the *minjung*. This implies that Jesus is different from but identifies with the *minjung*. Kim continues to be in solidarity with the *minjung* of this world who struggle against neoliberal globalization.[185]

Protestant theologian Suh David Kwang-sun, born in North Korea, moved to South Korea at a tender age. He shared the *minjung* experience of being harassed during the military dictatorship. As a *minjung* theologian he followed Ahn to a certain point, However, he goes beyond Ahn and asserts that the stories of the *minjung* and Jesus are identical only on the metaphorical level.[186] The *minjung* suffered, just as Jesus suffered, but they are not the same. This view is different from the dalit view that the dalit Jesus literally went through dalit experiences. Suh places more importance on the spirituality Jesus learned through his theological education in the desert. Suh asserts that Jesus' spirituality of love and grace, voluntary poverty, and liberation politics culminated in the cross. To Suh, the cross is the point where spirituality and politics converge.[187]

Although *minjung* theologians explicate their Christologies with particular nuances, they agree that the suffering of Jesus is the core of Christology, for it unveils the immorality and sin of the powerful against the *minjung*. Ahn Byung Mu and Suh Kwang-sun understood that women are among the *ochlos*. They have seen the role of patriarchy in the suffering of women as the "minjung among the minjung."[188] Currently the director of the Asian Christian Higher Education Institute of the United Board for Higher Christian Education in Asia, Suh consciously connects the issues of women in the discussion on education in the pluralistic world of Asia. Yet, the task of articulating Christology from *minjung* women's perspective remains the job of women. In totality, *minjung* theologians converge at the point where they see Jesus from the historical perspective and recognize him as a secular person, liberator, and friend of the *minjung*, who "provides the key to understanding Jesus as the living Christ of the present."[189]

Christology of Struggle

In the Philippines, theologians sensitive to context emerged with a theology of struggle that addresses the plight of the people. While liberation is the ultimate vision, the theology of struggle focuses on the lifestyle of constant struggle as the goal and main facet of Christian spirituality. The theology of struggle gives importance to the historicity of Jesus. It confronts the question of where to find Jesus and how to follow Jesus. The historicity of Jesus is significant because it is only in Jesus' humanity that we understand the Christ as liberator. The human Jesus went through a life of struggle.

Filipino Roman Catholic theologian and artist Karl Gaspar lived and worked with poor communities and had been a political detainee himself. He lifted up the reflections of a Filipino nun, Sr. Asuncion Martinez, on the image of Jesus that the theology of struggle resonates with and seeks to follow. It takes the Christ who is engaged in the struggle. The theology of struggle does not take the image of the cute Santo Niño, or the "sweet face of the Sacred Heart," or the "resigned Nazareno." It is Jesus the Christ who was poor, who struggled to cleanse the Temple, who was crucified for political charges, and who was a "failure in life but a victor in death."[190] Gaspar notes the inability of the Christology of struggle to make a connection with Filipino indigenous spiritualities and cosmic religiosities. He acknowledges that it may still be the task of the theology of struggle to bring genuine inculturation to the Philippines, considering that it is the most colonized and most Christianized country in Asia. Without this genuine recognition of the religious plurality and without a profound effort to engage with these religions at its core, the Christology of struggle will be inadequate.[191]

Considering himself a student of the Bible, Carlos H. Abesamis, a Jesuit priest, considers Third-Worldness and Asianness to be inseparable in doing theology. Though he trained in Europe with the renowned Karl Rahner, his immersion in communities of struggling people in the context of poverty and injustice challenged Abesamis to see Jesus "by and through the eyes of . . . the awakened, struggling and selfless poor, who want to create a just, humane and sustainable world."[192] He calls this the third look at Jesus. To Abesamis, Jesus stood on the same ground where the poor people stand, and Jesus is truly the bearer of the good news to the poor. Jesus continues to beckon people to alternative lifestyles of acting out the good news he proclaimed.[193] Jesus was the "first activist in the Christian history,"[194] one who accompanied struggling women, men, and children on their journey and engaged in conversation with them at different stations and locations. This challenges an advocate of a Christology of struggle to take seriously the praxis of immersion in the suffering and struggles of the people. Concurring with Abesamis, Julio X. Labayen, activist Catholic bishop of Infanta, lifts up the exploited but struggling peasants, workers, fisherfolks, tribals, and squatters as the reflection of the "new face of Jesus."[195]

A pastor of the United Church of Christ in the Philippines (UCCP), Luna Dingayan articulates a Christology of struggle that sees the resurrection event in the rising of the suffering people. To Dingayan, "the extraordinary Christ was found in the ordinary Jesus." Jesus the Christ is present in the struggle of the people, and is continually struggling to make each person a new being.[196] In agreement with Dingayan, Levi V. Oracion, also of the UCCP, reiterates the Matthean affirmation that Jesus is God with us.[197] Feliciano Cariño, who at separate times served as general secretary of the National Council of Churches in the Philippines and of the Christian Conference of Asia, notes that a person can only follow Jesus by being with the struggling people.[198]

It must be pointed out, however, that the Christology of struggle hardly addressed the struggles of women against patriarchy. Patriarchy and sexism are still deeply ingrained in the colonized Filipino consciousness, even among politically progressive theologians. Abesamis, Dingayan, and Oracion are among the few Filipino males who have attempted to say something about the problems affecting women and children. However, they have not gone deeply into the analysis of gender issues and patriarchy.

CHRISTOLOGY AND ASIAN RELIGIONS: TOWARD AN EYE-TO-EYE ENCOUNTER

Early Attempts at Cross-Textual Approaches to Religious Plurality

One approach to religious plurality is to do a comparative study of religious traditions. Raymond (Raimundo) Panikkar, a product of an interreligious, intercultural, and interracial marriage, his father being a Hindu Indian and his mother a Catholic Spaniard, did this but also went beyond. Delving into his works is like going into the thick forest of technical terms—Buddhist, Thomistic, secular, and particularly Hindu. His efforts in comparing the religious traditions may be considered an early attempt to a cross-textual approach to religious plurality. He coined the term *cosmotheandric*, which comes from three Greek words that mean "cosmos," "divine," and "human," all put together in one entity. Panikkar uses this term to construct a Christology that seeks to make a connection between Indian religions and Christian faith. Panikkar's starting point is the realm of philosophy, which he thinks is a common ground for a conversation between Hinduism and Christianity. Taking the Thomistic method[199] and following Paul's approach in Acts 17:22–31, this Roman Catholic priest draws our attention to the "unknown Christ of Hinduism." Some critics assert that Panikkar's reinterpretation of Isvara to fit him into the traditional understanding of Christ is conflated and forced.[200] *Isvara* is the Sanskrit word for "Lord" or "powerful one," who is "desired by all those who seek to escape from suffering."[201] Panikkar, however, need not make Isvara a Christian because, to him, Isvara is already the Christ embedded in the heart of Hinduism. Christ, though an unknown reality in Hinduism, is actually present in its heart as the principle of life that gives light to every soul in this world.[202]

The phrase "cosmotheandric Christ" immediately suggests that Panikkar sees in Christ the union of the cosmos, the divine, and the human. Christ, the central symbol of life and truth in the Christian faith, is the one—not the same—Mystery that draws all other human beings.[203] Panikkar sees a correspondence between the place of Isvara (Lord God), the revelation of the Brahman in the Vedanta, and the place of Christ in Christian thought. The Vedanta, for example, sees Isvara as "the first issue of the unfathomable womb of Brahman,"[204] just as the New Testament sees Christ as "the image of the invisible God, the first born of all creation" (Col 1:15). This correspondence makes it possible for Christianity and Hinduism to provide loci for Isvara and Christ respectively.[205] Panikkar's Christology is grounded in his understanding of the trinitarian unity of the cosmotheandric and the Isvaric principles that articulate a cosmic, divine, and human manifestation. Thus, in both traditions, it is not difficult to see Christ as the living symbol for the totality of reality. Christ, as the totality of reality is—not has—many names, and each name is simply a new dimension and revelation of the reality of the undivided Mystery. From this vantage point one can appreciate that Christ the Logos is not just the meeting point for Hinduism and Christianity.[206] Rather, Christ is the theandric point of convergence for all realms; the meeting place of humanity and the Absolute Mystery, the embodiment of divine Grace that leads humanity to God. Panikkar holds that when Christians meet and accept Hinduism as it is, they find Christ already there.[207] Every being who meets this Mystery has the capacity of christophany—the revelation of the Christ-principle.[208] No one has the monopoly on either Christ or Jesus of Nazareth, and because "whatever God does *ad extra* happens through Christ,"[209] there is no reason why people cannot attain unity in Christ.

Panikkar suggests pluralism as a way of relating with Asian religions. In pluralism one accepts differences and celebrates commonalities; one does not aim for uniformity or dualism. In pluralism one accepts the reality that there is no way that humanity will ever know everything but holds onto that cosmic trust that gives space for creative tension and peaceful coexistence among human beings, religions, and cosmologies. Moreover, pluralism welcomes the Logos and appreciates myths, which "makes thinking and belief possible."[210] In spite of this view, Panikkar still seems captive to Karl Rahner's concept of the anonymous Christian in relation to Hinduism. He does not see any need to rethink the classical Christology that hinges on the concepts of obedience and disobedience. While Panikkar speaks of the importance of experience and of the call to be a new way of being in this world, his disinterest in the historical Jesus gives rise to weaknesses. Like the Indian inculturationists, Panikkar has not paid attention to the social realities of Asia, its impact on the life of people, and the crucial intersecting issues of gender, class, ethnicity, and race.

The Relevance of the Cosmic Christ in Asia

In Asia, an eye-to-eye encounter means the meeting of two entities who acknowledge each other to be on the same level. It is a meeting of equals. This is a vision of some theologians. One who recognizes and appreciates the beauty of religious plurality does not seek to absorb the other into one's religion, Rather, such recognition and appreciation bring openness to understanding the other better, to being enriched, and for one's own faith to be strengthened. Many Christians who believe they have the monopoly on God's love and revelation find this eye-to-eye encounter difficult. However, some appreciate the necessity of interreligious conversations, especially when issues and problems that affect the well being of the Asian people—regardless of race, religion, and culture—are at stake. Thus, some Asian theologians have moved beyond the discourse of inculturation and contextualization to gain deeper insight into the challenges the Christian faith has to face in the midst of a pluralistic world.

In this vein Catholic priest Tissa Balasuriya of Sri Lanka has shaped his Christology, which is reflective of his interest in interreligious dialogue. His involvement with social justice issues and his openness to religions of Asia led Balasuriya to assert that Asian Christology should open more space for dialogue with other living faiths.[211] He weaves the social, cultural, and religious concerns in doing theology. Trained in economics, he brings into his theology the issues of the suffering of peoples and the degradation of the earth perpetrated by the oppressive structures that the powerful few have created. Thus, Balasuriya proposes a cosmic Christology that could be the basis for a planetary theology.[212] He sees Jesus as the cosmic Christ, one who manifests the universal and the christic in the reality of people's suffering worldwide and of the destruction of the earth. Jesus of Nazareth exemplified the supreme example of commitment to human liberation. Balasuriya criticizes traditional Christologies that have contributed to the formation of guiltless greed and arrogance among white "Christian" cultures in Europe and America. He cites the notion of Christ the victor as an example of a Christology that became useful in justifying imperialist conquest and plunder of the earth.

Moreover, Balasuriya's cosmic Christ is a critique of Christologies that hinge upon the notion that Jesus' death is a corrective to the sin of disobedience of Adam and Eve. This Christology justified the Christian colonizers' refusal to see the connection between the historical context of Jesus' death and the suffering inflicted on the colonized peoples by the colonizers.[213] In this sense, religion is indeed an opiate that numbs the consciences of those who enjoy first-world convenience at the expense of the peoples they exploit. Balasuriya suggests that rethinking the assumptions of the myths of paradise lost and of the fall of humanity will liberate Jesus from being an "ontological savior of humanity from irremediable enmity with God."[214] It will also liberate God from the image of an offended God sulking about the fall of humanity. Christians must face the connection between the life and death of Jesus and his commitment to human liberation toward an abundant life. Yet, though Jesus is the Christ, Balasuriya asserts that Christ is wider than Jesus of Nazareth. The revelation of Jesus as the cosmic Christ gives us deeper insight and understanding into the ongoing growth, or evolution, of the whole universe and of human history. Christ is the principle of universal human solidarity.[215] Revelation is a continuing process, and one can discern it in the christic dimension of all realities. Balasuriya envisions that the liberation of Jesus, Christology, and humanity from narrow concepts and myths of paradise lost and original sin will make theology humble and "Jesus-like."

Balasuriya acknowledges that humanity originated from God, but that origin does not make humanity perfect. Its tendency to do evil results in an "accumulation of historical and structural sin."[216] Balasuriya seems to follow the tragic heuristic in his understanding of humanity. This view challenges humanity to be self-critical of its statements and actions and to be more accountable for its complicity in bringing out the face of evil that it sees and experiences. In this light

Christians need to focus on the best of Jesus' life and teachings that manifest the Divine and the salvific practice of loving God and loving others as one's self.

In line with Balasuriya, Protestant theologian Stanley J. Samartha also viewed Jesus as the cosmic Christ. Samartha belonged to the Church of South India and was the first director of the Dialogue Program of the World Council of Churches. The overarching issue that Samartha tries to address is the necessity for interreligious dialogue both in India and in Asia as a whole. He aims to arrive at a theocentric Christology by advancing the understanding that God reveals the Godself through Jesus the Christ to people in many ways unknown to human beings. Christ incognito is already present in significant areas of the Asian (Hindu) life and thought. This unbound Christ is the cosmic Christ, whose presence and teachings are neither a possession nor a monopoly of the Christian church.[217]

Balasuriya and Samartha insist that there is no need to waste energy in dissecting the nature of Jesus the Christ. No one can ever claim to know how a coexistence of the human and divine nature happens in one person, and no intellectual formula can exhaust the fullness of God's mystery in Christ. We must, therefore "respect the realm of Mystery that is beyond human understanding."[218]

THE IMPORTANCE OF CHRISTOLOGY IN ASIA

Christology is the heart of the Christianity. A Christology that does not speak to Asian peoples' lives makes Christianity meaningless and irrelevant. Thus, it is vital to the Christian faith and practice. The christological trends discussed above are inadequate because they have their own limitations. The inculturated Christ, whether the unknown Christ or the acknowledged Christ of religions, remained Gnostic and metaphysical—oblivious of the social realities that an ordinary Asian person faces every day. The Christ of most contextualized Christologies stressed social realities but pushed the Asian cultures to the periphery and remained Western at heart. As we have seen above, there are definitely some exceptions. Considering the limitations of Christologies constructed by Asian male theologians, I will describe the kind of Christology that may truly be called Asian.

Christology from People's Gut-Level Experiences

First, if Christology is an articulation of one's response or reaction to an encounter with God through Jesus the Christ, then it has to start from the experiences of the Asian people, the majority of whom are poor and non-Christian. The Christologies of the missionaries, as well as those of inculturation and indigenization, ignored the Asian peoples' struggles for fullness of life. They were so full of words that people could hardly hear the voice of or see the face of Christ. Samartha's alternative, "bullock-cart Christology," may move slowly, but its wheels turn on Asian soil and it speaks to the daily life of the majority of the Asian people.[219] The imagery of the bullock-cart graphically suggests the situation of the many Asians who continue to suffer exploitation and poverty.

Aloysius Pieris considers the Christologies of indigenization and contextualization inadequate because the former seemed to trick Asians to accept Christianity[220] and the latter did not take Asian culture seriously.[221] What matters to him is not so much the Asianness of Christ but the "Christness of those categories of Asians who alone can reveal his Asian features."[222] Thus, he appreciates Christologies that envision the Christ of Asia as dalit, the *han*-ridden Christ, the breast-feeding *Christa*, and the third-world Christ of Asia who dwells among the humble of the earth as they strive for human liberation.[223] To Pieris Jesus "remains the absolute norm in Christology" because Jesus "corrects our preconceptions about what it means to be divine and what it means to be human."[224] He asserts that Jesus became the Messiah only at the moment he humbled himself to be baptized by John the Baptist in the Jordan River.[225] An Asian Christology follows what Pieris calls the "two-fold ascesis" or the liberative practice of Jesus, namely, his struggle to be poor and his denunciation of Mammon in the struggle for the poor. This constitutes the meaning of the cross and salvation for Asian people.[226]

In light of Asia's religious multiplicity, Pieris calls for a Christology that recognizes the liberative core of religions and engages in a core-to-core dialogue with the non-Christian Christ, thus stretching Christology's boundaries of orthodoxy.[227] Pieris believes that this double ascesis is a point around which Christology could develop without competing with other religions. In fact, on this basis Buddhism and other Asian religions can forge a symbiotic relationship in their journey. Both can walk the path of practicing voluntary poverty and agapeic engagement in resisting imposed poverty. The fact that pockets of basic human communities in Asia have practiced this twofold ascesis shows that this option is possible.[228] The symbiotic relationship of religions wherein religions challenge each other is a unique approach to the liberationist aspirations of the poor, without negating their cosmic religiosity.[229]

Reimagining a Liberated and Liberating Christ

Second, Christology in Asia will have to rethink some themes that hinder, rather than foster, dialogue and block a liberationist direction. The theme of the uniqueness of Christ, for example, will definitely not work as a starting point for a dialogue among religions. As discussed earlier, dialogue among religions will fare better with the soteriological dimension as the point of convergence. Such dialogue is anchored on faith in the human effort to "arrive at liberation" and on the humility of people to acknowledge that final liberation or salvation, the "absolute future," is beyond human endeavor.[230] This point of convergence will perhaps help reduce fears of syncretism,"[231] heresy, or unorthodoxy that traditional Western Christianity impose to stifle fresh christological expressions. Furthermore, in christological articulation Christians must view the uniqueness of the title Christ not in terms of Jesus as the "exclusive medium of salvation for all" but in light of the absoluteness that the word *Christ* conveys. The Christ may even take a non-Christian character, because we need to remember that "Jesus is Christ, but not all of Christ is Jesus" (*Jesus est totus Christus, non totum Christi*).[232]

Pieris reminds us that the term *Christ* is only a category invented by believers who made use of culture-bound concepts in their effort to "capture the ineffable mystery of salvation" that the person, life, and teachings of Jesus communicate.[233] It is only in the continuing embodiment and praxis of liberating efforts by the followers of Jesus that Jesus' Christhood is experienced. Thus, an Asian Christology cannot proceed meaningfully if it takes the humanity of Jesus lightly. Only a historical Jesus, an embodied Christ, can show the love and compassion that can liberate the oppressed and suffering peoples of the world. Samartha notes that this step will lead to a Christology that is "spiritually satisfying, theologically credible, and ethically helpful to people in the religiously plural world."[234] This christological criterion finds its basis in the kingdom of God as the focus of Jesus' life and teachings.

The Gospels are clear about Jesus' preferential option for the poor and the marginalized, and they challenge the privileged to walk the christic path with Jesus.

Christology also needs to rethink the theme of revelation in relation to the humanity of Jesus. All contextualized, liberation Christologies give importance to the humanity of Jesus of Nazareth. Yet, some of them still tend to share the claim that God's revelation happened in Jesus the Christ once and for all. Samartha argues that this understanding is a "stumbling block" in Asia[235] and that it compromises the basis of monotheistic faith. Theistic faiths use the word *God* to designate Ultimate Truth, Ultimate Reality, or the Transcendent. God was indeed present in Jesus of Nazareth, but Jesus was not "ontologically the same as God."[236] In other words, this once-and-for-all idea stifles the christic presence of the Divine in created reality. Revelation is a never-ending story. God does not stop speaking after the historical Jesus-event. Nor can we confine God's revelation solely to scriptures and the Christian tradition. Balasuriya rightly points out that we need to discern the christic revealed in history, nature, religions, ideologies, movements, and even ourselves.[237]

Many Christologies, including Samartha's, bask in the notion that Jesus' death on the cross was an act of obedience to God's salvific will, that it was Jesus' "voluntary" and "vicarious" "historical decision to take upon himself the sin of others."[238] However, this whole concept needs rethinking and redefinition. The discourse of obedience is problematic when connected to oppressed peoples' experience of abuse of power. It is all the more problematic in relation to women's and children's experiences of sexual abuse and harassment in society and in church. For it to be truly liberating, it is not enough for Christology to go through the double baptism in the "Jordan of Asian religiosity and in the Calvary of Asian poverty."[239] It is not enough for theologians to examine class, caste, ethnicity, and race in our christological formulations. Christology must give equal importance to the analysis of gender, sexism, and patriarchy. The majority of Asian male theologians is silent on issues unique to women, and the theologians who do speak about them do so only marginally, never in any depth. This is at least partly due to the fact that no man can truly speak for women in Asia. Asian women must speak for themselves and thus articulate their own Christologies.

At Home in Asia: Which Christ? Which Jesus?

Which Jesus, which Christ, then, will find a home in Asia? Is it the unknown Christ of Asian religions? Is it the acknowledged Christ of Hindu renaissance? Is it the incognito, the unbound, the cosmic Christ? Is it the Jesus of biblical history? Christologies are human attempts to make sense of Jesus the Christ in the midst of life's realities. They are never absolute. I can only attempt an answer from the insights gleaned from Asian realities. I am convinced, though, that it is not the Christ who claims to be unique, who claims to be God's revelation once and for all. I contend that the Christ revealed in the praxis of the followers of the Gospels' Jesus is most likely to find a seat in many Asian homes and hearts. This is the Christ found in the liberative efforts and redemptive communities of the suffering peoples—the *minjung*, the dalits, and other Asian peoples who are struggling for justice, freedom, and full humanity. One needs to remember, though, that the Jesus who was "God's defense pact with the non-persons of the earth"[240] in biblical history was not a Christian. Yet, the christic praxis of this non-Christian Jesus continues to be God's story mediated in the lives of the Asian poor, who are mostly non-Christian. It may be possible, therefore, that the one who will stay and feel at home in the vast continent of Asia is the non-Christian Christ.

In their search for a Christianity that makes sense in their contexts, Asian theologians began to take a look at Jesus the Christ through Asian eyes. Asian women theologians affirmed much of what the Asian men said in their efforts to indigenize and contextualize Jesus. Yet, Asian women found the Christologies of their male colleagues inadequate. These Christologies did not address the multiplicity of women's oppression and suffering. Very few Asian male theologians addressed gender issues or wrote extensively about them. Exceptions are Aloysius Pieris, Tissa Balasuriya, C. S. Song, Stanley J. Samartha, Suh David Kwang-sun, Sebastian Kappen, and Michael Amaladoss.[241] Some acknowledged their inadequacy to address gender issues.[242] Most of the Asian male theologians, however, chose to ignore the realities of patriarchy, sexism, and androcentrism embedded in Christianity as well as in Asian cultures and religions. Their androcentric concepts and sexist language have, in a negative way, alerted women to the role of language in the formation of concepts and in the perpetuation of a patriarchal world view. This awareness has led to the emergence of women's voices in the Asian theological world.

The Emergence of Asian Women's Voices

Asian women have heard the voices of women from other continents. They have listened to the white feminist debates over the maleness of Jesus. "Can a male Christ save women?"[243] Was Jesus a feminist? If he was, does he not simply gloss over patriarchy that seeks to impose the oppressive and traditional interpretation of *imitatio Christi*?[244] Does a surrogate Jesus have salvific power for black women who bear the suffering brought about by surrogacy and exploitation? Asian women heard the voices of the women among other minority groups in the United States, the Latinas in South America, and African women in protest over the totalizing claims of the male theologians. What is salvific about sacrificial obedience and of Jesus' death on the cross?[245] These concepts have been used by those who have power to control and abuse women, children, and other vulnerable peoples. The history of patriarchal Christianity has been littered with crucifixions of the "sacrificial lambs," those who challenged the prevailing doctrinal orthodoxy. On the one hand, Asian women resonate with these women as they point out the inadequacy of Christologies that did not take into account their experiences of oppression because of their gender, class, race, ethnicity, and culture. On the other hand, Asian women also criticized their white sisters, whose claims on women's experience seemed to have a propensity to erase the identities of women of color.

Perhaps the seeds of Asian feminist theologies were sown long ago by Asia's brave but unknown Christian women. But beginning in the latter part of the twentieth century, Asian women have made substantial contributions to the understanding of Christology. Women are indeed rising. We hear the voices of Dulcie Abraham from Malaysia and biblical scholar Hisako Kinukawa, along with Yoshiko Isshiki and Satoko Yamaguchi, from Japan.[246] I am not able to describe the contributions of women from all the areas of Asia. I am going to focus only on representative theologians from India, Korea, and the Philippines, as well as theologians from Hong Kong, who address Christology from a postcolonial perspective. I believe that these women, in one way or another, stand on the path opened by Marianne Katoppo of Indonesia, whose 1979 book, *Compassionate and Free: An Asian Woman's*

Theology, signaled the emergence of Asian women's voices. Asian women's Christologies are marked by their unique contexts and experiences within the vast continent of Asia. By embracing the reality of their differences and celebrating their commonalities, Asian women have forged solidarity in their common experience of suffering. By virtue of their locations, Asian women's christological approaches are diverse. However, they recognize that there are threads that connect Asian women's common dreams and vision; their own liberation from patriarchy is intertwined with their vision of the ultimate liberation of the marginalized and oppressed, and fullness of life for all.

Chapter 2

Do Indian Women Find Jesus in the Ganges?

In light of women's experiences, there may be a need to reject some of the traditional images of God/Christ that have been upheld as "sacrosanct" for ages. . . . The process of deconstruction of Christology . . . points out to the need to affirm the life and ministry of Jesus.

—EVANGELINE ANDERSON-RAJKUMAR,
"ASIAN FEMINIST CHRISTOLOGY"

On the occasion of the ordination of three priests in Dumaguete City, my friend, a news reporter, interviewed the cardinal. "Why does the Roman Catholic Church not ordain women?" the news reporter asked. The cardinal's answer was simple: "Priesthood is the highest expression of discipleship. The twelve disciples of our Lord were all men. Jesus did not call women to be his disciples. That is why the church cannot ordain women."

On another occasion a group of women lobbied for the election of a woman pastor to the top position of leadership in one Protestant church conference in Negros Oriental. Upon realizing that the woman was going to win the election, the theology professor who was there was upset. He lashed out at the women and scornfully asked, "What can women do anyway?"

In a congress of Asian theologians a man was given the task of introducing the members of the panel. He introduced the male speaker enthusiastically, but when it was time to introduce the female speaker, he turned to her and said, "Please introduce yourself." During that same meeting a man from India derisively told an Indian woman that "women really do not do theology."

These vignettes point to the reality of discrimination against women in church and in theological circles. Furthermore, they bring to the surface many issues on gender, sexuality, and power. Without Christology, God-talk cannot be called Christian theology; Christian theological discourse will always be entwined with Christology. Based on this view, the above stories direct our attention to the reality that there are many Asian male theologians who need to revisit their Christologies in relation to their understanding of the female human being. In spite of Asian men's openness to liberationist and ecumenical theologies that impelled them to construct Asian Christologies, male theologians have not addressed at length the multiplicity of the women's experiences of oppression and suffering. True, some men write reflections on the issues that affect women. This is a positive sign that seems to indicate that more men are now in solidarity with women. However, this should not give us the impression that all is well in the theological area. If men write about women's issues, I suggest that they should make it clear that their reflections are done from their male perspectives. Men need not pretend to write on behalf of women. They should not take the microphone away from their sisters.

Very few Asian men have taken seriously the issues of gender and sexuality in relation to power in their theological reflections and praxis. Many Asian male theologians have chosen to ignore the realities of patriarchy, sexism, and androcentrism embedded in Christianity and in Asian cultures and religions. A male-centered or androcentric Christology inevitably promotes patriarchal norms and sexist attitudes toward women. Moreover, these attitudes are reinforced by many Asian men's captivity to the Euro-American, middle-class, white, male theologies that are not only patriarchal, androcentric, and sexist, but sometimes misogynistic as well. Thus, an androcentric Christology is not only inadequate but also enslaving.

Women in Asia come from different social locations and cultures. Yet, suffering brought about by sexism and patriarchy becomes the tie that binds together the majority of Asian women. Suffering enkindles struggle and resistance; it also brings Christology to the center of nascent Asian women's theologies. Asian women bring a variety of approaches to their Christology. Their Christologies are marked by their unique contexts and experiences within the vast continent of Asia. By embracing the reality of their differences and celebrating their commonalities, Asian women have forged solidarity in their common struggles. Asian women's christological approaches are diverse, yet there is a common thread that connects their vision, that is, the hope for the ultimate liberation of all marginalized and oppressed women and for fullness of life for all peoples.

In this chapter I focus on the Christology of the women from the vast subcontinent of India. The first section focuses on the early christological formulations of Indian women and the impact of the women's situation within the caste system in their Christologies. I also discuss the contribution of women who are outside the caste system, namely, dalit and tribal women, and their struggle for women's ordination. The second section examines the Indian women's concept of connecting Jesus' blood with women's menstruation as life giving. The last part examines the Indian women's interpretation of Jesus the Christ as Shakti, the creative feminine principle.

INDIAN WOMEN'S EARLY CHRISTOLOGICAL FORMULATIONS

Jesus and the Vedic Tradition

In many cultures the river is literally and symbolically a giver and sustainer of life. In Asia great ancient civilizations and religions emerged from the banks of the Indus River, Ganges River, Hwang Ho (Yellow River), and Mekong River. Rivers feed and nourish India, making it a riparian civilization. Hindu feminist Vandana Shiva tells us that people in ancient times dedicated temples to the holy rivers and their sources.[1] The great Ganges, often called Mother Ganga, is one of these holy rivers. Metaphorically, do Indian women have access to the waters of the Ganges? Do Indian women find Jesus on the banks of the Ganges? Living by the holy river and admitting to a predilection for water, Vandana Mataji, a Roman Catholic religious sister, indirectly tells us that she meets Jesus in the "beautiful, gently flowing Gangaji," constantly beckoning to her unceasing *Om*. *Om* is the sacred sound of that which is transcendent and triune, believed to contain the essence of the Vedas. Hinduism and Buddhism consider *Om* a "sort of primordial mantra, signifying the manifestation of the Absolute."[2] Drawing from the Vedic tradition, Mataji considers water a vehicle that reveals the Savior:

> In the Rig Vedic hymn (vii, 49) to the divine water, one almost sees a prefiguring of the Lord Jesus in the waters. . . . Christ standing in the Jordan waters might be taken as a sign and fulfillment of all the washings, bathings, purifications—for the sins of all men, of all times.[3]

Mataji intimates that the most important event in Jesus' life was his baptism. It was the moment of his self-consciousness. The waters awakened Jesus to his *atman*, his true self. Making a connection between the Jordan and the Ganges, she notes:

> Anyone who has intelligently witnessed *Sannyasas-dikshas*—the initiation ceremony—by the banks of Gangaji or any sacred river will know and understand something of the real, inner meaning of the baptism of our Lord.[4]

Baptism awakened Jesus to his self-consciousness of God, to his being the revealer of God. Obviously, Mataji does not make a distinction between the person of Jesus and the Christ. Mataji frames her Christology within the trinitarian framework. She connects Jesus with water as the symbol of the Spirit and of the Shakti of God. Jesus is the source of the living water. Whoever drinks from him will not only have his or her thirst quenched but also will become a "living stream," like the Samaritan woman.[5] However, Mataji did not pursue this direction to break new ground. She detoured to follow the path of the classic male Indian theologians like Upadhyaya. Jesus is not only an ascetic or a *sannyasi* par excellence, who renounced the world and the small self. To Mataji, Jesus' awakening was toward a consciousness of being the Chit of Satchitananda. In classic Indian theology, Satchitananda is the Vedic notion closest to the Christian concept of the Trinity. In this understanding, God the Father is Sat, the pure Being, omnipotent and all-loving. Jesus is the Chit. And the Holy Spirit is the Ananda. Such a Gnostic Christology inspired Mataji to pursue a contemplative type of spirituality based on the Indian simple traditional Ashram lifestyle. She believes that Christ inaugurates Christian liberty, which, to Mataji, means freedom from sin and death, freedom from enslavement to self-interest and falsehood, freedom from wealth, from law, from prestige, from fear, and from sensual lust.[6] Mataji, however, did not make a connection between her understanding of Christian liberty and of the ethical dimension of Jesus' teachings on the essence of the kingdom or reign of God. She claims that the person of Jesus is far more appealing to the Indian than the kingdom. Consequently, her Christology seems to turn its gaze away from the suffering of poor, the dalits, and the tribals. Her writings give us the impression that she has ignored the cross that the sociopolitical and cultural realities of Indian society have forced Indian women to carry.

Jesus and the Women's Search for Humanhood

Late in 1984, three years before the publication of Vandana Mataji's *Jesus the Christ: Who Is He? What Was His Message?*, sixty-two women from all over India gathered in Bangalore for an ecumenical consultation to "discuss their theological response to issues confronting women such as domestic violence, rape, prostitution, to name a few."[7] The report on this gathering was published in 1986 in *Towards a Theology of Humanhood: Women's Perspectives*. Stella Faria, a Protestant, described this meeting as "auspicious and prophetic," because Christian women gathered for the first time, in a spirit of sharing and mutual concern, to address issues that are crucial to Indian women.[8] In this consultation Leelamma Athyal claimed that Mariology must be understood in the service of Christology, as it has a bearing on Athyal's understanding of incarnational Christology and the humanhood of women. To Athyal, Jesus was "at the same time both Mary's son and God's son." She stresses that the narrator of the virgin-birth story intended to explain the incarnation and person of Christ.[9] Indeed, Athyal claims that the humanity of Jesus the Christ is a woman's contribution. She argues that this affirmation rules out the notion of women's inferiority:

> Mary alone, without the help of a male, could provide to God what was needed for him to become "human." Jesus was not any less "human" for his having been a descendant of a woman alone, and his full humanity was what a woman could contribute![10]

In 1989, five years after the Bangalore gathering, Monica Melanchton, a Protestant Old Testament scholar, wrote an article on women and Christology. In commenting upon the endless debate on the nature and person of Jesus, Melanchton insisted that there is no way a finite human mind can comprehend the infinite. Unlike Vandana Mataji, Melanchton focused on the life and teachings of the historical Jesus; a Christology that ignores the life of Jesus the Christ, she says, will always be inadequate. She warns that the maleness of Jesus, if stressed as a precondition of Jesus' reconciliatory work, is problematic; that is, if maleness is constitutive of Jesus' role as "God with us," then Jesus could not represent the whole human race. Maleness is not constitutive of Jesus the Christ, and one should not identify the resurrected Christ with the male principle either. Women can only embrace Christ as representative of a new humanity if the humanness of Jesus is the basis for Christology. Taking the notion of *anthropos* as an inclusive category, she stresses that Jesus' humanity, not his "Jewishness, maleness, or any other such characteristic," is christologically important.[11] She points out that characteristics such as obedience, faith, love, concern, and so on are human, not male, and are christologically significant. Melanchton was one of the earliest voices to articulate Christology from an Asian women's perspective. This is her important contribution to the nascent Asian women's theologies.

To problematize the use of virtues such as obedience, love, faith, and others remains a challenge for women. This is important because vanguards of the tradition in the past centuries interpreted these virtues in a manner that served the patriarchal culture that marginalized women. In India the continuity of patriarchal Hindu tradition with patriarchal Christology in depriving women of their personhood also needs to be explored. This investigation may help us see the connection between the suffering of Indian women and the traditions in Indian society that instill subservience of women to men in the home, church, and society.[12]

THE IMPACT OF WOMEN'S SITUATION IN INDIAN WOMEN'S CHRISTOLOGIES

Indian Society, Women's Cross

The vastness of India contributes to the multiplicity and complexity of the situations Indian women face. India is a little more than one-third the size of the United States, but in 2001 it had a population of over one billion (compared to a population of under 300 million in the United States). The literacy rate is only 52 percent, and at least one-quarter of the population cannot afford an adequate diet. India's natural environment is precarious. The country's leaders bought into the fallacies of globalization, a process that makes the Indian economy subservient to the capitalist market. India is entrenched in debt because of its import-oriented economy and because its economic policies are tied to the dictates of the IMF and the World Bank, especially through its structural adjustment program (SAP). In 2001 its foreign debts rose to US$100.3 billion. The SAP gives high priority to debt services and military spending. In short, India has all the features of a neocolonial, third-world country. Religiously, India is very diverse, with 84 percent Hindus, 11 percent Muslims, and 2 percent Christians.[13] The rest are the Sikhs, Buddhists, Jains, Parsis, and adherents of indigenous or tribal religions.

Patriarchy in Culture and Religion

Anyone doing theology, or Christology, in India ought not to ignore the "third-worldness" of India and its religiosity. One should also not fail to notice the plight of the majority of the population composed of women, dalits, and tribal peoples. The Indian woman stands at the intersection of, or rather, bent under the interconnected burdens of caste, religion, gender, class, and ethnicity. The writings of most Indian women are full of case studies that point to the multiple oppressions and exploitation women suffer.[14] The experience of patriarchy that perpetuates violence against women is a thread that runs through class, religion, caste, and ethnicity. Interlocked with patriarchy are clusters of problems, namely, the dowry system, girl-child murders, female feticide, and bride burning. In the twenty-first century the dowry system still encompasses all social and religious groups, except perhaps among the tribal communities. Whether it is a love marriage or an arranged marriage, the bride's family must pay a dowry—money, jewelry, appliances, and real property—to the groom. The more educated and the higher the caste of the groom, the bigger the dowry the groom's family expects the bride to give. To add more insult to a woman's dignity, the practice demands that the more educated the woman, the bigger the dowry she must offer to "purchase" a groom.[15] Yet, contrary to the market economy, wherein the purchased item becomes the property of the buyer, in India's marriage market the woman—the buyer—becomes the property of the purchased husband. It is tempting to say that the old Filipino practice of the groom giving a dowry according to the demands of the bride's parents is a little better, but in effect this practice is also tantamount to selling the bride. In both cases the woman is at the mercy of patriarchal practices that treat her as a chattel or a commodity.

Rose Paul, a Roman Catholic religious sister, notes that the patriarchal church encourages dowry practice among Christians because, like a sales agent, the church collects a share of the dowry. Overall, she sees the problem as woven into the whole fabric of the "feudal, cultural, religion, social status, economic and political conditions."[16] The situation of women in India is far more despicable, because bride burning may result if the bride's family cannot pay the dowry. The perpetrators usually make the crime appear to be suicide. In many cases mothers-in-law figure as conspirators in dowry deaths. The dowry system has a domino effect. It triggers the practice of female feticide, female infanticide, and the business of reproductive technologies. It also, as Protestant feminist theologian Evangeline Anderson-Rajkumar notes, props up consumerist values of the men and their families, as well as reinforces the socialization of women to attain their ultimate goal and identity as a married woman.[17]

In spite of some legal gains in laws and courts, patriarchal traditions continue to deny women property rights. These traditions frown upon divorce and remarriage. Legislation changes tradition slowly.[18] While society has outlawed the practice of *sati* ("virtuous widow"), which encourages the widow to jump into her husband's funeral pyre, society continues to impose restrictions on the widow's social life. Rape—marital, gang, and custodial—is common. The abominable religious practice of *devadasi*—a system wherein parents dedicate their daughters, some as young as seven years old, to religious prostitution in the name of God—also destroys the life of young girls. Upper-caste men come to the *devadasi* for sex at a very low price, and the parents collect the payment.[19] Upper-caste people are not supposed to associate with the lower-caste people, yet some upper-caste men easily abandon their so-called purity to exploit a *devadasi*, who usually belongs to a lower caste.

Capitalizing on the notion of obedience and sacrifice, Indian culture and religion impose all these burdens upon the Indian woman, regardless of what caste she belongs to—Brahmin, Kshatriyas, Vaishya, or the lowest caste, the Shudras. To make things worse, Hindu converts have integrated these practices into their newfound Christian religion, which itself is not free of sexist and patriarchal concepts. Kamal Raja Selvi, a dalit activist, laments over the irony of the Indian culture, because the men worship goddesses yet oppress the women around them. She writes:

> [Men] have to maintain the myth of male-domination, for their convenience. It is true there are many women goddesses to be worshipped. They can cite the goddesses Meenaskshi, Kali, Parasakthi, Lakshmi and Saraswathi and others. He can call woman "the light of the house," the educator of the whole family and the source of knowledge. He can name the rivers after women, Ganga, Kaveri, Narmada. His literature can proclaim the freedom of women. He can call his country "Mother land," his language "Mother tongue." But at home, in actual life, she is little more than an unpaid servant, a child-bearing machine.[20]

In response to the problems that the dowry breeds, Rose Paul challenges each Christian woman, as well as the whole church, to follow Jesus as a person who works for the reversal of an unequal and unjust order of society. She stresses that the order of Indian society is determined by discrimination according to social class, caste, creed, and gender. She suggests that one image that Jesus used for himself—the vine—can inspire believers to think of unity with him. The concept of Jesus as the vine, she goes on, negates the dualism, hierarchy, and subordination that patriarchy advocates. Besides the image's value in shaping a Christology that is neither hierarchical nor anthropocentric, it is equally valuable for ecofeminist spirituality. Rose Paul adds a caveat in talking with women, though. She warns that the struggle to end the oppressive order so that women may attain full "humanhood" is not easy. Women have to share Jesus' suffering and crucifixion. The ultimate hope lies in women's resurrection to an altered just society.[21]

Jesus and Women's Rights

Omana Mathews of the Mar Thoma Church examined the situation of women within the bounds of abusive marital relationships. She found that the Christian tradition's view of the body is not helpful for women. Like most Indian women theologians, she asserts that theology must redefine the concept of the body. Theology needs to understand the violation of women's bodies from the perspective of incarnation, of Jesus' becoming human.[22] She sees that, in many cases, divorce is the only way out of a marriage with an abusive husband. Jesus is an advocate of women's human rights and heals women of their sufferings. Mathews points to Jesus' encounters with women, which were always moments of affirmation, healing, and empowerment. Jesus lifted up women from their brokenness and the humiliation imposed by a patriarchal culture. In agreement with Mathews, Elizabeth Joy of the Orthodox Church in India points out that Jesus' acts of affirming and healing the women from infirmities were Jesus' way of making people understand that a woman's body is sacred, not a commodity. Unfortunately, instead of celebrating the body as a site of mutual respect, love, honor, and dignity, men treat women's bodies as a site of control and domination. There is hardly any recognition that the bodies of women and of the marginalized peoples are part of Jesus' wounded body. Joy asserts that believers can only affirm their faith in God by sharing the suffering of Jesus and the abused and by reclaiming the body as a site of liberation and freedom.[23]

Jesus and the Suffering of the Women among Outcastes

The principle of purity and pollution heavily marks the Indian culture, an influence of the Brahmanical caste system[24] that is rooted in the Hindu *Varnashrama dharma*. Literally meaning "color and stage of life," the term *varnashram* in Hinduism refers to the original concept of four classes and stages of life.[25] This dualistic principle creates a divide between those who are supposedly pure—the ones who do rituals and intellectual work—and those who do manual labor. According to the *Varna*, Brahmins are the purest, the *Bhoo-devas* or "gods of the earth." Their ranks include the priests and scholars. They are merely 5 percent of the total Indian population. Next in rank are the Kshatriyas, or warriors, followed by the Vaishyas, the traders. Each of these two caste levels makes up 1 percent of the population. Landowners compose 10 percent of the population. Having access to wealth through land, they join the upper castes in controlling power, wealth, and prestige. Seventy percent of the population comprises poor Shudras, dalits, and tribals. At all caste levels women's "place" is always the lowest rung within the caste hierarchy.[26]

The dalits are outside the caste system. Hindu society considers them rubbish. Upper-caste people treat them with religion-sanctioned deep contempt and cruelty. Anyone who understands the evils of slavery, apartheid, and racism will understand the plight of the dalits. Like racism, discrimination continues to wreak havoc in the lives of one-fourth of India's population. Indian law and constitution had abolished the category of untouchable, but Hindu religious tradition continues to perpetuate the discriminatory practices associated with it. The sinful notion of untouchability finds a parallel in what African theologian Engelbert Mveng called anthropological poverty, that is, "the despoiling of human beings not only of what they have, but of everything that constitutes their being and essence—their identity, history, ethnic roots, language, culture, faith, creativity, dignity, pride, ambitions, right to speak . . . we could go on indefinitely."[27]

The sinful notion of untouchability is a burden, a cross that the Hindu caste system imposed on the dalits. Yet, the crosses that society has forced dalit women to carry are heavier. If the upper-caste women's place is the lowest in the hierarchy within their respective castes, and if the dalit man is regarded as a non-person, outside the caste system, the dalit woman is the most oppressed person. Religion not only condones but also sanctions the exploitation of dalit women's closeness to bodily processes and to Mother Earth. Moreover, male church leaders, such as priests, perpetuate this exploitation in the name of Jesus. With their denigrated, sexually abused bodies and desecrated souls, women "stand naked in view of the 'civilized' history" as the embodiment of the mystified and glorified suffering servants.[28]

Jesus and Dalit Women's Struggle for Survival

Survival is a basic issue among dalit women. Interwoven into their struggle for survival is the necessity for land and water, but society deprives them even of these basics. Instead of helping these most oppressed of the oppressed, the Indian government's participation in the capitalist scheme of globalization and mechanization has pushed dalit women deeper into the abyss of poverty. Kamal Raja Selvi points out that government projects and concessions result in deforestation, which affects dalit settlements and has pushed dalit people into areas that are even more inhospitable.[29] Powerful upper-caste men involved with such projects usually subject dalit women to various kinds of harassments, including rape, to humiliate their communities. They also subject tribal women to rape and humiliation to bring the tribal peoples to their knees.[30] N. G. Prasuna reports that in Madhya Pradesh villages, each dalit family had at least one female member raped and defiled by Thakur upper-caste men. Women are always in danger. While upper-caste men look upon dalit women as fair game, dalit men, who cannot contend with their upper-caste oppressors, also tend to make dalit women their scapegoats.[31] If a male-dominated and caste-dominated society, such as Indian society, considers dalit men impure because of the blood of untouchability that runs through their veins, Hindu society traditionally sees dalit women as doubly impure because of the blood of untouchability that runs through their veins and because of their menstruation. Women are not only the "dalit of the dalit,"[32] or the "slaves of slaves," but they are also deemed to be the most impure of the impure. Based on such ridiculous reasoning, many Protestant churches in India exclude seminary-educated dalit women from ordination.[33] Aruna Gnanadason, a Protestant, insists that women's oppression is a sinful situation.[34]

Affirming Gnanadason, N. G. Prasuna describes the system of the male-dominated and caste-dominated society as "eating the flesh and drinking the blood of dalit women."[35] Socioeconomic class, usually a built-in system within a caste, aggravates the situation of women. N. G. Prasuna's words echo the eucharistic formula of Jesus consecrating the bread and wine as he pointed to his body to be broken and his blood to be shed; the churches need to understand these words in the context of the harsh reality of the patriarchal sacralization of women's suffering. The women's suffering, like the suffering of Jesus the Christ on the cross, exposes the evil of patriarchy embedded in the political, economic, and social system of Indian society.

Disobedience as a Paradigm of Resistance

In their brokenness, dalit women long for a God who stands with them. They acknowledge they have found God in Jesus, whom they see as their liberator. S. Faustina, a dalit writer and activist, rejects the notion of obedience in traditional Christian teachings, saying that this "virtue" is detrimental to women, dalits especially. She argues that dalits must redefine the concept of obedience from the perspective of resistance to evil. Citing women's encounters with Jesus in scripture, she challenges dalit women to defy unjust traditions in order to be healthy and whole. She believes that women must be acquainted with the Jesus who was neither docile nor self-sacrificing, yet who was modest and courageous enough to shake the existing order and to inaugurate a just society. This is necessary, Faustina insists, in order to kindle the "fire of righteous anger" in the dalit women.[36] Faustina identifies righteous anger as a resource for resistance. Faustina's challenge is close to what American feminist ethicist Beverly Wildung Harrison calls "the power of anger in the work of love,"[37] that is, the profound rage at unequal and unjust relationships that stirs one to work for change in society. Harrison holds that the radical love of Jesus, a love that seeks mutuality and reciprocity with the excluded ones, fuels such anger against exclusivistic, oppressive structures and relationships.[38] In the same vein Faustina calls on dalit women to look at Jesus as a model of righteous disobedience. Jesus broke the existing unjust norms of his society regarding ethnicity, religion, and gender by associating with outcasts. When Jesus transgressed stifling traditions to restore the "stolen dignity of the oppressed and the marginalized people," he also gave life back to women and empowered them "to be sensitive to get involved with life-giving activities."[39]

To be sure, Indian women do not want people to think that they want to remain victims. N. G. Prasuna tells us that dalit women understand that neither the dalit men who ignore them nor the feminist movements that often forget them can liberate dalit women from their lot. Yet, unlike those who ignore them, Jesus, who seeks and values the little ones, inspires dalit women to rise up. They must work for their own liberation, raise their voices, and resist oppression in order to free themselves, along with their communities, and to secure resources for their livelihood. Prasuna stresses that the survival of dalit women is integral to the survival of the earth.[40]

Jesus and the Ordination of Women

One of the arenas of struggle for seminary-trained women everywhere is the matter of ordination. The churches have their battery of "classic" theologians to defend their stand against women's ordination. Their arguments range widely. They include the notion that woman brought about the fall of humanity, that women are incapable of discerning spiritual matters, that women are misbegotten males, that Jesus had no women disciples, and a host of other reasons. This "phallocentric Christianity," to borrow Mary Daly's terminology,[41] excludes women from the ordained ministry because of its fear of women as the "other."

In one of her earliest writings Monica Melanchton asserted that women should not allow the male-dominated church to smother and distort God's intention for women and to use such notions to hinder women from ordination and from meaningful participation in the church and community life. Contrary to the church fathers' usage of the word *anthropos* to mean only the male members of the human race, Melanchton takes the Greek word *anthropos* to mean men *and* women. Understandably, Melanchton's reinterpretation of the word functions to support her argument that Jesus' maleness is insignificant in relation to women's ordination.[42] To Pauline Chakkalakal, the idea that only a male can represent Christ "is theologically suspect."[43] Insisting that Jesus did not institute a cultic hierarchy of priesthood, Chakkalakal argues for the ordination of women from the perspective of Jesus' incarnation. Jesus is definitely the model for priesthood, but the essence of such priesthood is not his maleness. It is his sense of calling, his capacity to share the lot of the weak and the suffering, and his pastoral sensibility that define Jesus as a shepherd. Love and service, not masculinity, define the theology of priesthood.

Christology and Language

Language, in its variety of forms, has a very important role in doing Christology. It is a challenge for Asian women to consider the role of language in doing theology, especially when a foreign language such as English is used. Language is a symbol for the concept we seek to express. Since words and concepts about women were constructed based on patriarchal and androcentric norms, women must reinvent and redefine concepts. A case in point is the discourse of a theologically trained woman who reported the results of her case studies. As cited by Chakkalakal, this woman lamented over the futility of women's theological training if these women "are not being *used* by the Church . . . as full time workers" and that "many theologically trained *spinsters* [struggle] to make a living as they are not being *used* appropriately by the churches."[44] I understand what this woman wanted to say. However, some of her words point to the baggage of patriarchal socialization that women have internalized. I believe that women theologians do not want the church and society to treat women as objects "to be used." This demands a commitment among women not to reinscribe in their work sexist language and derogatory concepts that present women—or men—as objects.

Tribal Women and the Struggle for Self-Determination

Another voice in India that is hardly heard in the churches comes from the tribal women. Tribal peoples of Northeast India generally share the burden of India's economic problems.[45] Politically, the Indian government has been trying to push for a National Integrity Program that would "Indianize" the tribal peoples. Yet, the tribal peoples' desire is to gain independence and to chart their own destiny. Tribal peoples have been deprived of ancestral lands, historical landmarks, job opportunities, and basic human rights for self-determination. Mizoram and Assam (Bodo Land), for example, tried to seek independence from Hindu India, but the Indian government responded with suppression and militarization. Moreover, infiltration and occupation of the remaining tribal lands by people from outside India have triggered violence.[46] Nirala Iswary, a Bodo woman, feels that her people have become refugees in their own homeland. Rather than protecting the tribal peoples from the encroaching forces, the government's response has leaned more toward ethnic cleansing.[47] These forces, pressing upon tribal peoples from both sides, seem determined to wipe these people out from the face of the earth. Tribal women theologians lament that the situation of the tribal peoples goes unreported.

Like anywhere else, militarization always involves strategies of rape, looting, and hamletting to subjugate peoples. These assaults inflict the most wounds upon women, forests, and the earth itself. Iswary gives a voice to the tribal women, who cry out for liberation: "Come to our rescue before we totally disappear from the face of this earth. Bodos are also human beings created in God's image."[48]

Belonging mostly to Mongoloid stock, tribals do not share the Hindu religion. They have distinct cultures and traditions. They resisted as unacceptable the Indian government's move for the integration of the tribals into Hindu society. Protestant theologian Lalrinawmi Ralte of Mizoram and other tribal women theologians view the government's integration program as an invitation for them to become Hindu and to make them "part of the outcaste, or the untouchable."[49]

To Ralte, this act of cultural imperialism and religious supremacy finds reinforcement in the Hindu caste system. Contrary to some Indian theologians' view that Hinduism is the most tolerant religion, tribal women think otherwise. Raimundo Panikkar says that Hinduism "believes it has room even for Christianity within its own multiform structure."[50] Ralte disagrees with Panikkar's view and argues that the caste system has crept into the ethos of other religions that seek to coexist with Hinduism. A case in point is Indian Christianity. Most Indian women writers who examine the condition of women within the churches validate Ralte's observation that casteism is generally present in Indian Christianity.[51] One can only note that Hinduism and Christianity have liberating elements distinct to each one's character, but they also share commonalities that affect women: their patriarchal character that exploits women in the name of obedience, sacrifice, loyalty, and love.

Tribal Women's Call for Solidarity

Feminist theologians in India, therefore, need to be engaged in a dialogue not only with fellow Christians but also with Hindu women. Together, they may be able to open a path to a spirituality that is life affirming and life giving. Chakkalakal, Dietrich, and Gnanadason are explicit about this need to do theology in dialogue with women not only from the Hindu tradition but with women from other traditions as well. One of the Hindu women with whom Asian women could fruitfully engage in dialogue is Vandana Shiva. An ecofeminist who has a passion for life, she has explored a path to an earth spirituality and activism.[52]

Recognizing the crucial role of Christology in forging solidarity among Christian women, Chakkalakal insists that Asian women must do Christology with women of other religious persuasions.[53] Gnanadason agrees, but she stresses that women must do theology without "religious labels," thereby "respecting the liberation strands of all faiths and encouraging the search for protest elements in all faiths."[54] The invitation of Ralte for women theologians to be in solidarity with the tribal women in their journey of doing theology that focuses on survival begs for a response. She insists: "Survival is our life. Survival keeps us going. Survival is our point of integrity. Come join us as we celebrate our survival."[55]

Women and Patriarchy in the Tribal Church

Old Testament scholar R. L. Hnuni of Mizoram identifies the triple burden tribal women have to carry within the domestic sphere. Unlike Hindus, the tribals, such as the Mizo, welcome girls for their labor in weaving, household chores, childcare, and in *jhum* cultivation when they grow up.[56] As in most patriarchal societies, only sons can inherit and own property in Mizo culture. Despite recent revisions of such customs, depriving women of their right to own or inherit property is still practiced widely. The seeming social freedom of tribal women to mingle with men is not a measure of liberation. It merely hides the reality of their marginalization. Society imposes upon women an "eat less" ideology, a practice that results in widespread cases of malnutrition among women. Even in the tribes of Khasi-Jaintia and of Garo Hill, which claim to be matrilineal, the men still view the women with contempt and beat them.[57] In these hill tribes a man can easily cast his wife off if she strikes back at him. A "proper" woman should not sit opposite a man, and a wife should not eat before her husband has been served. Traditional tribal proverbs reveal these cultures as sexist and patriarchal. Rather than putting an end to patriarchal practices and discourse within the tribal cultures, Christianity reinforced them with its androcentric theologies.

> Women and crabs have no religion.
> A woman's wisdom does not cross the brook.
> A wife and a broken fence can be easily changed.
> The words of women and the horns of the female
> *methun* [water buffalo] are of no use. (Kuki)[58]
>
> If a hen crows, the world is over. (Khasi)
>
> If a hen crows, and a woman preaches,
> the world is over. (Christian Khasi proverb)[59]

Christian educator N. Limatula Longkumer of Nagaland stresses that in Northeast India "the role of women in the church is worse than in secular society. . . . Women were not given leadership in the church."[60] To illustrate this, she cites the Presbyterian Church in Northeast India that refuses to ordain women, so only men can serve the church. Since no women are ordained, and since the church emphasizes a hierarchical ordained ministry, no woman can serve as secretary of church organizations. To drive her point further, Longkumer underscores a common practice among Khasi Presbyterian churches to have a man act as secretary of women's fellowships.[61]

It is understandable why Longkumer, like other tribal women, connects Christology so closely to her understanding of the church as she challenges it to be transformed. If Jesus Christ challenged a traditional system in order to usher in God's new order of freedom in community, what does it mean to say that the church is the body of Christ? Moreover, the view that Jesus is the healer recurs in tribal women's theology, as in Longkumer's. Jesus is one who empowers women, R. L. Hnuni asserts, by exposing the "absurdities" of patriarchal privilege in religion and by showing an example of an inclusive ministry. Jesus tore down the walls of religions and cultures that dehumanize and deprive others.[62] Jesus' attitude toward women was revolutionary, and his life and teachings are the most significant theological sources for the empowerment of women. In interpreting the Lukan story of the bent-over woman (Lk 13:10), Hnuni insists that Jesus' concern for life transcends religious laws and that he knew that it was "social and cultural sin"[63] that brought illness to the woman. Satan is the system that binds women and forces them to bow their heads in submission to male dominance. Jesus saved women from human oppressions, but Hnuni also insists that the acts of the resurrected Jesus were more significant for women because "the human Jesus conforms to the Jewish patriarchal tradition" by choosing only men as his "twelve official (recorded) disciples." Jesus' praxis of restoring women's wholeness and empowering them necessitated a step of taking a "radical and revolutionary action against the Jewish religious and social norms." More significant for women, Hnuni further notes, is the "resurrected/divine Jesus" who chose women "to be his first disciples and first messengers of his resurrection."[64]

Hnuni points out Jesus' posture of lifting up and recognizing the capacities of women in his time, particularly as the first witnesses of the resurrection. However, by bracketing the terms "resurrected/divine Jesus" as distinct from the "human Jesus," Hnuni seems to imply that the human Jesus was devoid of or lacked divinity. Consequently, this term implies the same for the rest of humanity. Moreover, Hnuni, an Old Testament scholar, runs the risk of being misunderstood to suggest anti-Semitic interpretations. Like many Christian feminist theologians, she comes close to stepping on a landmine of anti-Semitism with her discourse on Jewish norms. Like other theologians, Christian feminist theologians can easily fall into the temptation of placing a negative label upon Judaism. But scripture provides evidence that Jesus valued his Jewish tradition and had no intention of breaking away from it: "Do not think that I have come to abolish the law or the prophets; I have come not to abolish but to fulfill" (Mt 5:17). Mindful of the feminist anti-Judaism trap, Elisabeth Schüssler Fiorenza argues that "any feminist impulse detectable in the Jesus movement must be derived from Judaism, since Jesus and his first wo/men disciples were Jews."[65] While this reminder will be a helpful guide to Asian women in their theological journey, they need to recognize the enslaving elements of every religion.

MAKING CONNECTIONS: JESUS' BLOOD AND WOMEN'S MENSTRUATION

> For the sake of holiness and our safety, we kindly request women being [*sic*] menstruation not to enter the temple.

These words were written on the billboard posted at the gate of a Hindu temple in Bali, Indonesia.[66] This statement confronts everyone with the stark reality that religions in postmodern times continue to uphold taboos that exclude women because of the natural monthly biological process of menstruation. This brings us to the issue of blood in religion, particularly Jesus' blood and women's menstruation.

Blood. Everybody knows what blood is. We know that it is a red fluid that flows through vessels called veins, arteries, and capillaries. This fluid carries oxygen and nutrients to all parts of the body. In both scientific and spiritual senses, blood is life. Socially and politically, blood takes on another sense as it comes to mean race or lineage. The symbol of blood is ubiquitous in Christian art and literature. It is typically associated with the blood Jesus shed on the cross. In relation to women, the gospel speaks of blood only in terms of illness, such as the story of the woman who had been bleeding for twelve years (Lk 8:43–48). Blood in the Judeo-Christian tradition is something that pollutes. The Hebrew scriptures use the words *gaal* and *chareph* in connection with blood and bloodshed to mean "to defile, profane, and pollute."[67] Women's blood during menstruation and birthing is particularly dirty because it is associated with the female sex. Yet, as a theological theme, menstrual blood is still a newcomer. This is evidenced by the scarcity of theological writings that focus on blood in connection with menstruation.

Women's Blood in Culture and Religions

Studies in the area of women and religion, however, have explored the theme. These studies reveal that in many cultures menstruation has a double meaning. Blood is both sacred and taboo. Some male-dominated societies have viewed menstruation negatively, but many primitive hunting and gathering tribes have given menstrual blood a positive religious meaning as a symbol of life. Thus, for a girl and her people, the onset of menstruation is an occasion for celebration.[68] In African religions blood is powerful. This pervasive symbol of women's powers evokes in men ambivalent attitudes toward women. The fear of women's powers associated with the mystery of menstruation have driven some tribal communities to control women by instituting taboos and prohibitions, such as confinement in menstrual huts during a woman's period.[69] The taboos imposed on menstruating women by society are certainly repressive. Yet, Rosalind Hackett, who studies African religions extensively, asserts that one can detect underneath such repression a "tacit symbolic affirmation of the implicit divinity and power of women."[70]

Mercy Amba Oduyoye of Ghana examined women's leadership participation in relation to menstruation in African societies. In Akan communities men fear the mystery of menstruation. This mystification has a negative impact upon women's participation and leadership in African churches. In some churches menstruating women are prohibited from taking communion or are refused entry from the main church building; they can, however, send in their offering, sing hymns, and read a text within worship. On the one hand, free-flowing menstrual blood is a sign of nature's hospitality and paves the way for the arrival of the ancestral spirits. On the other hand, one should not touch menstrual blood because it is a pollutant. Menstruation is life giving, but it is also associated with death and is believed to have sufficient potency to render all prayers and rituals ineffective. Perhaps, this explains why Akan men have "deep-seated fear of menstruation and women."[71]

In ancient Japan, notes Michiko Yusa, a religious studies professor, menstruation was considered sacred because it was associated with life force. Menstruation is a positive sign for a woman. She can become a medium *(miko)* or bride of a deity *(kami)*. Yusa claims that the negative attitude toward menstruation and the strong sense of ritual uncleanness "originally came from India with Buddhism, and assimilated into the Shinto sensibility of cleanliness."[72]

Reclaiming Menstruation as Symbol of Life and Creativity

Indian churches and Indian society consider women impure because of menstruation. Dalit women become doubly impure for not only having come from untouchable "stock" but also because of their monthly biological cycle of menstruation. Elizabeth Joy points out that Christian dalit theology ignores the role of blood in determining the plight of dalits. Indian society brands these people untouchable because of their bloodline. Bloodshed resulting from violence inflicted by upper-caste oppressors, and as a consequence of dalit resistance against such forces, has marked dalit communities. Joy suggests that the positive image of blood in the eucharistic formula needs to be stressed to "counter argue" the concept that dalits are pollutants in Indian society. She grounds her argument upon the understanding that if the blood of Jesus purifies the dalit, so blood purifies individuals. In the case of menstrual blood, one need only connect it with the powerful, new-life-giving, and redemptive image of Jesus the Christ's blood. Joy points to an analogy between Jesus' bleeding body and women's capacity to procreate. Women must explore this connection, she says, because Christian traditions have barred women from ordained ministry because of menarche. For dalit women, flesh and blood connect with pathos, the epistemological paradigm dalit theologians have chosen.[73] Joy concludes:

> If Dalit theologians, a firm position do not take
> And Dalit religious tradition they mercilessly forsake
> Thus it will not be a genuine Dalit Theology
> Lacking in Dalit women's pathos, its epistemology.[74]

Aruna Gnanadason has observed that in ancient Indian culture blood is a powerful symbol of creativity. She points to the existence of temples and shrines dedicated to the supreme power of the feminine and the presence of devotees who dress in red to symbolize blood as proof of this claim. She cites, for example, the Khamakya temple in Guwahati, Assam, where the central focus of the religious ceremonies is the *yoni*-shaped symbol that has a blood-like flow.[75] Extolled as the sacred area, the *yoni-yantra*, according to Indian author Ajit Mookerjee, is the triangle, the "immemorial sign" of woman, the "gateway of cosmic mysteries"; it represents the Great Mother, the source of all life.[76] Gnanadason suggests that Christian feminist hermeneutics should retrieve the empowering elements of India's past and reclaim the powerful symbol of women's creativity that draws inspiration from blood. Understanding menstruation as part of the reproductive process, Gnanadason says that blood cleanses and prepares the environment for new life: "Women who have an intimate experience of what the 'birthing of new life' means by the life-cleansing blood that they shed each month, have always throughout history been engaged in protecting and nurturing life."[77]

Gnanadason is not explicit in connecting women's menstruation with Jesus' blood. However, the imagery she brings before us alludes to the blood of Jesus that Christian theology traditionally interprets to have a cleansing effect. Unlike the traditional Christian notion that "Jesus washed our sins through his blood," Gnanadason stresses that blood is the powerful element that sustains, protects, and nurtures life. Because of this emphasis, I infer that she would relate the "birthing of new life" with Jesus' blood as a powerful symbol of creativity and life. I believe it is in this same vein that Womanist theologian JoAnne Marie Terrell speaks of the power of blood to give new life to people who have lost meaning in their lives. She cites a gospel singer's account of her delivery from drug addiction through Christ's agency. In her testimony the singer declares that "there *is* power in the blood" of Jesus.[78] In the name of Jesus' blood this singer claimed a new life and redemption from the experience of social alienation and self-destruction.

Ambivalence characterizes religious views on the subject of blood. Blood can be either sacred or polluting. Generally, religions consider the blood that is shed for rituals of sacrifice sacred, but religious views usually do not connect women's blood and menstruation with life. Instead, most religions view menstrual and birthing blood as pollutants. Nevertheless, women generally have a deep understanding of the connection between blood and life, blood and fertility. In India the patriarchal culture does not view the blood women shed as a result of rape, abortion, or domestic violence as connected with the sacredness of life and blood. Gabriele Dietrich, a naturalized Indian citizen, alludes to the connection between Jesus' blood and women's menstrual blood by graphically portraying the paradox of women's lives as life givers whom society abuses in many ways. A woman's blood cries out to resist the violence that patriarchy inflicts upon women—society-imposed abortions, rape, invasive medical practices, militarization, temple prostitution, wife beatings, exclusion from religious functions, and much more. In her poem she writes:

> I am a woman
> and the blood
> of my sacrifices
> cries out to the sky
> which you call heaven.
> I am sick of you priests
> who have never bled
> and yet say:
> This is my body
> given up for you
> and my blood
> shed for you
> drink it.
> Whose blood
> has been shed
> for life
> since eternity?
> I am sick of you priests
> who rule the *garbagriha*,
> who adore the womb
> as a source for life
> and keep me shut out
> because my blood
> is polluting.[79]

In describing the suffering of women, however, Dietrich does not resort to hate and violence. She merely continues to bleed from her womb and from her heart. Yet, with a hint of a day of reckoning, her poem ends with these words:

> I am a woman
> and my blood
> cries out.

We are millions
and strong together.
You better hear us
or you may be doomed.[80]

Jesus and Women Shed Blood to Give Life

In Dietrich's poem both Jesus and women shed blood to give life and to renew life. Dietrich notes that, unlike the bloodshed that drains life from the body as a result of violence, menstrual bleeding is a "precondition for human procreation and spacing of birth."[81] Giving life is actually both a biological and spiritual experience. In her later writings Dietrich is more explicit in connecting women's menstruation with the eucharistic symbol of Jesus' blood shed on the cross. She expressed this concept in her blessing over the bread and wine:

Five loaves and two fishes in the hands of the child
He gave them to Jesus happily
He blessed, broke, and gave them
He made the hunger of 5,000 people to go.
The blood of Jesus and the blood of women shed
together
tells [*sic*] us to work for the life of the world
after blessing, having given to drink,
he asked us to live as disciples.[82]

Dietrich cites the popular Filipino interpretation of the feeding narrative as a miracle of sharing rather than a story of Jesus making food magically appear. She urges Christians to see a connection between the miracle of sharing in the feeding of the five thousand and the miracle of women sharing their lifeblood to give new life. The Eucharist is a sacramental sharing. This communal action ideally points to a society in which no one goes hungry and no one will have too much.[83] Indeed, the Eucharist is an antithesis to the socialization of Indian women to feed others first, to eat last, and to eat less. Thus, Jesus' blood and women's menstruation are sacramental, a communion in celebrating life. Dietrich points to the irony of Indian people's refusal to imagine a female Christ on the cross, clad in a loincloth. They associate this image with pornography, as if Indian society does not strip women naked of their dignity all the time. India's increasingly consumerist society exposes women's bodies in movies and in advertisements, including family-planning posters that show "women's insides turned outside."[84] The patriarchal culture's hypocritical double standard strips women of their humanity and refuses to see women shed blood in their daily life struggles. Indian women are calling the church and the believers of Jesus the Christ to consider the connection between the life-giving blood that Jesus shed and the life-creating blood that women shed. This is a challenge that women coming from the patriarchal cultures of Asia need to consider seriously. To reclaim the power of the blood of women's menarche will certainly liberate women and help them regain their self and dignity. Women from other parts of the world affirm this view, as Janet Morley demonstrates in her Eucharistic Prayer for Christmas Eve in which she expresses beautifully the connection between Jesus' blood and women's menstruation:

> Come now, dearest Spirit of God,
> Brood over these bodily things,
> And make us one body in Christ.
> As Mary's body was broken for him, and her blood shed,
> So may we show forth his brokenness for the life for the
> world,
> And may creation be made whole through the new birth
> in his blood.[85]

CHRISTOLOGY AND THE LIBERATING IMAGE OF SHAKTI FOR INDIAN WOMEN

Asian Christian feminists must draw from the well of traditional sources of God's revelation to interpret Christian doctrines.[86] This is the challenge Stella Baltazar and Aruna Gnanadason put forth. Considering women's experiences of domestic violence, Baltazar, like other feminists, pinpoints the source of the problem. She calls the foundation that supports the perpetuation of oppressive traditional family culture and the privatization of women's lives "patri-kyriarchy." She argues that it is necessary for women to define themselves, their roles in society, and their goals in life in order to resist and to prevent violence perpetrated against them and against nature.[87] Women can do this by reinterpreting their cultural traditions and primal stories, and, in light of these primal traditions, reinterpreting the Christian faith. In demonstrating how this is possible, Baltazar has developed a christological construction that identifies Jesus the Christ with Shakti of the Hindu tradition. Who is this Shakti?

Shakti, the Creative Feminine Principle

Lina Gupta, a Hindu scholar from India, explains that Shakti is the feminine creative principle underlying the cosmos. The word *shakti* means "power" or "energy." Shakti is also called Devi, a word rooted in the Sanskrit *div*, "to shine." Devi is the self-manifested one who shines despite all obstacles. Shakti has many names and embodiments. However, she retains her identity as the symbol of life-giving powers of the universe, as the one who is truly liberated. Since Shakti is the eternally existing feminine principle of creation, all creation has a spark of her creativity and femininity. As an embodiment of Shakti, the goddess Kali dances a destructive dance that communicates her response to an oppressive existing order as well as her vision of how things should be. Through her post-patriarchal reinterpretation of Shakti and Kali mythologies, Gupta looks at Kali more as the "fountain of creative energy" that saves the world from all forms of oppression. Although Shakti is the feminine principle embodied by the goddess Kali, Shakti cannot be confined in one particular image. Ultimately, Gupta insists that "neither masculine nor feminine image, [nor] language . . . contains the final truth. . . . They are both aspects of the same, single reality."[88]

In a land where goddesses, along with gods, are worshiped, it is reasonable to wonder why women are oppressed in India. Where is Shakti in all the suffering of women and female children? Where is Shakti, the Great Mother, in the violation of women's personhood? Where is Shakti in the plunder of nature for profit? K. Rajaratnam of India explains that the invading Aryans subjugated the powerful goddesses of the ancient Indus civilization through the process of "sanskritization." This process involved the absorption of the goddesses into the Hindu pantheon and their relocation to a lower level by making them wives of the Hindu gods. The process of "spousification" not only turned the goddesses into models of subservience, but it also resulted in the creation of the subservient Indian woman as the "ideal woman" defined by the Manusmriti code. This code effectively installed the caste system and consequently condemned women and the lower castes to the status of the ritually impure.[89] Obviously, though, the patriarchal Hindu religion could not get rid of Shakti. As a local goddess Devi defied sanskritization and emerged as the semi-orthodox Tantric Shakti, embodied by Kali and Durga. Today, in South Asia, one can still find thousands of devotees of Kali, whom they usually call Ma' Kali. Yet, again, we may ask, where is Shakti in the suffering of women in the face of patriarchy and ecological degradation?

Gnanadason asks these questions and opines that modernity has banished Shakti into the unconscious "under the onslaught of patriarchal religions" and the Eurocentric "scientific" cultures. Nevertheless, Gnanadason recalls for us the words of Swami Vivekananda, a nineteenth-century Hindu prophet, who predicted that the hope for all creation lies in the "resurgence of the Mother into the consciousness of the world's population."[90]

Jesus the Christ, and Shakti the Creative Feminine Principle

In the Christian tradition the one who gives us hope and raises us from death is Jesus the Christ. This is the starting point for Stella Baltazar's Christology. She suggests that reinterpreting primordial stories and Christian tradition enables women to become life creating. By acknowledging the dynamic energy and source of life, women will have access to the life-affirming, life-sustaining, and life-transforming power who is Shakti. Jesus the Christ is Shakti. Baltazar does not become mired in the debate about the maleness of Jesus. She categorically states that gender is not the important issue: "The question for us is not how to make Jesus become a woman. Rather, the transcended Christ can be the embodiment of the feminine principle, the Shakti, the energizer and vitalizer. It is a serious limitation to express the resurrected Christ in purely male or patriarchal terms. Only women can liberate him from this gross limitation."[91]

Does Baltazar follow the path of Indian Gnostic Christology? No, for she does not limit her understanding of Jesus the Christ to the metaphysical realm. On the one hand, she certainly gives importance to the historical, human Jesus who taught us the prayer that pleads for the wholeness and holiness of the world. Jesus taught a prayer that reimaged God as one who is as close to us as a father or a mother. That God is against any form of violence—whether hunger or the infliction of pain on others. This prayer calls the believer to embrace the opportunity to fulfill the highest potential of the human being: ensuring justice and equality; sharing and partnership; and living according to a sense of stewardship and interconnectedness with all creation. Baltazar says Jesus' prayer is an appeal to reclaim the original identity and image of human beings as the children of God. On the other hand, she goes beyond the concept that only the male Jesus can embody the Christ and reveal God. She liberates Christ from the patriarchal grip, saying:

> With his bodily death the maleness of Christ, too, dies. The risen Christ must be liberated from the violent male language and this only women can do. Drawing from indigenous and primal religions, we need to make the resurrection of Christ become actual in our culture. In this way Indian culture, too, will experience a transformation by making alive an Indian cosmology of wholeness and interconnectedness which is truly the liberative potential of the cosmic Christ.[92]

Baltazar has opened a new path in understanding Christology from Asian women's perspectives. The notion of Jesus the Christ as Shakti is compelling in that Shakti is the creative principle or creative energy present in all things—both in humanity *(purusha)* and nature *(prakriti)*. One need not worry if the names and images Asian women attribute to Jesus do not coincide with classic, Western, patriarchal notions. Ultimately, Asian women must not allow anyone to define or to limit their experience of God to a particular mold, and, as Baltazar warns, no one should impose his or her experience of God on others as if it were universal. After all, she says:

> God is multiple in communion.
> God is unity in diversity.
> God is universally local.
> God is transcendentally immanent.[93]

Jesus the Christ and Shakti as Wisdom Incarnate

Monica Melanchton is in full agreement with Baltazar. Women can liberate Christ from male-oriented moorings and interpretation, Melanchton suggests, by seeing God as Wisdom, and, consequently, by recognizing Jesus as Wisdom Incarnate. In the book of Proverbs,

Wisdom is the feminine personification of God's presence and activity. Wisdom gives life and wholeness; she is the tree of life, with the implication that she is the source of fertility. Wisdom governs order and stability; she is the master designer; she is the Word (Prv 3:13–20). Wisdom was with God, active in creation, and thus, Melanchton asserts, creation is the result of God in solidarity with Wisdom, "the female principle."[94] Can we identify Wisdom with Shakti? Melanchton does not categorically mention Shakti in connection with Wisdom (*hokmah* in Hebrew and *sophia* in Greek). Nevertheless, the connection is evident in the juxtaposition of characteristics and tasks of Shakti and Sophia. Melanchton only clearly connects Jesus with Woman Wisdom (Prv 1:20–33; 8:1–21): Jesus was a street preacher, one who gathered the lost, confronted injustice and evil, fed the hungry, and empowered the weak and the downtrodden. Jesus is the Wisdom of God, whom God "sent in one form that she might be with human beings, and in another form that she herself might be a human being."[95] Ajit Mookerjee explains that Shakti, also as Kali, is the Great Wisdom who "nourish[es] new life with the blood-nectar from her neck."[96]

Shakti, as Wisdom and as the creative principle, inspired the women of the Chipko movement to hug the trees and protect the forest from wanton destruction. Itwari Devi, a local village elder, affirms that the women who initiated the Chipko movement have drawn energy from Shakti in their struggle against the mining operations in the Nahi-Barkot area. Hindu ecofeminist activist, physicist, and philosopher Vandana Shiva has observed that women like Itwari Devi have "a kind and level of knowledge that no western trained technocrat can have access to. . . . [Their] participation in nature is the source of a different kind of knowledge and power, which opposes the knowledge and power that is causing destruction."[97]

The Importance of Shakti Christology

Reclaiming Shakti in constructing a Christology is liberating to women. It also opens up spaces for conversation between Christians and Hindus in India, especially among women. The role of Shakti in Chipko women's struggle to protect a forest demonstrates how a Shakti Christology can open the door to future dialogue with the oppressed Indian people as they seek inspiration and empowerment in their project of resistance against the growth of Mammon in India.

Gnanadason thinks that Shakti, as a spiritual energy, is the "essence of great religions in Asia."[98] This statement coincides with Hans Koester's suspicion that Shakti worship is the primal religion of Asia, as indicated by the non-Hindu features of the practices of Shakti worshipers or the Shakta. Koester, a Shaktism scholar, has observed three significant features of Shakti worship practices. First, the Shaktas do not pay attention to the caste of the worshipers in their rituals. Second, as part of their ritual worship, the Shaktas eat meat and drink wine that they offer to Shakti, who calls them around the table of fellowship. This practice is reminiscent of Hokmah (Wisdom) inviting her children to the feast (Prov 9:1–9). Just as Hokmah and Shakti call their children to the banquet, Jesus calls people from all corners of the world to celebrate life around the table of fellowship. Third, Koester further notes that a "unique feature of Shakti-worship" is the "participation of women in the ceremonies."[99] Jesus, indeed, is both Hokmah and Shakti, who gathers her brood under her wings, the one who calls people to unite and to celebrate the banquet.

A Christology that embraces Shakti leads to some important reflections. First, it is not androcentric. It could, therefore, inspire the prevention of violence against women, children, and vulnerable peoples. Shakti empowers women in their struggle for full humanity. Shakti enables feminist theologians to reclaim their cultural heritage in reimaging the Sacred, especially the feminine dimension of the Divine. Finally, a Shakti Christology challenges Christians to transcend images, concepts, and language that are imprisoned in the patriarchal norm.[100] Melanchton stresses that lifting up Woman Wisdom and identifying her with Christ liberates Jesus from androcentric dogma. The imagery of Jesus as Wisdom Incarnate also allows for the acknowledgment and celebration of women's creative power—that women contribute to the sustenance of life in all its socioeconomic and political dimensions.[101]

Second, it is not anthropocentric. It helps human beings reflect in humility that they are latecomers into this world, and Wisdom demands that human beings respect the reality that their survival is inevitably intertwined with the survival of the planet. Kwok Pui-lan of Hong Kong affirms Melanchton's Wisdom Christology when she hails the advantages of employing the philosophical and popular notion of Shakti to interpret Christ. She notes that Shakti links Christology to ecofeminist spirituality among Indian feminists who come from various traditions.

Third, Shakti Christology potentially empowers people to fight racism. Shakti explicitly affirms people of all colors. Although Shakti sometimes appears as the white goddess, the iconography of Shakti usually portrays her as black, dark as the night. All colors belong to the created world, her domain.[102] The image of Jesus the Christ as Shakti is the antithesis of Christ the victor, ruler, and king who dominates powerless humans, nations, and the planet. Just as women in their daily lives come into close contact with seemingly small but crucial things in life, Jesus the Christ, as the Shakti-Wisdom of God, affirms the "small things" of life.[103]

Fourth, as Gnanadason notes, Shakti, if seriously considered as the foundation of Asian spirituality, makes sacramental the relationship between humanity and creation. Shakti has reemerged and stirred Asian women to new ways of seeing things and new ways of living. Asian women are finding the courage to question oppressive traditions. They are moving away from notions of freedom and power motivated by self-gratification. They are now more conscious of their responsibility to the oppressed and to all of creation. In Shakti, Asian women find God, the God that Jesus reveals to us.[104] Jesus the Christ is Shakti and allows women to discover a new spirituality in Asia. This potential is manifest wherever a new community affirms womanhood and many forms of motherhood; where women have come of age to define themselves; where women critically participate in liberation struggles; where women celebrate commonalities as well as differences among peoples; and where women look to indigenous traditions for God's revelation. Finally, a Shakti-Wisdom Christology puts Jesus the Christ within a paradigm that is pluralist and spacious for dialogue. Thus, it empowers women and all oppressed peoples to rise up and struggle for the well being and liberation of the created world from injustice and denigration.

Do Indian women find Jesus in the Ganges? They do, but not in the usual image of Jesus as traditional Christianity has defined him. Removing sexist, patriarchal, kyriarchal lenses from their eyes, Indian feminist theologians have released themselves from the bonds set by the Nicea-Chalcedon formula to rewrite what Jesus the Christ means for them.

Chapter 3

Korean Women

Meeting Jesus at the Foot of the Salt Mountain

Is it possible to understand multiple Christs
or to recognize communal Christs?
If Jesus became Christ, what made him so?

—CHUNG SOOK-JA,
"BECOMING CHRIST: A WOMAN'S VISION"

A university-educated Korean woman became an initiated shaman. She conducted a shamanistic ritual to bless the founding of the Korean women's liberation organization and celebrated women's power by dancing on a sharp sword while holding her infant daughter. At another time she "performed another *kut* in front of a factory while women workers demonstrated against multi-national corporations" to exorcise the powers of capitalism, the oppressive multinational corporations, and military dictatorship.[1] Some people believe that the spirit of the mountain Baek-Du guides her work toward the unification of the two Koreas. Baek-Du is traditionally called Chosen, meaning "morning calm" for Koreans. The name also refers to Korea's position east of China and in the northeastern part of Asia.

In the indigenous shamanistic tradition of Korea, salt has the power to drive away evil spirits; therefore, it is a positive symbol. A mountain that turns into a salt mountain, albeit symbolically, evokes great significance within one who witnesses it through a vision or a dream. Especially to the marginalized, such a vision means good news and signals hope. When she was pregnant, Kwang-Myung had a dream. In that dream, she saw Mudeng Mountain of Kwangju turned into a salt mountain. To her, the transformation of Mudeng into a salt mountain heralded a good future for the baby she was carrying in her womb.[2] Through dream, she experienced an epiphany of the Buddha and the blessings of the good spirits. Kwang-Myung eventually became a Christian, and one wonders if she met Jesus at the foot of the salt mountain too.

Mudeng Mountain witnessed the bloodbath that marked the struggle of the oppressed people, the *minjung*, for justice and democracy. In the 1980s, this "city of youth" became the site where people, young and old, protested against government repression and demanded democratic governance. Here, the South Korean soldiers cut off the breasts of young women they captured, stabbed the bellies of pregnant women, and killed at least two thousand young people during the Kwangju Uprising against the repressive government of Chun Doohwan.[3] Here at the foot of Kwang-Myung's Mudeng Mountain, women saw Jesus in the suffering of the people, but they also found a glimmer of light as Mudeng turned metaphorically into a salt mountain.

In this chapter I intend to show that Asian women are capable of doing Christology creatively once they free themselves from the blinders of traditional patriarchal constructs. To do that, I examine the emerging Christologies in the writings of South Korean Christian women. I give an overview of the impact of religion and culture on the lives of Korean women. Then I discuss *minjung* women's understanding of and relationship with Jesus as interpreted by Korean women theologians. From there, I proceed to examine the Christian Korean women theologians' understanding of the cross in relation to *han-puri* and their notion of Jesus as the priest of *han*. Finally, I examine their concept of the Woman Jesus and the symbolic Woman Messiah.

THE COMFORT WOMEN: BREAKING THEIR SILENCE AND NAMING THEIR PAIN

In reading the story of Korea one must not lose sight of the stories of women's experiences. A horrible chapter in the history of Korea is the story of the exploitation of Korean women by forcing them to provide "comfort" to foreign troops. At the turn of the twentieth century, Japan, after many prior attempts, succeeded in gaining control and occupying Korea. When Japan made Korea its strategic base during its aggressive campaign against China in 1938, Japan conscripted Korean men into the army. They forcibly took young Korean women to become sex slaves for the Japanese troops. These "comfort women" appeared in military report statistics as "war supplies."[4] Although the Japanese government has adamantly withheld military documents, a study conducted by a Korean feminist group estimated that more than 200,000 Korean women became comfort women from 1932 to 1945.[5]

Jong Ok-Sun was seventy-five years old when she mustered the courage to tell of her five-year ordeal at the hands of the Japanese army. In 1934, when she was fourteen years old, the Japanese police stationed in Phabal-ri, Phungsan County, kidnapped and raped her before turning her, along with other girls, over to the Japanese army barracks. An average of fifty imperial soldiers "used" or abused each girl every day.

> Everyday [*sic*] many visitors came. If girls cried out, rags were put into their mouths. When resistance continued, soldiers threatened to kill them by pointing the blade of a dagger at their private parts. In this way, my body was bruised and my legs got injured. One day four years later, eight Japanese officers appeared naked and started making lewd advances towards me. After doing all manner of inhuman acts, they thrust the shaft of a dagger inside my private part. Unbearable, I bit them [*sic*]. They took me out, tortured me with water, and hung me naked upside down from a horizontal bar. And then, they forced an iron club inside my mouth and whirled it round to break all my teeth. Not satisfied with this, they placed my lips inside out and tattooed on them with a stamp full of needles, and continued tattooing on my breasts, backs, legs, stomach and even on my private part. When I lost my consciousness, they threw me in the garbage dump.
>
> Of course, such a tragedy is not confined to me alone. The "comfort woman" life forced by the Japs brought death as well as unbearable physical and mental agony to many Korean women. Though many years have passed since then, physical and mental scars still remain. No matter how the Japanese Government may pay compensation, they can never wipe out the deep-rooted grudges and scars left in my heart and on my body and, moreover, the history of the crimes committed by the old Japanese can never be concealed or erased.[6]

The war is long over, but the comfort women continue to suffer the wounds it has inflicted on them. In spite of testimonies of Japanese nationals, some of them doctors, who had witnessed the plight of the comfort women during the war, the Japanese government continues to refuse to make a public apology to the victims.

The war is long over, but a system that oppresses women goes on. Women suffer, this time, under the *kisaeng* system of South Korea. In the past decades the *kisaeng* system has involved kidnapping women and putting them in brothels to entertain aristocrats and local officials. Today the *kisaeng* system serves the tourism business and earns dollars for both the perpetrators of this practice and the government that flourishes while women become sex objects for foreign men and victims of sexual violence.[7] They contract sexually transmitted diseases, including HIV and AIDS. The South Korean government has sacrificed more than 200,000 Korean daughters to feed the appetite of those who benefit from prostitution. Ironically, it has transformed more than twenty thousand Korean women into prostitutes just to entertain US troops, troops that stay in the military bases in Korea.[8] These troops' sole purpose is to keep the two Koreas divided.

The prostitutes or sex workers—estimated at between 500,000 and one million—make up one-seventh of South Korea's total workforce.[9] Lee Mi Kung insists that the "very seeds of prostitution lie not in the bankruptcy of [the] individual or social value system [of women], but in the structural contradictions of the South Korean society."[10]

THE IRON GRIP OF PATRIARCHAL RELIGION AND CULTURE

Lee Oo Chung, a New Testament scholar and activist, notes that the coming of Confucianism, particularly the Chuja school, into Korea from China brought the fast development of the notion of class as well as the patriarchal "ethics of subordination."[11] The Confucian book *Mingan Kenyusu* instructed women to cultivate the virtue of subservience. It instilled the idea that the king is the sky, the people are the earth, and man-woman relationships should reflect this understanding: that man is the sky, and the woman is the earth. In the context of marriage the husband is the king to whom the woman must bow; she must serve him with respect.[12] Infused with Confucianist values, Korean society deprives women of their moral agency, dignity, and humanity. It persecutes, discriminates, and limits their world to the family. It socializes women to think of marriage as the ultimate fulfillment of their lives. A woman's calling is to do her wifely duties, while a man's calling is to tread the path of the sages. When a girl marries, she ceases to belong to her family. Henceforth, she is supposed to belong to her husband's family. Yet, even though she becomes an outsider to her own family, she does not gain a place on her husband's family tree.[13] A married woman retains her maiden name, but rather than a mark of liberation it is an indication of her marginalization and oppression. Comparable to the law of Manu in Hinduism, Confucianism's code demands triple obedience from women: as a daughter, she must obey her father, as a wife she must obey her husband, and in her old age, she must obey her son.[14] Disobedience requires punishment in various forms. According to a Korean proverb, "A woman becomes a fox if she is not beaten up for three days."[15]

Society expects lower-class men to work like beasts of burden. Yet, women are even more miserable, because they have the additional burden of living in their parents-in-law's house. The women express their sufferings in *kayo*, a genre of folk song, or *minyo*, a women's song of protest against oppressive institutions and cultures that focuses on women's daily struggle for survival. Through these kinds of song, a woman can at least express resistance to her father-in-law's abusive power. Take the case of a daughter-in-law who must find a way to ease the demand of her husband's parents that she pay for the silver cup she accidentally has broken. She may not be able to say it directly to her parents-in-law, but to vent her pain, she responds by composing a *minyo*:

> As your son and I departed from my house, we said goodbye to my family holding hands warmly. Then are you saying that the silver cup is that important? When stars rose high into the night and no one was aware, I offered my whole [being] to my husband, your son.
>
> If you compensate my broken virginity, I will compensate your broken cup.[16]

Patriarchy has made some women collaborate with men in oppressing other women. Mothers-in-law and sisters-in-law tend to abuse the wife of a son or a brother by giving her too much work. The daughter-in-law becomes a slave of the family. The tradition of *minyo* has become a venue for women to reveal their experiences of oppression by other women. Consider this *minyo* from the Kochang area. It points to an overworked woman's fatigue and struggle to avoid violence from the women in her husband's household:

> Sleep, Sleep! Don't come!
> The sleep coming to my eyes will cause much talk and
> fault finding.
> Take out my sleepy eyes and hang them on the orange
> tree;
> When I come in and out of the house
> I see the tree nodding sleepily.[17]

Korea's patriarchal culture is a product of the Korean cultural and religious mix of discriminatory practices that have burdened women with suffering. Yet, the Japanese occupation of Korea from the turn of the twentieth century until the Second World War proved even more devastating for Korean women. The Korean girls whom the Japanese had taken as sex slaves and the Korean people whom the US atomic bombs "melted" in Hiroshima and Nagasaki were mostly poor, lower-class Korean people—the *minjung*. Even after those catastrophes, the nightmare of war was far from over for Korean women. A decade later the competition between the former Union of Soviet Socialist Republics and the capitalist United States dragged their country into the Korean War. By 1953 Korea was divided into two parts—the North and the South—by a demilitarized zone along the 38th parallel. The division has kept more than ten thousand families separated for more than half of a century.[18] Thousands dreamed, hoped, and worked for the reunification of Korea, but many died heartbroken by the pain of their separation from their wife or husband, sons, daughters, fathers, mothers, and friends. In their lifetime their suffering found no redemption. Those brokenhearted people have yielded to death's embrace, and many of their remaining relatives live on to become part of the *minjung* people of Korea.

KOREAN WOMEN UNDER THE CLAWS OF THE TIGER

South Korea quickly recovered from the war and rose to become one of the four economic tigers of Asia. Its recovery, however, came at a price: the sponsorship of the US government and its Bretton-Woods agencies that dictate and control the economic policies of the country. To this day, the presence of US military bases in Korea symbolizes foreign control. In recent years the Korean tiger has joined in the race of globalization and has fully engaged in a consumerist economy, even to the extent of threatening its foreign master. Its *chaebols*—Korean conglomerates whose component corporations are usually engaged in diverse and unrelated areas of production—reach consumers all around the world through the proliferation of their appliances, electronic gadgets, cars, and beautiful garments.[19] Families usually own *chaebols*. All products carry "Made in Korea" labels. What most consumers do not know is the story behind those "Made in Korea" labels: the life stories of struggling *minjung* workers, especially women *minjung*. These people have not been able to live a humane life because the Korean government has protected the interests of its *chaebols* and foreign multinational companies in order to project its image as an emerging economic tiger. The South Korean government has conceded to the regional economic council and to world trade rules that govern a quota game. Quotas affect not only the workforce but also come at the expense of the farmers. Korean farmers suffer from the devastating effects of the government's import-export economic policy as well as its low-grain-price policy.[20] Farmers have found themselves buried in debt for their agricultural investment while their products struggle to compete with imported farm products. The tiger has taken a toll on people's health, life, and future. Young people flock to the cities to seek job opportunities. The phenomenon of migration of people from the rural areas to the cities increases the population in the slums. Children at a tender age must face the harsh realities of life in Korean society.

An often-quoted poem entitled "My Mother's Name Is Worry"—written from the point of view of a child—records the oppression and suffering that urban poor women continue to face at the nexus of sexism-class-culture. The twelve-year-old Korean slum girl who wrote the poem remains anonymous. Nevertheless, she lives in all the slum areas of Asia. Listen to her cry:

> In summer, my mother worries about water;
> In winter, she worries about coal briquettes,
> And all year long, she worries about rice.

In daytime, my mother worries about living;
At night, she worries about the children,
And all day long, she worries and worries.

This is why my mother's name is Worry.
My father's name is Drunken Frenzy,
And my name is Tears and Sighs.[21]

Women workers in the factories are victims of poor working conditions, low discriminatory wages, sexual abuse, and unfair labor practices that include union busting, arrests, torture, and dispersal of picket lines and protest rallies accompanied by tear gas and bullets. To make the women's situation worse, supposedly progressive male unionists display their sexist and androcentric fear of sharing power by discriminating against women's unions. Women's dexterity and capacity to pay attention to small details have usually been valued by the factories, especially in microchips production. However, these women rarely find promotion to supervisory jobs because companies traditionally reserve those jobs for men.

The situation of women workers has steadily worsened with the advent of globalization, which is interlocked with the reign of technocracy. The power and knowledge of science and technology, when combined with the power of capital and the military, create a formidable, oppressive system. This system encompasses all of human life. The new gods of this globalized technocratic-military-capitalist world crush women's lives. While journalist Jennifer Veale thinks of the Internet boom as a "godsend for women in Korea," she fairly cites the observation of Kang Sun Mii of the Center for Women's Studies at Ewha Women's University in Seoul that as South Korea has advanced technologically, the condition of women workers has declined.[22] "Progress" pushes women to the periphery more than ever before. Indeed, not many women have opportunities to learn the skills and knowledge required to work with such technology.

Meanwhile, multinational companies and *chaebols* are setting the "ripe old age" for retirement of women at twenty-six. This is based on their assumption that beyond that age, women would be raising children. Women's refusal to go along with the social practices and patriarchal work culture in the corporate world usually characterized by "late-night drinking and golf weekends" ensures that women do not get promotions. Women in the corporate world suffer prejudice at different levels. Mi Hae, a twenty-nine-year-old communications worker, does not see bright prospects for her work:

> I'll probably never get a promotion. . . . No women in this company have, at least beyond assistant general level. . . . I can't think of a single woman at that level. Management doesn't want to give women any real responsibilities, but they say they can't promote women because they haven't been tested.[23]

Nor is life rosy for a married worker. Once she goes home, a married woman worker does not get to rest. The life of Mrs. Ku Cha-myong, as portrayed in the poem below, written by Ko Chong-Hui, gives us a glimpse of the burden a married factory worker has to carry. This woman seems to bear the whole world on her shoulders. Yet, hers is only one story among the many stories of ordinary Korean women who struggle to survive:

> Mrs. Ku Cha-myong, a working mother and wife,
> who has a seven-month-old baby,
> Begins to doze as soon as she boards the shuttle bus in
> the morning
> Warmed by the morning sun,
> She dozes all the way from Ansan, Kyonggi-do to
> Youido, Seoul.
> Nodding to the front and nodding to the sides.
> Horn blasts cannot wake her,
> The seasons flit past the window,
> And azaleas and chestnut blossoms smile;
> But Mrs. Ku Cha-myong dozes away, like a sleepy
> Buddha.
> Yes, the first ten minutes
> Are the ten minutes she suckled her baby last night.
> And the next ten minutes
> Are the ten minutes she served medicine to her mother-
> in-law.
> That's right, and the next ten minutes
> Is the time she spent putting her drunken husband to
> bed.
> At the beginning and end of each working day
> She dozes and shakes like a pansy flower.

The flowers on the dining table bind women fast to
their duties,
But from every roof over every kitchen
A family's welfare sustained by a woman
Is shooting an arrow of refusal
Towards the sleep of death,
Unnoticed by anyone.[24]

THE IMPORTANCE OF STORIES IN KOREAN WOMEN'S THEOLOGIES

There are a number of reasons for using stories from the experiences of Korean women extensively. First, Korean women's theologies emerged from the interweaving of their own life stories with their interpretation of the experiences of *minjung* women. Second, the Korean *minjung* themselves prefer stories rather than abstract logic that is fabricated from the desk of the elite culture. The *minjung* women treasure stories that "embrace the living wisdom drawn from concrete life situations."[25] Generally hardworking, the *minjung* look at nature as the mother of life, which sustains and provides them companionship in their struggles for survival. They weave their life stories, songs, dances, and art forms into the fabric of their religiosity and spirituality. Taking this perspective opens up the world view of the *minjung*, as well as their religiosity. Third, the *minjung* have difficulty believing in an abstract God. Their indigenous myths and stories tell them that the deities were previously human beings who did noble things for their fellow beings, went through suffering, and come out victorious from life-risking ordeals. Thus, after their death these good human beings were exulted and became gods and goddesses.[26] An example of this is the story of the first ancestor goddess of Shamanism, Princess Baridegi.

> Princess Baridegi, whose name means a deserted or abandoned child, was the youngest of the seven daughters of King Ogu the Great and Queen Byong-on. Frustrated that his wife had once again not borne him a son, the king ordered his servants to put the girl baby in a jade chest and to sacrifice her to the Dragon king of the sea. However, a golden turtle rescued the chest and carried it on its back to a mountain. A couple found the chest and raised the baby. Time passed. After a time, the king and the

> queen got sick. Only the spring water from the western paradise could heal them. Since the six daughters refused to search for the healing spring water, the king ordered his servants to search for the Baridegi princess. Upon knowing that her original parents were dying, the Baridegi princess wept in sorrow. To make the long story short, the Baridegi princess set out on the journey, went through many tough ordeals, and endured great sufferings to find the spring water that could save her parents. She successfully brought back the healing water and revived her parents. When she died, she became the goddess of healing and the first ancestor of the Korean shamans.[27]

The story shows that the pre-Shamanism culture of Korea was also patriarchal. Yet Baridegi, a victim of patriarchy, showed a different way of living by taking steps towards forgiveness, reconciliation of relationships, healing of broken bodies, and restoration of life. Being the daughter of a king, whom ancients considered divine, she too was considered divine. Yet, she also experienced abandonment, suffering, and hardship—the life common to most regular human beings. In the course of her ordeals she humanized a patriarchal giant and blessed dead bodies of childless women.

Choi Man Ja points to the similarity between the Baridegi myths and the story of Jesus, who gave himself for all human beings.[28] It is not surprising that the historical figure of Jesus, who suffered, was tortured, and died because of his acts of great love for the poor and the oppressed, is a compelling figure for the *minjung*. It is certainly easier for them to understand, at the very least, that the human Jesus became God after his death because of his good teachings and compassion for the suffering people.

EMERGING CHRISTOLOGIES OF KOREAN WOMEN

Jesus and *Minjung* Women's Struggle for a Meaningful Life

In order to understand *minjung* women, how they see and relate to Jesus, a deeper understanding of the term *minjung* will be helpful. *Minjung* comes from the word *min*, "people," and *jung*, "mass." Thus, *minjung* means a mass of people. Park Soon Kyung, a feminist theologian, explains that this term belongs to a family of related terms, including *minjok*, "nation" or "people"; and *minju*, "democracy."[29] The *minjung* are people whose political, economic, and sociocultural rights and opportunities have been taken away. They are the mass of despised, oppressed, and exploited people who belong to the lowest rung in the hierarchy of the Korean society. However, the term carries additional meanings. Recalling his stay in the interrogation center with other professors and Christians during the martial-law days in 1980, Suh David Kwang-sun says that the *minjung* are "present where there is socio-cultural alienation, economic exploitation, and political repression." He stresses that the *minjung* include ethnic groups that are discriminated against, the colonized nations or races, oppressed women, suppressed intellectuals who work in behalf of the oppressed, and exploited workers and farmers.[30] The self-understanding of the Korean *minjung* is much broader than the Marxist concept of the proletariat.[31] Many Korean theologians involved in the democratization struggles in South Korea claim that they have met and seen the face of Jesus among the *minjung*.

Taking into consideration Suh's definition of *minjung*, Korean women theologians who experience sociocultural alienation, economic exploitation, political suppression, and patriarchal domination and discrimination are counted as *minjung*. Such a definition has also expanded the traditional understanding of *minjung* as those that belong to the masses of ordinary people.

Minjung women, like their male comrades, have found Jesus among the *minjung*. Oh Cha-gyo, a former garment factory worker turned evangelist, says she "found Jesus the Laborer *(Nodongja Yesu)* among the workers."[32] Another *minjung* woman worker imagines Jesus dressed in a factory-worker's uniform and helping her. She has found her Christ in the workers, the *minjung* women.[33] What these *minjung* women are saying about Jesus, therefore, is not new. Yet, *minjung* women have a nuanced view of Jesus that makes their perspective distinct from that of *minjung* men. Although, as Koreans, they share the same history, the women carry with them a long history of subjugation that the men have not experienced. Women know the added burden of oppression because of their gender. That is precisely why the women assert that they are the *minjung* of the *minjung*. The systems of oppression—such as those fostering economic, political, social, and racial discrimination—are themselves built upon the discriminatory cultural foundation of the patriarchal religious traditions of Confucianism, Buddhism, and Christianity. Korean women have had to tackle these multiple layers of oppression and suffering that society has imposed upon them. Women are at the bottom of the heap, Korean feminist theologians agree.

The image of Jesus as the abandoned one resonates among *minjung* women. *Minjung* women factory workers cry, "How could God allow our efforts to secure our rights to be crushed?" In the *minjung* women's cry, Oh Cha-gyo hears Jesus among them crying out, "My God, my God, why have you forsaken me?"[34] The *minjung* woman's cry does not evoke in her the necessity to preach about Christian suffering and humility. Preaching about humility, usually interpreted as subservience, is no longer relevant for *minjung* women workers. Oh Cha-gyo believes that women have suffered long enough "for the sins that the privileged people committed."[35] She does not explain to *minjung* women workers the complicated doctrines of God. Oh Cha-gyo simply finds Jesus as a worker among the *minjung* women workers.

Just as Jesus suffered on the cross involuntarily, *minjung* women workers experience suffering because of the sins that the powerful and the privileged continue to commit. The suffering of the *minjung* is a result of the sinful acts of the powerful, the intentional acts of imposing suffering on *minjung* women. Pae Pok-sun, who has worked with prostitutes, reports that these women *minjung* reject the church's Jesus, who comes only to tell them that they are sinners. These women surely need God, but they do not need a condemning God. They welcome a Jesus who comes to visit them as his friends, one who understands their suffering bodies and souls and embodies God's compassion for them.[36]

As I reflect on the situation of many women in Korea and in Asia, I find Engelbert Mveng's broader definition of poverty, "anthropological poverty," relevant. It is deeper and broader than economic and political poverty, because it is about the "despoiling of human beings . . . of everything that constitutes their being and essence."[37] Mindful of Mary's Magnificat (Lk 1:46–55), Korean women theologians are convinced that the oppressed and powerless women *minjung* are crucial players in Korea's history of salvation, a history that they hope will ultimately include national reunification. Thus, they have resolved to stand in solidarity with the women *minjung* of the Third World to work for social transformation.

The Importance of Shamanism in Korean Women's Christology

Without factoring in Shamanism, Choi Man Ja advises, one cannot speak knowledgeably of the *minjung* people, especially of *minjung* women. She contends that one must understand Shamanism in order to find the very pulse of the Korean people's lives and to enter into their world view. Shamanism is the air that Korean *minjung* women breathe. Korea's folk music, dance, and plays trace their roots back to the *minjung*'s original religion, Choi says.[38] Shamanism as a religion emerged naturally from the *minjung*'s longing to live a life free from calamities and filled with blessings. The people's deep connection with nature led them to believe in an abundance of spirits and deities in the cosmos that gave them inspiration and hope of prosperity. Shamanism is resplendent with environmental spirits; spirits of the dead ancestors and of human beings who became gods and goddesses; the spirits of foreign religions that came to Korea; and ghosts.[39] Although the number of female deities in Korean Shamanism is debated, there is a good number of goddesses. One study says the majority of the deities in Shamanism are female. Some Korean Shamanism scholars believe that in the southern culture the primitive images of gods were female.[40] These studies also suggest that the actual number of female gods has declined over time, especially in the north. As Korean culture changed over the centuries, the patriarchal images of gods replaced the original feminine images of goddesses.[41]

Shamanism is pervasive in Asia, and Korea has held to this tradition. Shamanism is a *minjung* belief that revolves around the shaman or the *mudang*, the priest of Shamanism. These priests are usually women who stand out from other women. Korean Shamanism has no hierarchy, no prophets, no temples, no scriptures, and no dogma. In other words, it is not an institution. The *mudang* is the only important figure in it. Its ritual life involves the dance and music of the *mudang*, and her utterances come from the spirits and gods. The shaman presides over the *kut*, the shaman ritual of driving away calamities and of inviting the blessings of the spirits.[42] This ritual manifests the essence of the Korean people and of their culture. One may also understand Shamanism as a religion of *minjung* women because the majority of the participants of the *kut*, particularly the *han-pu-ri*, are women, and 65 to 70 percent of the *mudangs* are women.[43] Some scholars do not consider Shamanism to be a religion but merely a "phenomenon of the *mudang*" or "custom of *mudang*" *(musok)*. Suh David Kwang-sun and Choi Man Ja, along with Korean feminist theologians, argue that the *musok* or "custom of *mudang*" itself fulfills the qualifying notion of religion to have a "contractual obligation with a divine being."[44] Choi Man Ja believes that a distinctly Korean feminist theology will be able

to stand on a solid foundation only if it reclaims the strong feminine images of God in the Korean myths and culture that are rooted in Shamanistic tradition.

The Cross and the Relevance of *Han-pu-ri*

As Suh puts it, Shamanism is a religion of *han*.[45] Chung Hyun Kyung quotes Hyun Young-Hak, who offers a graphic and encompassing description of *han:*

> Han is a sense of unresolved resentments against injustice suffered, a sense of helplessness because of the overwhelming odds against injustice suffered, a feeling of total abandonment, a feeling of acute pain of sorrow in one's guts and bowels making the whole body writhe and wiggle, and an obstinate urge to take "revenge" and to right the wrong all these constitute.[46]

Han accumulates in the body and the spirit, and the *mudang*'s task is to exorcise the *han* in order to restore the person to wholeness. If *han* is a collective feeling of the Korean *minjung*,[47] the situation of the *minjung* women discussed above makes them the "embodiment of the worst han."[48] *Han* overflows in women's bodies and minds because of the oppressive combination of Korea's patriarchal religio-cultural system and the people's experience and memory of colonialism and neocolonialism, militarism, globalized capitalism and of the poverty these "isms" bring. All these are components of the cross that *minjung* women daily carry. The life of the comfort women also illustrates how Korean society forced them to carry a horrible cross. In Jesus' context the cross signified state power and state violence not only against criminals but also against dissenters. The cross also symbolized innocent people's sufferings brought about by the sins of those who abuse power. The cross is a symbol of humiliation and suffering. Like the cross of Jesus, the cross that women carry is a result of a social and political system that lacks concern for the weak and lowly.

Poet Chang Jung-Nim expresses this view in a poem. She sees the crucified Jesus in the lives of women whom the Japanese used as "public toilets" and who were "betrayed by the fatherland," Korea. Chang calls South Korea the "fatherland"—a male-dominated country whose hypocritical concept of morality rejects the comfort women as "dirty and shameful" and whose men push the women away only to protect male honor. Chang sees the suffering comfort women on the crucifix, an allusion to the image of the crucified Jesus. She writes:

> Who can wash all of your bloodstained body?
> Who can stitch together your torn heart
> and bring it to its last resting place?
>
> You were crushed underfoot sooner than the fatherland,
> You were forgotten sooner than the liberation,
> You who are the flowers of history's tears.
>
> Who can lull your revenge-filled heart
> to sleep, in its last resting place?
> You! You are the victim, fallen, as war plunder,
> as public toilets. You are like a *pakkokt*.[49]
>
> You, pain-filled crucifix of earth,
> You blossom anew like flowers trampled under weed,
> You challenge us, who are burdened with shame and resentment,
> You touch the fatherland who betrayed you, filled with anger.
>
> We want to give you a secure shelter,
> come back, and rest, when you
> are no longer a long-haired sixteen-year-old virgin.
>
> Today we want to construct a memorial for you
> so that no more women will fall victim to colonial brutality.
> You are innocent. You are our mother.
>
> Now wrap up your wings.
> No longer waver from side to side.
>
> You who are the crucifix of Korea
> Repose in comfort
> You who are the flowers of Korea's tears.[50]

Chang interweaves her reflection on the crucifixion of the women from the perspective of the Christian faith and from within the Shamanistic tradition. *Han-pu-ri kut* is a ritual that releases the *han*.

Christians need to rethink why they keep the cross and what it means for them. Considering *han-pu-ri*, Christians may keep the symbol of the cross to remind them of their task to expose and stop all forms of violence. This is necessary because perpetrators of violence almost always try to erase their sin from people's collective memory. The Japanese government continues to refuse to make a public apology to the women it has sinned against. South Korea, Chang's fatherland, also tried to bury the memories of these afflicted women in order to avoid shame. The result is that the spirits of the comfort women are restless and full of *han*. To release the *han*, the evil must be named. Today, the cross must be seen as it is—an instrument of torture and death. It stands for the state-endorsed sexual violence against the comfort women. It brings into the open the evil of patriarchal domination that encompasses the old and new forms and faces of militarism and colonization. The cross as part of Christian *kut* (ritual) confronts us with the memory of Jesus' violent death. Thus, setting up a memorial is an act of naming the evil. Chang knows this and assures these *han*-ridden spirits that women today will make not only a memorial but a *kut* to release the *han*. Moreover, Chang knows that the *kut* only marks the beginning of *han-pu-ri*. The people must take concrete action to seek justice for the comfort women. Such "secure shelter" will put the torn, revenge-filled hearts at peace.

Of particular importance to Korean feminist theology, therefore, is the *han-pu-ri kut*. Chung Hyun Kyung makes this point clear and asserts that feminist theology in Korea must take *han-pu-ri* as its purpose and norm.[51] Suh David Kwang-sun, who must be referring to *han-pu-ri* in describing *mudang kut*, notes that psychological studies view this ritual as a process of dramatized counseling that powerfully uses the principles and steps of "projection, catharsis, transference, consolation, admonition, release, or salvation."[52] Chung explains that, from the *minjung* perspective, this ritual provides a chance for the voiceless, *han*-ridden ghosts to tell their stories. While addressing both the individual and the collective needs of the *minjung*, the ritual challenges the community to do something to remove the source of oppression and pain for the ghosts as well as to comfort or to negotiate with the ghosts.[53] In other words, *han-pu-ri* is an opportunity for community therapy, repentance, and healing both for the living and for the ghosts. The poem "You Are the Crucifix of Korea" illustrates this point. Constructing a memorial for the *han*-ridden ghosts of comfort women means, for the poet Chang, fighting colonialism.

The *minjung* women of the present strive to break the cycle of its violence.

Jesus the *Mudang* of *Han*: Appropriating Shamanist Tradition in Christology

Drawing from Shamanism as Korea's indigenous religion, the image of Jesus that emerges most strongly is that of a priest of *han*, a *mudang* who heals and restores hope and wholeness to women who have accumulated too much *han*. Under the weight of the cross of sociopolitical, religio-cultural, racial, and gender oppression, *minjung* women are in pain mentally, emotionally, and physically. Jesus will only be significant to them in relation to their longing for liberation and salvation from *han*. This is precisely what a Korean *minjung* woman said in response to Filipino Catholic theologian Virginia Fabella's query on the significance of Jesus. The *minjung* woman declared, "If Jesus Christ is to make sense to us, then Jesus Christ must be an exorcist of our *han*."[54] It is easy for the Korean women to accept the Jesus of the Gospels, Chung Hyun Kyung notes, because of his healing ministry.[55] In other words, what Jesus did—how he related to the poor, the hungry, the despised, and the sick in his time—is exactly what the *mudang* does for *minjung* women. Park Sun Ai Lee affirms the statement of the Korean woman whom Fabella encountered, saying that the Jesus story in the Bible makes Korean women understand that the power of Christ is "life-giving and enabling to the powerless and oppressed" and exorcises all forms of satanic bonds that keep them from experiencing life.[56]

As discussed earlier, Korean feminist theologians are aware that *minjung* women rooted in Shamanism have difficulty understanding a personal God who becomes human to save the world. In fact, "there is almost a complete lack of a framework in shamanism to understand Christology"[57] in terms of Jesus' passion, death, and resurrection. Nevertheless, this lack has not hindered *minjung* women from reimaging Jesus from their perspective. Shamanism has no concept similar to the Christian understanding of the historical Jesus,[58] but the women understand that Jesus as a human being became God after his death, like Princess Baridegi, who became the first shaman and the goddess of healing after her death. Poet Chang Jung-Nim also illustrates this in her poem, cited above. In Shamanism the hope for new life, identified by the Christian vision as the resurrection, comes through the metaphor of beauty in the flowers that spring from the *minjung*'s struggles.

Kim Grace Ji-Sun demonstrates the longing of a Korean woman in diaspora to be in touch with her culture in light of her Christian faith. A theologian, Kim seeks to address theologically the *han* of Korean women in North America brought about by two patriarchal traditions: the Confucian culture that encompasses Korean life, and the racist white American culture reinforced by an androcentric Christian tradition. She recognizes the value of her culture's way of releasing *han* through *han-pu-ri*. Like Chang, Kim certainly does not consider the ritual sufficient if people take it as an end. The ritual must stir the spirit to stop oppressive traditions. She recognizes that a Christian ritual needs to connect to Christ, who not only confronts evil, heals, and restores people's self-worth by releasing their *han*, but also accompanies women in their suffering and empowers them to move toward their liberation as well as that of others.[59]

Korean feminist theologians do not see *han-pu-ri* as an end in itself. What happens after the *han-pu-ri* is equally important. *Minjung* women who convert to Christianity still find *han-pur-ri* an important process through which to resolve their problems. They recognize the parallelism of the ministries of the *mudang* and of Jesus. Jesus is the *mudang* who dances the cosmic dance to bring *sahlim*. *Sahlim*, according to Lee Oo Chung, encompasses "living, humanization, existence," but *sahlim* is not separable from the concept of *muht*, which means "vitality, freedom, and harmony of the whole."[60] To Chung Hyun Kyung *sahlim* is a cosmic dance that is life giving. She describes it as dancing inside us to the tune of the rhythm of the universe, the "synergetic dance" of the erotic and detached, of fullness and emptiness, of claiming power and renouncing power, of social analysis and spiritual liberation. *Sahlim* keeps life in balance.[61] This Shamanist concept, which Chung Hyun Kyung articulates in her "Sahlimist Manifesto," is no different from Jesus' understanding of the fullness of life (Jn 10:10).[62] Jesus the *Mudang* teaches us the dance and challenges us to be *sahlim* dancers in our contemporary world. From an ecofeminist perspective, Chung Hyun Kyung also shows the connection of the Cosmic Christ with Jesus' *mudang* dance in the *han-pu-ri* that makes things alive on the cosmic level.

THE CHALLENGE OF RECLAIMING THE ETHOS OF SHAMANISM IN CHRISTOLOGY

From the vantage point of interfaith dialogue, and using Chung Hyun Kyung's work as a springboard, Akiko Yamashita of Japan criticizes the method of the *minjung* feminist theologians:

> I could not agree with her because her methodology is too Western and uniquely Christian-centric. When I did a field research among Korean *mudang* (shaman), I heard of their indignation toward Christians. One of their complaints is: "They now take everything from us as if theirs, especially our music and its instruments." The *Minjung* Church, the Women's Church and those related progressive organizations have started making use of traditional people's arts in their worship service. I don't think this is bad, but just making use of *shamanism*, influenced by a Western postmodern boom while ignoring the real shamans, is no better.[63]

If by "Christian-centric" Yamashita means that Korean feminist theologians like Chung Hyun Kyung and Choi Man Ja are heading toward inclusivism, I do not see it that way. Yamashita seems to have a curious, if not distorted, perception of Chung's method as "too Western." On the contrary, Chung has elicited criticisms from Western and traditional theologians because her method is too Asian, shamanistic, and is deemed to have signaled the "surrender" of Christianity to paganism.[64] I affirm Yamashita's concern about Western people taking other people's cultures and appropriating them as their own while ignoring the contexts that gave rise to these spiritualities. One should even be critical of Western people's act of "selling" these cultures and spiritualities as exotic commodities to bored Christians in the West. This is what the New Age did to African, Asian, and Native American spiritualities.[65] People may find meaning in practicing the rituals, but they often fail to make the slightest effort to connect with the realities of the lands in which these spiritualities originally emerged and took root.

This is not what Korean feminist theologians are doing. The biographies of these women, and some men too, tell us that many of them risked their lives in their participation in Korea's socio-historical struggles. Rather than taking away the power of the shamans, Korean feminist theologians claim their connection with a tradition that patriarchal Western theologies have pushed to the margins. They only reclaim the ethos of Shamanism that has been part of their collective consciousness. They have drunk from the well of their ancestors the water long despised and polluted by their colonizers and the elite class of Korea. Drawing from the well of their heritage has helped them make sense of Jesus in their *han*-ridden society. In effect, Korean feminist theologians are sending a message to those who claim a monopoly on theological discourse: they are breaking free and removing the blinders that Western and patriarchal theologies have placed before their eyes. Chung challenges Asian women to dig into their heritage, yet at the same time she warns them that this Asian anthropology requires recognition of the "multiplicity of the religious heritages that live and interact within and among Asian bodies" and, in her context, among Korean bodies.[66] She cites herself as an example:

> I'm not doing just an interreligious dialogue with Buddhists, Confucianists and Taoists, because all of them are within me. . . . I feel like my bowel is *shamanist*, and my heart is Buddhist, and my right brain is Confucianist and my left brain is Christian. I need an archaeology of spirituality within me because at every layer I can see all these people screaming and shouting at each other. This is like a symphony of gods. I call it a family of gods.[67]

Because Korean feminist theologians are in touch with their cultural roots, they see Jesus the Christ in new, meaningful ways that give them courage to struggle against oppressive forces.

Yamashita's concern may serve as a precautionary signal, a warning to women not to fall into the trap of commercialized spirituality and religion. Given the reality that Shamanism is the bedrock of Korean women's consciousness, though, I am convinced that in each Korean woman is the spirit of the *shaman* waiting to be set free. Jesus empowers each woman to reclaim and to realize that dormant *mudang* spirit so that in solidarity women do the task Jesus has commissioned his followers to do. It is only a matter of acknowledging it and allowing it to surface. However, Yamashita's warning should not hinder women in Asia from reclaiming the liberating dimensions of their religio-cultural heritage.

JESUS THE MOTHER, THE SYMBOLIC WOMAN MESSIAH, AND WISDOM INCARNATE

For three decades Western feminist theologians have been mulling over the question of Jesus' maleness. The sexuality of Jesus is precisely the location of power that patriarchal Christian men have claimed for themselves and have used to dominate others. For centuries men have used Jesus' sex as a normative criterion for redemption, education, leadership, ordination, and a host of other things that men want to keep to themselves. In challenging this norm Rosemary Radford Ruether posed what has become accepted as a foundational theological question in Christology, "Can a male savior save women?" In an effort to redeem Jesus from patriarchy, Ruether has asserted that Jesus' ability to be the liberator "does not reside in his maleness" but in his capacity to "embody the new humanity of service and mutual empowerment."[68] Mary Daly asserts that the only way to "release the memory of Jesus from its destructive uses" and from "enchainment" to the role of the scapegoat is to recognize the "new arrival of female presence, once strong and powerful, but enchained" by patriarchy.[69]

Without ignoring the issue of Jesus' maleness in christological discussions, Korean women, who have endured tremendous suffering under oppressive social and cultural systems, have drawn strength from their own traditions. They have not remained focused on this issue, which is largely a Western feminist concern. As they have gone through the crucible of Korea's recent turbulent and painful history, Korean feminist theologians have opened their eyes to new christological possibilities. They have seen the liberating gifts that Korea's rich culture and tradition offer them, and they have used these gifts accordingly as resources in their christological constructions.

Jesus as the Image of a Mother

Ahn Sang-Nim, an active leader of women in the Korean church, contends that a living theology need not be the monopoly of the academicians.[70] She has rejoiced in the nascent Korean feminist theology that has lifted up the status of women in the Korean society, a society that is so oppressive to women. In the 1980s the issue of motherhood became a theological theme for Korean women. This theme arose in light of Korean family laws created by the male-dominated National

Assembly that maintains the patriarchal system and does not see the connection between those laws and the *han* of women who have been their sacrificial victims.[71] Thus, she proffers a Christology of motherhood without romanticizing the traditional Confucianist view of motherhood. When a woman in scripture cries aloud, "Blessed is the womb that bore you and the breasts that nursed you!" (Lk 11:27), Jesus' response may seem a blunt rebuttal as he replies that the ones who hear and keep the word of God are blessed. Yet, to Ahn Sang-Nim, in saying this Jesus did not negate the personhood of women. Instead, his response indicated Jesus' rejection of the traditional notion that women are "childbirth machines" whose bodies are merely instruments to perpetuate patrilineal interests. Lisa Isherwood points out that Ahn Sang-Nim's Jesus is one who values the bodies of women. This perspective is in stark contrast to traditional Korean and Asian societies' prevalent view that female bodies are sex objects, baby makers, and fodder for economic growth.[72]

Ahn Sang-Nim draws her theology of motherhood from her understanding of the Matthean text that tells about Jesus lamenting over Jerusalem: "Jerusalem, Jerusalem, the city that kills the prophets and stones those who are sent to it! How often have I desired to gather your children together as a hen gathers her brood under her wings, and you were not willing!" (Mt 23:37).

She builds her motherhood Christology on an understanding of God that highlights the creativity of Korean women in their christological constructions. Drawing upon the feminine images of God in the Hebrew scriptures, and seeing God through the lens of a woman's experience of birth pangs, she exclaims, "Ah, God is like a mother!" and declares, "I came to understand why God came to earth, to human beings, telling them how much God loves them."[73] Ahn's emphasis is clear though: Jesus offers us the image of a mother who longs to embrace her children, one who calls the wayward Jerusalem to come under her wings. Ahn goes on to describe this motherly Jesus as the Christ who is "the Creator God, our Redeemer and Liberator, and the Comforter who defends and takes care of us."[74]

A mother must be creative to provide for her children's nourishment and to redeem them from waywardness. Based upon this understanding, she declares, "I am saved." Yet, when speaking about the cross, Ahn Sang-Nim turns around and follows the seemingly traditional line, "Jesus died for me on the cross and promised me a new life through his resurrection."[75] Said in the context of a society that has stunted the development of women's self-worth through sexist socialization, Ahn Sang-Nim's self-affirmation has encouraged women to break free from the socially imposed chain of self-negation. She affirms herself saying, "I am created in God's image and I am [as] important as anybody in this world."[76] For Ahn Sang-Nim, this motherly Jesus is also the giver of the Holy Spirit and of new life. A fresh life in the resurrected Jesus Christ means being able to remove the "rock of poverty, disease, and suffering of the powerless, who have been exploited and oppressed by the powerful of this world," as well as "removing thousands of years of an old patriarchal culture."[77]

In suggesting that women must highlight the spirituality of motherhood in developing Asian women's theology, Korean feminist theologian Park Sun Ai further widened the path to a new way of seeing motherhood by making a connection between motherhood and Christology:

> We mothers live and experience in the process of birth, the core of Christian theology, crucifixion, and resurrection. Our parallel experience is the deadly suffering of labor pain and the immeasurable joy of having given birth to a new life. And [a] mother's care for her children is unconditional and undiscriminating. Even if the child is less talented than the other, she would feed and clothe it the same [as] the more talented one.[78]

To Park, motherhood is women's lived experience of the core of Christian theology—the birth, crucifixion, and resurrection of Jesus the Christ. Put in a different way, she points to the metaphor of motherhood in Jesus the Christ who suffers the pain of labor to give new life to the world. While she seems to have skipped a segment of the story between birth and crucifixion, she fills that space with the story of how Jesus as a mother cares for her children without discriminating against any of them, and in an unconditional way. Jesus paid attention and gave love to the unloved and to the sick. Jesus cared for the sheep that society abandoned. Surely, one cannot afford to romanticize the suffering that mothers endure in childbearing and child rearing or gloss over the reality that some mothers participate in perpetuating the violence of patriarchal cultures. Far from it, Park is saying, rather, that Jesus embodied the mothering characteristics of the Divine, who nurtures, cares, and provides for all her children. That is why Park became fascinated with Jesus' attitudes toward women and his liberating message, especially so with his mother-discourses.[79] Jesus exemplifies a personality that has a balance of feminine and masculine characteristics.[80]

In the same vein, Lee Oo Chung sees the suffering Jesus in the faces of mothers who have lost their children at the brutal hands of the police or the military. Lee Oo Chung hears Jesus saying, "The sorrow in my heart is so great that it almost crushes me" (Mk 14:34) in response to the heartrending wails of mothers whose children are struck down in their prime because of illness brought on by poverty. Whatever the cause of the suffering, whether the social system or individual evil, Lee recognizes that the cost of bearing the suffering is high. Jesus is the compassionate mother who shares the pathos of her child.

To illustrate the pain of a mother, Lee tells the story of the beautiful bell housed in the National Museum of Kwangju, Korea. Because the Buddhist bell maker could not produce a bell with a beautiful sound, the council came up with an idea of sacrificing a "pure young maiden" for the cause. The soldiers of the Shilla kingdom took a village girl and threw her into the pot of molten lead and iron used to cast the huge temple bell. While other people could enjoy and praise the unequalled beauty of the bell's sound, for the mother the sound only echoed the girl's piteous cry, "Emille! Emille!," which means, "Mother! Oh, Mother!" The cry she hears in the bell's tolling pierces her heart every time. Those in the neighborhood who knew of the sacrifice could not hear the sound of the bell without pain. "Only those who understand the sacrifice can feel the pain," Lee stresses.[81] In her reflection on this story and on Lee's writing, Chung Hyun Kyung points out that the image of Jesus as the suffering mother of the little girl demonstrates to the Asian women that redemption comes only through the One who shares the pathos of humanity.[82]

Jesus the Christ, the Woman Messiah

Korean feminist theologians have found the source for new Christologies in the compassionate mother image of Jesus the Christ. In this section I lift up the works of three Korean feminist theologians who have envisioned Jesus the Christ in different feminine christological images. Choi Man Ja speaks of Jesus as the Woman Messiah, the female Christ who sides with the oppressed and liberates Korean women from suffering. Using the Jubilee declaration of the Lukan account, Chung Sook-Ja reimagines Jesus as a Korean Woman Jesus.

The late Park Sun Ai Lee wrote about suffering women as scapegoats of patriarchy, who, like Jesus, become the lamb of redemption.

In an article written for an Asian women's conference in 1987, Choi Man Ja presented a new way of interpreting and reimagining Jesus the Christ as the Woman Messiah.[83] She starts by saying that Jesus was a judgment upon patriarchy and thus opened the path for the emergence of a new humanity. Jesus transcended the prevailing notion of relationships built upon the binaries of male and female, dominant and subordinate. This was evident in the mutuality that characterized his relationships with those who surrounded him. The risen Christ chose to appear first to a woman and, Choi reminds her Christian readers, Christianity stands upon the witness of a woman. Choi does not avoid the issues of obedience and vicarious suffering, aspects of Christology that feminist theologians rightly have criticized. Like other feminists, she recognized that the insistence of patriarchal Christianity on the redemptive value of obedience and vicarious suffering could put "women and children at risk within Christian homes," in workplaces, and even in churches and Christian societies.[84] In contrast, suffering, when it is not seen as an end in itself, can take on new meaning. For Korean women, the suffering that results from choosing to resist injustice and of exposing the evil powers of this patriarchal, technocratic, Mammon-oriented world can be fruitful and liberative.[85] Choi recalls that Mother Teresa preferred to speak of Mother Jesus and that women prophets in the early church received visions and oracles of Christ as a female figure. Along with Park Soon Kyung, Choi asserts, "Jesus is a symbol of the female and the oppressed," and thus, "we may call Jesus the woman messiah who is the liberator of the oppressed."[86] Choi also notes that the account in Acts 2:18 about the Spirit of Jesus being poured upon both women and men also portrays an inclusive Christ, one who transcends gender and who appears to people in many ways through the lives of the oppressed. Based on this understanding, Christians are free to "recognize the praxis of a female messiah," the female Christ who represents the new humanity whose praxis includes solidarity with the oppressed and liberation of women from the quagmire of suffering.[87]

Choi's Christology affirms the pneumatological Christology of another Korean woman theologian, Chung Sook-Ja, who is pastor of the Korean Women Church in Seoul, a church that has declared its solidarity with the oppressed. Chung Sook-Ja asserts that, as scripture attests, the resurrected Jesus appeared in totally new and different forms in the midst of people who suffered under the unjust conditions imposed by the male-dominated society and religion.[88] Given this scriptural witness, Chung Sook-Ja has conceived of a new christological image, Korean Woman Jesus, an image she has encouraged members of Korean Women Church to embody.[89] On the fifth anniversary of the Korean Women Church, she, along with two women, reimagined the Jubilee passage in Luke 4:1–18, especially the phrase "the year of the Lord's favor," through the christological image of a Korean Woman Jesus who announces a sabbath for the Korean people:

> Today we give birth to Korean Woman Jesus. . . . Our practice is rooted in Jesus' declaration of a Sabbath which exists for people. We are working to establish a church which truly follows Jesus. We are women who have been oppressed for 5,000 years, so we stand on the side of the oppressed.
>
> We are women who have been and are forced to serve within the hierarchical structure of churches, and so we will work to overcome those hierarchies. We are the women who can become pregnant and bear life, so we will continue to hold life precious.[90]

On that occasion, leaders and other worshipers declared themselves a part of the mission of Woman Jesus:

> The Spirit of God is upon us, Women Church,
> Because God has anointed us;
> God has sent us together all kinds of women in one place,
> from different denominations of divided churches,
> to share their experiences, to unite in the love of God,
> to protest structural evils and unjust situations,
> and to seek human liberation, women's liberation.
> God has placed us in this world
> to proclaim liberty to the captives who are caught
> in the bonds of materialism and capitalism,
> and sight for the blind who have closed their eyes
> in individualism and individual-churchism
> by stressing only a faith of blessing-receiving;
> to liberate oppressed women under patriarchy
> and authoritarianism and to proclaim the year
> of God's favor for the realization of peace in the world.[91]

To illustrate the connection between Jesus and Korean women, the Korean Women Church leaders presented a "drama worship" as part of the fifth anniversary celebration. Within this drama worship the leaders portrayed the temptations that Korean women face—to deny their wholeness and to abandon their own liberation—as parallel to the temptations Jesus faced. In the drama Woman Jesus is the main character. She sets out upon her mission. Along the way the devil, as the Father in the drama, tempts Woman Jesus first by the false image of the ideal marriage, a marital relationship in which women experience liberation as well as equality with men. In the second temptation scene the devil is cast as Company Owner and Woman Colleague. Company Owner urges a female worker to accept and to buy into her own oppression—low wages, lack of day care for children, no chance for promotion, compulsory retirement at twenty-eight, sexual harassment. Woman Colleague tempts Woman Jesus with items many Korean women highly value, such as nice clothes and cosmetic surgery. She offers Woman Jesus the false image of the beautiful woman as a successful woman who will influence men because of her seductive appearance. In the third temptation scene the devil takes the form of Male Pastor. Male Pastor tempts Woman Jesus to accept tradition and to wait prayerfully for change. He admonishes her to resist heretical and anti-traditional views about women. In response to these temptations Woman Jesus refuses all offers of political, economic, and religious power. In the closing scene Woman Jesus rejoins the company of women "to stand up to watch and protect God's order of creation," to "participate in the mending of creation as true mothers who love all lives, and as God's daughters who follow the life of Jesus of Nazareth," and to "become partners to walk this same road."[92]

In looking at the responses of Korean women to the oppression in their lives, as dramatized in the Korean Women Church play, Choi sees two groups: women who suffer oppression and do nothing but endure their suffering, and women who suffer yet work to liberate themselves and other women from oppression. Suffering is their common ground.

Another Korean theologian, the late Park Sun Ai Lee, spoke of Korean women as the "lamb bearing the sins of the world." Men have made women scapegoats who must bear the local and global sins of the world, including their own oppression. Park suggests that these contemporary scapegoats must become instead the lamb of redemption. Park envisions this transformation as possible only if women create a sustained "spiral of scientific analysis, organization, effective action, theorizing, and theologizing in the creation of a new life model and new human relationships."[93] Through this spiraling process women as the "most suffering of the suffering lambs" achieve "imminent and potential eschatological redemption for all."[94] They become what Choi refers to in another christological image as the Woman Messiah. Women who suffer oppression yet who take steps to uproot the system, she says, are the true disciples of Jesus. In their praxis, they image a new facet of the Body of Christ, the Woman Messiah. In Choi's words, these "women are the true praxis of messiah-Jesus in Korea."[95] Unlike the patriarchal culture, whose view of redemption is narrow and inclusive only of men, Woman Messiah envisions a holistic redemption, reconciliation, and harmony for all creatures. Woman Messiah affirms the feminist value of giving birth to life, both literally or metaphorically, and of sustaining life.[96] The continuing challenge is for women to embody the Woman Messiah, for, like Jesus, women "have come to give life, life in its fullness."[97]

Wisdom Incarnate: Jesus through a Buddhist Lens

While she appreciates the Christology that draws wisdom from Shamanism, Kim Grace Ji-Sun also uses the lens of Buddhism to see Jesus from a different vantage point. She points out that in Buddhism, Prajna Paramita is the supreme Wisdom. She not only protects women and looks after them in childbirth, but she also heals children from their illnesses. The bodhisattva Kuan-yin, whose compassion goes beyond concern for human beings, symbolizes Prajna Paramita. She listens to the cries of the earth, of the animals, and of the plants, mountains, wind, rivers, and sky. Kim, therefore, finds Lady Wisdom (Sophia) in Prajna symbolized by Kuan-yin as an image more powerful than the masculine notion of Logos. To her, the grace of Sophia-Prajna in Kuan-yin brings liberation and empowerment to women who have suffered oppression and domination in a sexist, patriarchal, and racist society. From the Christian point of view Kim sees Wisdom incarnated in Jesus, who shows us the way to a life of goodness and truth.[98] Jesus embodies the grace of Sophia, the beauty of God-Wisdom.

OWNING THEIR STORIES, REIMAGING JESUS THE CHRIST

Korean women theologians demonstrate that removing the blinders of traditional patriarchal Christologies enables them to articulate their own understanding of Jesus the Christ. They are able to appropriate some aspects of Shamanism and Buddhist traditions in constructing a Christology that makes sense to them and gives meaning to their daily struggles and suffering. In the face of conservatism among many Korean churches, these Korean women's Christologies can open up new paths for Korean women as they journey with Jesus. What is the impact of Korean feminist theologies on these conservative churches?[99] Ironically, the very religious conservatism that has interlocked with intransigent social patriarchy has driven Korean feminist women theologians to reinterpret Christology. Consequently, Korean feminist Christologies are now available to challenge the Korean churches to reexamine their faith, to reread their bibles, and to rethink their Christologies in the face of the issues and problems that confront Korean society. Korean feminist Christologies can challenge the conservative, Westernized, technologically oriented churches to rediscover and to be in touch with the "vintage intoxicant of primal spirituality"[100] and the life-affirming dimensions of Korean traditions hidden deeply within their "shamanized" version of Christianity.[101] Korean feminist theologians are leading Korean women and men toward owning their stories and articulating their own encounters with Jesus the Christ, the symbol of the Great Mystery, God of many names.

In Korea religious traditions have come together in plurality and have seasoned each other in uniquely Korean ways. In Shamanism, salt is a symbol of cleansing and healing. The vision of a mountain turning into salt is symbolic of hope. Thus, the pregnant woman who, in her vision, met the Buddha at the foot of the salt mountain found hope for herself and her baby. Have Korean feminist theologians met Jesus at the foot of the salt mountain? Metaphorically, I would conclude they have. Their rereading and reinterpretation of the scriptures through the lenses of their cultural heritage and contemporary contexts have helped them reimagine the Christ. Their new images of Jesus the Christ have created the foundation for Christologies that can empower women to break free from the grip of the "death-wishing, virginity-obsessed," patriarchal and triumphalist Christologies.[102]

At the foot of the salt mountain Korean feminist theologians have met a Jesus who is liberating and life giving for Korean women. As a result, the Christologies of Korean feminist theologians are typically creative and celebratory. Their Christologies are also uniquely responsive to the concrete situations of many oppressed women in Korean society, especially the less privileged. At the foot of the salt mountain Korean feminist theologians have labored to give birth to life-centered Christologies. As their new creations mature, these imaginative women have offered both women and men in the Korean churches new paths they too can take to the salt mountain.

Chapter 4

Walking with Jesus in the Philippines

Singing and Dancing amid Struggle

Whipped and lashed desperately
by bomb-raised storms,
has not our Asian land
continued to bloom?
With the same intense purity and fragrance
we are learning to overcome.

—MARIA LORENA BARROS

THE BROWN SOIL THAT NOURISHED THE FILIPINO STRUGGLE

The Philippines boasts of its status as the only Christian country in Asia. Christians comprise 92 percent of the Filipino population, and a great majority of them are Roman Catholics. Christianity in the Philippines is a product of Spanish and American colonialism. The stamp of the colonial mentality continues to impress itself on the minds of a large segment of the Christian converts, especially among the elite and the privileged class. Like the bamboo trees that once flourished abundantly in the islands, the Filipino people are resilient and hardworking. They have endured tropical depressions and typhoons that frequent the seventy-three hundred islands of the Philippines. Over the course of nearly five hundred years, the people have struggled against and weathered waves of colonization that have brought political and economic storms that have battered the people's individual and collective lives. The people continue to suffer at the hands of the elite and corrupt Filipino officials who, like puppets, execute the sophisticated dance of death as their white masters' hands pull the strings. The role of the United States in declaring the mock Philippine independence from Spain on June 12, 1898, and its "liberating" the country from the "naked brutality of the Japanese" in 1946 marked the beginning of a new captivity of the Filipino people.

Songs of struggle and freedom emerged from people's experiences and their longing to break the shackles of poverty and oppression. The song "Bayan Naming Minamahal" (our beloved homeland) tells the story of the people's struggle:

Bayan naming minamahal	Our beloved country
Bayan naming Pilipinas	Our country, the Philippines
Ang buhay ay puhunanin	We will spend our lives
Makamtan lang ang Kalayaan	Just to attain freedom
Bayan naming minumutya	Our country, our gem
Kami'y handang magpakasakit	We are ready to sacrifice
Ang buhay ay nakalaan	Our lives we will set apart
Dahil sa iyo O aming bayan.	For you, Oh, our homeland.
Perlas ka ng silangan	You are the pearl of the orient
May likas kang kayamanan	Endowed with natural wealth
Dahil dito'y sinakop ka ng mga Dayuhan	Thus strangers sought to control you
Kaya dapat kang magtanggol	You should defend and resist
Lumaban ka O aming bayan.[1]	Fight, Oh, our country.

Theoretically, the Philippines had been freed from its colonizers. Yet, in this postcolonial era, the country is marked by its neocolonial character. In the Philippine context, inculcating a sense of nationalism is relevant and necessary. The experience of colonization has wounded the Filipino soul deeply. The Filipino mind is colonized. Moreover, in times like the present, when blatant deception, graft, and corruption are the order of the day for many leaders in the government, people, especially the middle class, who still have some options, think and feel that the Philippines is a sinking ship. To survive means to abandon this ship. This explains the massive exodus of Filipinos who emigrate. A sense of nationalism needs to be restored in the Filipino psyche. Rather than abandoning the ship, the challenge is to stand up and struggle for the well being of the country. The song "Tumindig Ka" (stand up) articulates this dream:

Iligtas mo kami sa panginoong	Save us from the master
mapang-alipin	who enslaves us
Pagkakapantay-pantay	Let equality
at hustisya ay pa-iralin	and justice prevail
Bugang tulad ng hangin	As the wind blows
ang bulaklak sa kabundukan	may the flowers bloom
Tulad ng apoy	Like the fire
ang tabak ko'y iyong linisin	You cleanse my bolo
Mangyari na ang loob Mo dito sa lupa	May Your will be done here on earth
Bigyan Mo kami ng tapang at lakas	Give us the courage and strength
sa pakikibaka.	to struggle.
Siya nawa.[2]	So be it.

This song is a prayer. It asks for the sovereign God to bless the struggle, for, indeed, the Philippine struggle for freedom is historically both a political and a religious undertaking.

It was 1996. The place: Dumaguete City. With other picketers I stood on the picket line and publicly protested an unjust situation in the university. Negotiations over the stipulations in the collective-bargaining agreement between the administration and the teachers had reached an impasse. The teachers had demanded just wages, fair working conditions, and non-commercialization of education. A strike was the next step. During the negotiations the teachers held vigils at the gates and on the grounds of the university "beside the sea." To ward off sleep, some women led the faculty and friends who had come to express solidarity and support in dancing and singing. At other times they sang hymns and listened to scripture readings or poetry that some members of the union had written. They shared more reflections, and prayed. Many poems and songs of struggle emerged from these experiences.

Song and Dance as Expression of Resistance

If a song is the language of the soul, dance communicates that language through the body. Thus, both songs and dances foster stronger bonds among people. Songs and dances are ways to commune with others, to release heavy emotions, and to heal. Singing and dancing are the most common expressions of life celebrated and victories gained. To some people, singing and dancing in the context of a union strike might appear strange. Yet, as Ma. Corazon Manalo, a religious studies professor at De La Salle University, explains, dance "brings to the fore the reality of unified living in the religious psyche as well as in the innate culture of Filipinos."[3] Just as dance may create moods and provide a sense of context that frames, prolongs, or may even cut off communication, dance can also enhance or destroy life.[4] In most cases in the Philippines, women dance to affirm life. Women often make pilgrimages to shrines dedicated to Mary, the mother of Jesus, and to other patron saints. At the shrines the women dance and plead for healing and good harvest. Barren women dance to be blessed with a child.

Filipinos use songs and dances to tell their stories, their dreams, and their everyday struggles. While tourists may enjoy watching peasants who seem to follow a rhythm in their movement while planting rice, those whose backs are bent the whole day to do the job for starvation wages sing, "Planting rice is never fun." When they sing about their huts made of *nipa* palm leaves surrounded by vegetable gardens, it is to put across the message that they have to work hard in order to survive. In the Visayas region the ancient tradition of *balitaw* (a genre of song sung responsively) illustrates Filipino creativity in using songs and poetry to exchange views and express feelings. Filipino dances also reflect the people's religious and cultural rituals, as well as their connectedness with their communities and nature.

Looking back at my own experience on the picket line, I see that the women's acts signaled the surfacing of the *babaylan* or *katalonan* within themselves, albeit unconsciously. The *babaylans*, as they are called in the Visayas region, or the *katalonans*, as they are called in the Tagalog region in Luzon, are the Filipino traditional religious functionaries. They used chants and dance to invoke the ancestral and ecological spirits, called *anitos*, to heal. They called upon the spirits to bestow favors: peace, survival, well being, and freedom from the evils that burden life.[5] During the teachers' strike, the women sang and danced in the midst of struggle in order to direct their energies toward justice, peace, harmony, and life. Filipino women, and the people in general, dance and sing in the midst of struggle. Somehow, songs and dances make them resilient, and they laugh and smile in the midst of their troubles and pain.

Understanding the Filipino Struggle

Filipino people value life. All other aspects of the indigenous Filipino society are entrenched in this life-centered culture that is characterized by face-to-face relationships. Belief in Bathala, God the Supreme

Being, and the spirit world connected the Filipino with the whole creation.

Yet Philippine society is in a quagmire of social ills. Many factors brought about the corrosion of Filipino society. One potent force was the long experience of Spanish and American colonization. Colonization and its new forms have altered the context and values of the Filipino. Western values and world views have seeped into the matrix of Filipino culture. These factors have encompassing and double-edged effects. While there are beneficial effects, the enslaving ones have strongly influenced the whole system of society, especially the political and economic systems. Free-trade globalization buttresses the neocolonial arrangement of subtle domination of the country. The dominant elites that protect foreign interests in the country enjoy the benefits of being installed in positions of power both in the public and in the private spheres. Accumulation of material wealth at the expense of the vulnerable and poor people has become an obsession of the already privileged. Graft and corruption in government is rampant.

The cumulative effect of globalization is visible in the violence of economic poverty. People's lives and well being are no longer held precious. Consequently, the nation is burdened with social problems. Poverty is the most critical indicator of Philippine society's illness. Social Watch Philippines, an independent group that monitors the compliance with obligations the Philippine government has promised in UN summits and declarations, declared in its flyer that the Philippines' level of poverty is alarmingly high and that the entire country should be "put under a State of Red Alert."[6] Poverty is interlinked with all kinds of other problems, such as those concerning land and ecology, food, shelter, clothing, education, healthcare, unemployment, the rise of crime rates, and many others. It is unfortunate that the predominant religious and theological persuasions tend to make the ordinary people turn their gaze away from the social issues and look forward to a postmortem heaven instead. These also reinforced patriarchy and *machismo*, even as the church remained generally silent about the increase in reported cases of gender-related violence against women and children.

The social problem is complex, the struggle multifaceted. The struggle is to help the Filipino people set themselves free from a cultural prison that makes them complacent about social issues. This includes appreciating and reclaiming the wholesome and liberating aspects of the Filipino indigenous culture and values. It also aims to help the Filipino people develop a sense of nationalism and defend national sovereignty, rather than selling out the country to foreign control. The ultimate goal of the struggle is to make *all* life flourish.

Poverty, Abuse of Power, and the Plight of Prostituted Women and Children

In commenting upon a study that pointed to many Filipinos' difficulty in relating to the image of the risen Christ, Laura Somebang-Ocampo, a Protestant, explains that this is so because the majority of the Filipino people continues to live below the poverty line. They have yet to experience Easter.[7] In contradiction to what affluent Christians usually suggest, people are poor not because of their indolence or because of a lack of piety that has made them undeserving of God's blessings. The Philippines' massive poverty is a systemic problem. Within this system women carry a double or triple burden. As men's frustrations grow in times of economic crises, men tend to target women as scapegoats. As they reflect on their own experience of violence, these women find the *Pasyon*, a dramatization of Jesus' trial and suffering, a genuine venue for them to "empathize with the suffering of Christ" and to be assured that Jesus the Christ understands their sufferings.[8] Patriarchal values aggravate their economic problems and result in more violence against women and girls. The trafficking of women for domestic and foreign markets as prostitutes, mail-order brides, and overseas workers has increased. The Philippine government allocates very little for children's health and education in its budget.[9] In fact, this system has prostituted Filipino children, especially girl children under eighteen, and women. Catholic theology professor Agnes Miclat-Cacayan has observed that because of "unbridled drive for profit," the Philippine government feeds its young children to its country's tourism industry, an industry that "devours the children alive."[10] Ignoring their own complicity, the leaders of the government and society have generally discriminated against women and girls who suffer the horrible consequences of prostitution: unwanted pregnancy, HIV and AIDS and sexually transmitted diseases, and even death. In the process the system has caused the breakdown of traditional values and communities.[11] Philippine society and government officials say nothing about the men who literally use the women and girls, and young boys in some cases, for sex. To add insult to injury, the system criminalizes prostituted girls and women. Filipino girls pay the price of this unjust, cruel system. Thirteen-year-old Aida of Davao City has asked: "Why are we the ones being pinned down by the *baranggay* [village] and police officers? What about our partners—the men who use us?"[12]

Another thirteen-year-old girl, Rosario Baluyot of Olongapo, Zambales, died of infection caused by a broken vibrator left inside her uterus by a European tourist who abused her. Taking advantage of the poverty of the Baluyot's family, the man, who was imprisoned briefly, dangled before them a bribe of twenty thousand pesos (about US$500) for an amicable settlement. The court eventually acquitted the man for lack of evidence.[13] His lawyer succeeded in arguing that there is no provision within Philippine law that criminalizes the act of his client. Obviously concerned more with the revenue that sex tourism brings, the government refused to learn from the Baluyot case and continues to sacrifice the lives and futures of young children on the altar of Mammon. One can only conclude that the Philippine government wants to outdo Thailand, the country that ranks first in Asia in the sex industry. Indeed, the Philippines is catching up, having the second highest rank in terms of the number of commercial sex workers; it is in first place for being corrupt.

Short stories—labeled fiction—often reveal the damning facts some people prefer to avoid seeing. For example, in F. Sionil Jose's novella *Obsession*, Ermi, a schooled and free-lance prostitute, sharply brings the facts to the attention of her client, the Yale-educated government technocrat Roly: "How can you be so dumb. We are not different, we are very much alike. Go before a mirror, Roly. Ask yourself how you have behaved during the last ten years, or even just during the last ten days. We are alike, I repeat. I sell mine—and you—you sell yourself."[14]

A closer look at the issue of prostitution reveals that the state shamelessly operates a nationwide brothel, where local and overseas-educated officials and technocrats serve as high-class pimps and as prostitutes themselves. State representatives, like Roly, essentially sell to the big capitalist countries not only their very selves, but also the women and children, the land, the whole country.

Globalization

In a very real sense only capitalists and multinational corporations benefit from neoliberal globalization, which promises growth by placing the highest importance on private capital. It is propelled by the neoliberal principle that advances the consolidation of "multifaceted power structures" and renders national governments inutile in fulfilling the task of protecting the welfare of the people.[15] Globalization may offer limited opportunities to the privileged class, but it does not improve the condition of the poor people.[16] Globalization widens and systematizes the oppression of workers, the marginalization of local farmers, and the desecration of life and of the earth itself.

Joseph Stiglitz, Nobel Prize winner and economic adviser to former US president Bill Clinton, witnesses the "discontents" of globalization in the developing countries. As World Bank's former chief economist, he argues strongly that the problem lies in the weak management of the globalization project by the international financing institutions such as the IMF, the World Bank, and the WTO. These international financing institutions promote the doctrine of the free market and work for the interests of its leaders rather than serving the poor.[17] It is clear that the capitalist principles adhered to by these institutions are in line with what Gordon Gekko in Oliver Stone's movie *Wall Street* propounds. Gekko declares, "Greed is right. Greed works." Neither fair nor just, the doctrine of free trade destroys people and demolishes life-sustaining communal values. The leaders of powerful nations and corporations replay the old bullying colonial game, only with more sophisticated tools and strategies.

The economic structure, the educational system, and the laws of the Philippines cater to the interests of the transnational corporations of neoliberal globalization. As a result, workers contend with oppressive working arrangements such as low wages and contractualization of labor. Some companies resort to brainwashing by playing aloud recorded salvation-as-pie-in-the-sky sermons during the workers' lunch time to cultivate docility and subservience among the workers.

Working conditions are usually harsh and gender specific, especially for women, whether they are working as factory workers, domestic helpers, sex workers, or office workers. Sexual harassment is common. The threat of termination due to pregnancy and the inadequacy or absence of maternity care encourage women workers to terminate pregnancies.[18] Like all other human beings, women need both physical and spiritual care and nourishment. Thus, there is a need for a Christology that address women's longing for well being as whole persons.

MAKING SENSE OF GOD-TALK OR CHRIST-TALK IN A TROUBLED LAND

Filipinos dream of achieving genuine peace and freedom, both from local oppressors and from local bureaucrats' foreign masters. The experience of being under foreign control for many centuries has made progressive Filipino theologians resonate with Latin American liberation theology. However, the long history of struggle against foreign domination—375 years under the Spaniards and 100 years under the Americans, interrupted briefly by the equally brutal Japanese occupation of 4 years—has led Filipino theologians to focus their reflections on what they call a "theology of struggle."[19] Edicio de la Torre, a Roman Catholic priest and long-time political detainee, is hailed as the "father of the theology of struggle."[20] However, de la Torre points to Louie Hechanova, also a Roman Catholic priest, as the first to suggest that Filipino theology should take the definition of a "theology of struggle, rather than a theology of liberation."[21] The argument behind the distinction is that, while liberation is also a process, struggle is the key component of a spirituality that goes beyond solidarity and takes a lifestyle and perspective of resistance.

Filipino Women's Voices Are Rising

In the cultural and political context of struggle, pioneer feminist theologians have emerged to articulate their own theologies. Even within their own academic context, these women—across class, religion, and ethnicity—continue to experience multiple oppressions because of their gender. It is important to note that Filipino feminist theologians and activists do not separate the struggle for women's liberation from the struggle of the 85 percent of Filipinos who live at or below the poverty level. In telling their stories many ordinary Filipino Christian women speak of life as a struggle for survival and as a faith journey. They see themselves as making this journey with Jesus, a journey punctuated by singing songs of resistance and dancing the dance of life and healing amid struggle. Their songs and dances reflect the concrete realities of life and articulate their hopes. An ecumenical group of women in the Protestant and Roman Catholic churches whose members engage in rereading the Bible and theologizing from women's perspective calls itself the Association of Women in Theology (AWIT).

The women take Mary's Magnificat as their own, a choice especially appropriate because the Cebuano and Tagalog word for "song" is *awit*. This organization has published *Dancing amid Struggle: Stories and Songs of Hope*, a collection of essays that reflects the journey of many women in the Philippines.[22]

The reality of patriarchy in society, fought within the context of the struggle against political repression and poverty, has motivated the women to refashion Christology. The male proponents of the theology of struggle in the Philippines have placed at the forefront of their methodology the issue of class. They have set aside the issues of race and ethnicity. Filipino male theologians talk about the struggle for freedom from dehumanizing forces, and yet they have tended to overlook their own complicity in gender oppression. They have viewed women's suffering mainly from the perspective of class struggle, a valid but inadequate perspective. Issues of sexuality and gender oppression hardly enter into their theological conversation.[23] Filipino feminist theologians have brought to the attention of their male colleagues the importance of gender and sex in theological method, factors just as important as class, race, and ethnicity. Certainly, some male theologians of struggle have acknowledged the gender-specific and gender-related abuses against women, such as rape. However, these men consider these issues mere "subsections" of the general condition of human rights violations and crimes against the person. A theology of struggle can connect the issues of prostitution and of comfort women to the overarching subject of imperialism. However, male theologians of struggle seem to have avoided the equally important issues of domestic violence, sexual harassment, and sexual abuse of girls and women in homes, workplaces, streets, mass media, and church. A prevailing notion common in the discourse among male theologians is that when social, political, and economic problems are resolved, the problems affecting women will surely be solved, and everything will be all right.

Some male theologians of struggle also tended to frown upon the attempts of women to retrieve the liberating elements of their own culture as well as those of the indigenous religious traditions. At its early stage, most theologians of struggle, especially among the Protestants, have rejected the value of religion unilaterally as human alienation, echoing the notion that religion is antithetical to faith. Prominent theologian Karl Barth distinguished religion as "the realm of man's attempts to justify and to sanctify himself before a capricious and arbitrary picture of God." Christian faith is anchored in Jesus

Christ, "the revelation of God as the abolition of religion."[24] Holding Christology as the benchmark of all knowledge of God and all theology, Barth's exclusivist affirmation closes the possibility of Asian and indigenous religions as venue for God's revelation. From another angle, male theologians of struggle also seem to be influenced by the materialist claim that religion numbs people's social sensitivity.[25] Yet, some Filipino feminist theologians have begun to retrieve elements of indigenous Filipino and Asian religions, myths, and traditions that are potentially empowering and liberating for women and for the earth. Even so, the leading Filipino feminist theologians, mostly Roman Catholics, agree that the feminist theology of struggle in the Philippines is still in its infancy.[26]

Theology has long been the turf of men. Although a good number of Filipino Catholic women have taught theology in colleges and universities, Protestants had only Elizabeth S. Tapia, an ordained Methodist pastor. As of 2002, Tapia was the first and only Protestant Filipino woman who had a degree in systematic theology and had taught theology in the seminary.[27] Members of AWIT, however, insist that although women in churches may not be writing theology, they are already *doing* theology as they articulate their faith in the praxis of the struggle against enslavement. Virginia Fabella, a leading Filipino Catholic feminist theologian, notes that women are just beginning to discover Jesus for themselves: "What we say may not be new; what is important is now we are saying it ourselves."[28]

The theological voices of Filipino women have not come out of a void. They have emerged from their struggle for wholeness of life in the context of the people's seemingly endless battle to survive. The struggle is a process, and it has taken place for centuries, since the moment invaders trampled our sacred shores. Filipino women resisted the colonizers in many creative ways. There was the mythical Princess Urduja, and a host of women priestesses who resisted colonization as faithful bearers of indigenous spirituality and tradition. Women like Gabriela Silang, Teresa Magbanua, Gregoria de Jesus, Melchora de Aquino, and many others struggled alongside their men for freedom from foreign domination. Except for issues of gender, culture, and ethnicity, the theology of struggle and the rising feminist women's theologies in the Philippines have common roots.

The nascent Christologies of Filipino women have emerged from within the Filipino people's historical struggle for freedom. Two Filipino communal practices—the *pasyon*, the dramatization of Jesus' trial and suffering; and the *lakbayan*, the people's march rallies—have been integral to people's resistance and struggle for survival. Another important women's articulation of Christology is the understanding of Jesus as the fully liberated human being and liberator. In spite of being influenced by the former colonizers' cultures, there lies in Filipinos a subterranean longing to be in touch with their indigenous roots. This yearning poses the challenge to explore and draw out christological reflections from the indigenous people's traditions, myths, and spirituality.

THE *PASYON,* THE *LAKBAYAN,* AND FILIPINO WOMEN'S STRUGGLE FOR SURVIVAL

Lydia Lascano, a community worker and a Catholic nun, has outlined two moments of Jesus' passion. The first moment is that of suffering, humiliation, and powerlessness at the hands of religious leaders who colluded with powerful Romans officials to protect their interests. The second moment is that of accompanying women in their struggle for freedom and empowerment.[29] Kwok Pui-lan of Hong Kong, in commenting on Lascano's work, has referred to these moments as the passive and active moments of Jesus' suffering.[30] Taking a clue from Lascano's outline, but on solidarity as a way of understanding the passion of Jesus, Myrna Francia and Margaret Lacson, both Catholics, along with Roy Chiefe, a priest, prefer to see the incarnation as Jesus' initial act of accompaniment. In the incarnation event Jesus accompanied the people in their struggle to have abundant life. They assert that the passion was only a continuance of that act.[31] This view is compelling because it sees the death of Jesus on the cross as an outcome of his ministry and his solidarity with those who suffer marginalization and oppression in society. This view understands the option of Jesus to leave the marginal comfort of his family's home to become an itinerant teacher-preacher-healer. Indeed, his ministry was, and is, an ongoing process of accompanying the outcasts of society.

Jesus' story of accompaniment and suffering inspired two Filipino processional practices, *pasyon* and *lakbayan*. These practices cannot be separated, for their fibers are closely interwoven in the lives of many Filipinos. Thus, we need to examine both as integral components of the whole picture of the Filipino people's struggle for the fullness of life in the Philippines. For the sake of discussion, however, let us first look at the *pasyon*.

Pasyon: A Colonizer's Tool to Tame the Soul

The *pasyon* is a tradition practiced especially among those who belong to the Roman Catholic Church. Filipino liturgical scholar Anscar Chupungco describes this religious practice:

> Indigenous to the Philippines is the chanting before home altars during Lent, or less frequently, at funeral wakes, of the verses of the *Pasyon*. The *Pasyon* is a book written in seven major Filipino languages consisting of 3,150 rhymed stanzas of five lines each. Though it narrates the history of salvation from the moment of the creation to the second coming of Christ, including apocryphal stories, much of it is a detailed account of and a prayerful meditation on the passion of Christ. Friends and neighbors drop in to sing a portion of the *Pasyon* and sit afterward for the meal, which still vaguely retains a sacral undertone.[32]

As one born into a Protestant family, my memory of the *pasyon* comes only from having watched my friends participate in the drama of reliving the story of Jesus' trial, suffering, death, and resurrection. The Lenten season is marked by processions. The longest, most colorful one highlights the drama at the end of the Lenten season. Devoted Catholic neighbors plant lighted candles on their windowsills and fences to signify their unity with those who walk in the procession. Bedecked carriages *(carrozas)* carry statues of beautifully garbed patron saints and are followed by other *carrozas* carrying the different images of the suffering Jesus. The *carrozas* are separated at intervals by columns of devotees—mostly women. These devotees carry candles, sing, and recite decades of the rosary. At the head of the procession a band plays mournful music. At dawn on Easter the procession proceeds to the church, passing through a palm-decorated arch, for the celebration of the *sugat* or *encuentro*, which means a meeting with or encountering of the risen Christ.[33] Although this practice varies from town to town, the core of the ritual remains the same. Stationed in each elevated corner of the arch are little girls wearing white robes and wings. As angels, they sing "Hosannas," while the "star" angel is lowered from the center of the arch to put a crown on the images of the risen Jesus and of Mary. The procession is part of the *pasyon*, and women who can sing the *pasyon* play an important role in carrying on the Filipino tradition of reading, singing, and reenacting the passion story of Jesus.[34] In the Tagalog region, the *pasyon* includes the reading *(pabasa)* and the dramatization *(sinakulo)* of Jesus' trial and suffering on the cross.

Spanish missionaries introduced such rituals in an attempt to dislodge the native spirit of the ancient rituals of the indigenous religious priestesses. Thus, the *pasyon* bears a significant stamp of Spanish colonization that included imposition of the conqueror's religion. Reynaldo Ileto, a Filipino Catholic historian, reports that the Spanish colonizers intended to use the *pasyon* to instill a soul-oriented spirituality and to develop a postmortem notion of salvation that would inspire subservience in the colonized Filipinos.[35]

On the one hand, the Spanish colonizers cultivated a Roman Catholic religiosity among the Filipinos, especially among the elites, that emphasized the image of the suffering Christ rather than that of the resurrected Christ.[36] Thus, many Filipinos remain "Good Friday Christians." The missionaries largely succeeded in instilling the attitude of docility among the people. Part of the strategy involved in domesticating the once-independent native women was the use of religious education to cultivate meek and subservient women. This Iberian image of a docile Mary is far from the singer of the Magnificat in the Gospel of Luke. By introducing the *pasyon*, the Spanish friars and the succeeding clergy coaxed women to endure suffering as Jesus did on the reasoning that such suffering was God's will and enduring it would make one saintly. A popular maxim among the people in the central part of the Philippines reinforces this notion: *Pag-antos aron ka masantos* (You must endure suffering so that you will become a saint). This kind of understanding of the *pasyon* assures the participants that they have a place in heaven after their deaths. In short, the *pasyon* provides a religious justification for women's passive acceptance of suffering from violence, abuse, and oppression.

The *Pasyon* as Resource for Resistance

On the other hand, by introducing the *pasyon*, the colonizers unwittingly provided Filipinos with a space in which they could express their free spirits and a medium to animate their resistance. The *pasyon* became a ritual that inspired them to wage their struggle for freedom. The *pasyon* has stirred up energy by giving natives a religious language with which to articulate their values, ideals, and dreams for freedom and liberation. Indeed, the *pasyon* has shaped the "style of peasant brotherhoods and uprisings during the colonial periods,"[37] including the millenarian movements that survive today. The *pasyon*, itself an expression of a domesticated Christianity, ironically became the earliest attempt of Filipinos to contextualize the passion narrative and relate it to their own lives. Much of the people's anticolonial language has drawn inspiration from the *pasyon*. Thus, the *pasyon* is not only a narrative and dramatization of the suffering, death, and resurrection of Jesus the Christ, but has embodied continually the life and passion of the oppressed Filipino people.

Filipino Women's Suffering and the *Pasyon* of Jesus

Some years ago the story of a battered woman who killed her children rocked the "friendly city" of Dumaguete. She killed her children to end their suffering from poverty and from the violence inflicted on them by their father, and then she committed suicide. As in most Roman Catholic homes, there was a small altar in her hut.[38] The altar had a picture of Jesus hanging on the cross and a rosary. One wonders whether she found solace and redemption in Jesus' death.

In another case Pasya, a strong woman who earned a living as a vendor in the pier area of the city, redeemed herself from suffering at the hands of her violent husband by fighting back. Finally, she accidentally killed her husband in front of her children as she defended herself. She too had an altar in her rented house in the slum area. There, Jesus continued to hang on the cross.

Belen struggled to survive. Her "yuppie" philandering husband left her for another woman who could bear him a son. Her husband's family scorned her, even though she was the one who had sent her husband to school. Left to raise her two children alone, she put up a fight in the courts to make her husband fulfill his obligation to support their children, despite knowing how ridiculously snail-paced the Philippine legal system is. Her Protestant mother-in-law told friends that Belen was ill due to *gabâ*, a curse, for she did not easily obey her husband's demands. Belen often wondered about the meaning of God's love in light of her suffering. Did she have to suffer to experience God's love? Did God's love make her suffering "special"? After years of fighting poverty and a three-year battle with cancer, Belen succumbed to death. She also had an altar in her home and regularly put fresh flowers at the foot of the image of Jesus hanging on the cross.

Many Christian women whose bodies and spirits are wounded find consolation in the thought that Jesus understands their sufferings. Such thoughts give them a taste of hope and redemption. The sight of Jesus enduring pain on the cross reminds them that they are not alone in the struggle to carry their burden and affliction. These experiences find expression in the poem of Netherlands-based Filipino Protestant Elizabeth Soriso Padillo-Olesen:

> The face of Jesus on the cross helps us to bear
> our walk on the valley of bones on a Holy Friday
> The blood and sweat of Jesus help us to clean
> Our own wounds and bear the pain inflicted on us.[39]

Wounded Healers

Most women find the healing of their pain possible only in the context of solidarity with other wounded spirits. They move from a sense of victimhood to seeing themselves as survivors and finally toward a transformative view of themselves as wounded healers. In seeing Jesus as the wounded healer, women heed Jesus' call for them to become healers.[40] The suffering Jesus, who, as the Christ, is in solidarity with the suffering people is not simply a memory of the past. In the lives of women wounded healers, Christ becomes real. Christ is alive, Lascano says, among the "militant, protesting Filipino women who have taken up the cudgels of the struggle for themselves and for the rest of the Filipino nation."[41]

In the struggle to be whole again, women connect all concerns about justice, peace, people, and the earth to one basic issue: the fullness of life. When women are able to identify their triple burden of economic deprivation, gender exploitation, and social victimization, their experiences of suffering can ignite the fuel of women's struggle for liberation. The songs of two women who call themselves Inang Laya (Mother Freedom) explicitly connect the issue of gender with the wider social and political issues. In their song "Base Militar," they call on women to join the struggle for freedom. They insist that the Philippine government must stop its madness of hosting American military bases; their presence only drags the Philippines into the American wars of aggression, and ultimately mocks the nation's sovereignty. Moreover, the "G.I. Joes" take advantage of the Filipino women and, in several instances, have shot people who wandered near the bases. When investigated, these soldiers gave the same lame excuse for the shootings: they thought the people they killed were wild pigs. Inang Laya sings:

Pampalipas libog ng mga sundalo	Used to relieve the lust of the soldiers
Pagbibigay hilig sa kanilang mga bisyo	Giving in to their hobbies and vices
Manyikang buhay na nilalaro,	As live dolls, they treat them as toys
Libangan lamang ng mga 'Kano.	Mere pastime for the American guys.
Sa base military ay walang katarungan	In the military bases there is no justice
Banyaga'y hari sa ating bayan	Foreigners are the rulers of our country
Baboy damo ang trato sa tao	They treat people like wild pigs
At walang karapatan ang mga Pilipino.[42]	Filipinos are deprived of their rights.

Inang Laya does not use "churchy" language. However, its songs echo deep theological questions related to the same issues the historical Jesus was concerned about: the value of human life, the goal of peace, and the ethically appropriate use of power. Jesus knew the paralyzing effect of any oppressive condition upon individuals and peoples. Just as he called the paralyzed man by the pool of Beth-zatha to stand up (Jn 5:1–15), Inang Laya urges the Filipino people to stand up against a system that robs them of their lives.

Eighty-five percent of Filipinos are living in poverty. More than half are women. These suffering women can be wounded healers when, in their own small ways, they work for the healing of the land and people.

The *Pasyon:* A Journey from Darkness into Light

The theology of struggle takes the context of suffering as its starting point, and the theology of Filipino feminist theologians is based in women's experiences of suffering. Feminist theologians examine their social context and investigate how Christianity's teachings about Jesus Christ contribute to their sufferings, specifically as women. Hope for the fullness of life is the ultimate vision within the overall struggle for societal transformation. Mary John Mananzan asserts that the starting point in doing theology in the Philippines cannot be other than women's suffering. She contends that the *pasyon* forms the core of that life of affliction and is connected to woman's emancipatory struggle: "But there are signs of hope. A political consciousness and social movements for change—and the continuing empowerment of women—have developed among its people, promising a true and lasting Easter Sunday."[43]

The *pasyon* confronts women with the reality that one passes over from darkness into light, from death to life. The flow of the paschal mystery culminates in Easter, and so a spirituality of struggle serves as a corrective to the Good Friday religiosity of Philippine folk Catholicism.

According to Virginia Fabella, Jesus' passion is an act of solidarity with the people in his time. The passion of Jesus is relived and experienced among the militant Filipino women who choose to struggle for themselves, for their sisters, and for the rest of the poor people.[44] It must be noted though, that there are also some middle-class and privileged women who choose to walk, in solidarity with the poor, along the path that Jesus walked. Many of them have professed that their faith in Jesus has enabled them to survive on a life-and-faith journey that entails their involvement in the struggle for the fullness of life.[45] This is affirmed by Catholic activist Victoria Narciso-Apuan: "What sustains me in my personal and communal journey is the thought that I have but one life to live and I must live it as intensely and as single-mindedly as Jesus did."[46]

Fabella points out that Filipino women's Christologies are not mere products of an academic exercise or the result of speculative activity to interpret Jesus. She asserts that Filipino women's Christologies are "confessions of our faith in this Jesus who has made a difference in our lives . . . and . . . active engagement in striving towards the full humanity Jesus came to bring."[47] Indeed, most Filipino feminist theologians who have been cited above have been and still are involved, in one way or another, in the struggle for justice and peace. Their Christology has emerged from praxis and embodied engagement with the issues of daily survival as women and as a people. To Lascano, this is what the story of incarnation is all about: becoming the "concrete expression of God's involvement in the historical process of humanity."[48]

Lakbayan as the Story of Women's Journey with the People

The Tagalog word *lakbay* means "to travel" or "to go on a journey." This is connected to another word, *lakbayan*, which is a contraction of a Tagalog phrase *lakad ng bayan*, where *lakad* means "to walk" and *bayan* means "people or nation." *Lakbayan*, therefore, means a caravan of people walking or journeying toward freedom and liberation. *Lakbayan* is a protest walk. During the height of the Marcos dictatorship in the Philippines, people organized *lakbayans* to vent publicly their opposition to the unjust acts and undemocratic programs of the government. *Lakbayan* was a way to campaign for public support for their cause in spite of the risks of government reprisals, which could take the form of harassment, arrests, and salvaging (extra-judicial killing). Usually synchronized nationwide, *lakbayans* might cover fifty kilometers or more. People walk for days, passing several towns and converging on the capital city, to hold big protest rallies where representatives of different sectors—fisherfolk, peasants, workers, professionals, students, urban poor, women, and church people—articulate their situation and struggles. They make demands of the government. Interspersed among the speeches are protest songs, dances, and prayers. The change of government leaders after the dictatorship of Ferdinand Marcos did not effect significant change for the betterment of people's living conditions.[49] Graft and corruption continue. The new leaders' desire for privilege and power and their class interests make them renege on their promises to the people. They surrender their political will to the pressures of their foreign masters. It is not a surprise that militarization continues to accompany the anti-people programs of the Philippine government. Militarization is usually aligned with the interests of globalized capitalism represented by transnational and multinational corporations.

The 1997 statement of the Philippine Church People's Response (PCPR) and Kasimbayan (Ecumenical Fellowship) on *lakbayan* is still relevant in the year 2006. At the time it was issued, people walked to protest against the government's program of strengthening the export-oriented, import-dependent economy to gain entry into the draconian WTO. The ecumenical movement and the people's organizations criticized state leaders who have made laws that cater to the interests of foreign investors and laws that are harsh in their application to the common *taó*, the ordinary people. In its *lakbayan* statement, PCPR laments: "Even our future is already mortgaged. He [Ramos] has opened the doors of the Philippines so that the big foreign capitalists will have unhampered access to our country's rich resources" (my translation). The next presidents, Joseph Estrada and Gloria Macapagal-Arroyo, have been no different. In fact, one seems to outdo the other in mastering the arts of deceit, graft, and corruption. Assured by their foreign masters of unfailing support, these government officials have shamelessly eliminated the gains of previous peoples' struggles for social, political, and economic reforms, including land reform.[50]

Lakbayan is a journey of the people, a concrete experience of what Lascano calls the moment of Jesus' passion, that moment of accompanying and doing what needs to be done. Accompanied by believing and doubting disciples, Jesus walked the dusty roads among the downtrodden poor, attended to the sick, and healed the despised lepers. He crossed paths with those who considered him an enemy and a troublemaker. The significant point in Lascano's reflection is her identification of the "enlightened Filipino women" as the ones who become Jesus' "incarnated challenge," the embodiment of Christ:

> Following Jesus' blazed paths, these enlightened Filipino women, who are immersed among the people and events of their times, are Jesus' incarnated challenge, the Risen Lord's question to the present inhumanity, blind rage, ambition, political masochism, corrupting greed and unfeeling complacency in the country. Where are these women who are "carrying the spice they had prepared"? They are behind the People's Reform Code to question the government land reform program. They are managing human rights desks, healing the sick, feeding the hungry, building basic ecclesial communities among the poor as well as among the open middle class and wealthy, teaching in classrooms or under mango trees or in tattered make-shift schools in remote barrios, facilitating prayer meetings. They are strengthening organizations being honed to continue the struggle in streets and byways where, united in purpose to give the country to its people, they will smile and laugh again.[51]

Women who have gone through the passion of Christ have transformed themselves. They have embodied the Christ who accompanied them as they walked with other suffering people who also bear the image of the crucified Christ. In other words, Jesus' *pasyon* is a day-to-day reality of the *lakbayan* among Filipino women as they strive for abundant life. Jesus' passion is incarnated in women "who suffer and therefore struggle."[52] Emelina Villegas, a Catholic nun, has observed that people endure suffering even as they struggle, because they have hope in the assurance Jesus gave when he said, "And remember, I am with you always, to the end of the age" (Mt 28:20b).[53]

Lakbayan, the Convergence of *Pasyon* and *Lakaran*

The seeds of *lakbayan* were sown in the brown soil centuries ago, when women and men walked long distances to the town centers to make known their sentiments about issues that concerned their communities. The seed is the *lakaran*, a variant of *lakad* (to walk) that also indicates that the walk is done by groups of people or communities for a particular goal. Teresita B. Obusan, whose research centers on Filipino religious culture, defines *lakaran* as a "pilgrimage towards understanding a little better our spiritual roots."[54] The pilgrimage is a process, and the process is as important as the goal.

Lakbayan takes nourishment from the concept of *lakaran*, formed during the time of the *Katipunan*, the revolutionary movement founded by Andres Bonifacio toward the end of the nineteenth century. *Lakaran* was an image of an arduous journey on foot from the darkness of Spain's control to the light of *kalayaan*, freedom.[55] Procopio Bonifacio visualized this image in a poem addressed to his fellow *Katipuneros:*

Lakad, aba tayo, titig-isa nag hirap	Walk on, lowly people, endure hardship,
tunguhin ang bundok	head for the hills,
kaliwanagan ng gubat	the bright forests
gamitin ang gulok at sampu ng sibat	use our arms and tens of spears
ipagtanggol ngayon Inang Pilipinas.[56]	We will defend Mother Philippines right now.

Reynaldo Ileto points out that the poem connects the Filipino revolution against the Spanish colonizers to the *pasyon* of Jesus the Christ. Jesus walked the journey to the hill of Calvary. In this *lakaran*-unto-death, in victoriously rising from the dead, the Second Person became fully the light.[57] In the *lakaran* of the *Katipunan* movement, the women did not serve merely as cooks and nurses. They also served as information gatherers and messengers—and as combatants. Isabelo de los Reyes, an advocate for the church's independence from Spain and for labor unions, wrote in 1890 that some women served as religious functionaries within the revolution. As priestesses, de los Reyes noted, they presided over the rituals of initiation of candidates into the *Katipunan* movement. These rituals included a *pacto de sangre*, a blood compact. As priestesses, these women also gave the blessings of Bathala, the Supreme Deity, to those who joined the revolutionary movement.[58]

Lascano notes that the *pasyon* did not just hone women's abilities to be disciples who accompanied the suffering Jesus. In contemporary times the women are not there simply to comfort those who suffer. They, themselves, carry the cross with Jesus and go through Jesus' passion as they suffer with the people:

> In the passion for social transformation, death takes on a new level of meaningfulness. . . . Today many Filipino women do not merely accompany Christ to the Calvary as spectators. They carry the cross with him and undergo his passion in an act of identification with his suffering.[59]

One may notice a similarity between the Filipino concept of *lakbayan* and the Hispanic/Latino theology that exclaims, "*Caminemos con Jesús!*" (we walk with Jesus). However, unlike the Hispanic theology of accompaniment that is about "learning to walk" in the United States as immigrants,[60] *lakbayan* is about people who walk with Jesus as internal refugees in their own homeland, negotiating a labyrinthine path within the same geographical location.

Lakbayan as a Symbol of Resurrection

Emelina Villegas examines culture and new forms of religious rituals and symbols that have emerged in the context of struggle. She operates from the premise that culture is a force for change. In funeral services of fallen militants, she has seen firsthand the strong power of resurrection emerging in the resolve of the living "to go on with the struggle with the assurance of victory because Christ himself had affirmed it."[61] In this sense *lakbayan* also becomes an expression of *luksa ng bayan* (the mourning of the people) over the symbolic death of *kagawasan* or *kalayaan* (freedom). Villegas points to the struggle as a symbol of the resurrection. People will continue to rise up to proclaim freedom. The Philippine delegates to the Asian Theological Conference (ATC) on liberation spirituality led by Fabella have observed that pastoral workers recognize the importance of integrating popular forms of religiosity. These pastoral workers, they say, "integrate the Way of the Cross with contemporary forms of protest and conscientization, such as the *lakbayan*, a people's march patterned after the Israelites' journey to the Promised Land."[62] The ATC delegates view the *lakbayan* as a metaphor for the Exodus, a march toward freedom from the bondage of oppression. Perhaps we could compare *lakbayan* to the march of the people who accompanied Jesus toward the city of Jerusalem (Lk 9:51; Mk 10:32–34). It is a journey of people from the periphery of society toward the geographical center of power in order to call those who are in positions of power to be accountable for their actions (Mt 21:6–16). Better still, *lakbayan* may be understood as a sign that points to the resurrection. The two disciples who walked down the road to Emmaus with a stranger did not understand the meaning of the resurrection until the stranger who walked with them broke bread and shared it with them. The disciples then realized that the journey signaled that Jesus lives as the Christ in their midst (Lk 24:13–36). The journey is Jesus' life. He claimed the freedom to live simply, to travel light, and yet to live a life of compassion for those who have less. He embodied the passion to celebrate love and life.

If a Christian symbol arises from the story of the people, then *lakbayan* is a symbol "that carries the Jesus story unfolding in history, incarnated in the dreams, hopes, and yearnings of peoples."[63] Women have walked the *lakbayan* in the *pasyon* of the struggle. Some have stumbled along the way. Some have grown weary. Some have found inspiration in the thought that Jesus has always walked with them, and they have heeded Jesus' call for a "total commitment and detachment," a call that prods them to reexamine their lifestyles, choices, and relationships against the measure of God's yardstick.[64] Ruiz-Duremdes affirms that Jesus the Christ "moves Filipino Christians to accompany the oppressed in their journey toward a friendlier tomorrow that starts with a reversal of social structures of injustice obtaining in our country."[65] Thus, *lakbayan* is intertwined with the *pasyon* story—a story of Filipino women's journey with the people. The people who go on with this journey continue because they have hope in the resurrection story. The resurrection is a challenge to transcend the darkness of pain and to start a fresh new life. Padillo-Olesen urges women to listen to the mystical call of the resurrection, which beckons them to leave their symbolic graves.

> Come out of the grave
> You cannot lie in the grave forever—
> in the grave of despair, hatred,
> fear, anger, cold and greed.
>
> You cannot forever shut your
> eyes from the beauty of nature,

the warmth of sunshine
and from the existence
of your other fellow humans.

Dance in the morning
Easter has come
Jesus has vanquished death
Problems we can overcome.

Celebrate the joy of Easter morning
Experience Jesus walking with you
in the narrow byways in life
alive, talking, walking with you
side by side in flesh and blood.[66]

In the realm of the people's collective struggle, the resurrection is the hope and vision for the nation to break free from captivity and to move toward a new heaven and new earth. Resurrection urges one to be in touch, yet transcend, the experience of pain and death. The song "Banagbanag" (dawn) articulates the crucified people's passion, hope, and vision for the resurrection:

Sud-onga ang adlaw sa kahapunon
Natina sa dugo ang nagkuyanap
Nga landong
Sud-onga ang nasod
sa iyang kagabhi-on
Naduhig sa dugo
ang atong yutang tabunon
Hataas ang gabi-ing
atong pagtukawan
Hataas ang dalan nga
atong pagalaktan
Sa tumoy sa pangandoy
may langit nga bughaw
Ang nawong sa sidlakan
mapahiyumong kahayag
Mosidlak ang adlaw,
ang bulawanong silaw
Mobanagbanag ang bag-ong buntag
Mo-abot ang gisa-ad
nga bag-ong ugma.[67]

Behold the setting sun at dusk
Blood tinted the creeping
darkness
Behold the nation
in its darkest night
Blood has drenched
the face of our brown soil
Long will be the night
of our vigil
Long and far will be the road
that we will walk
Yet at the end of our dreams
We see the blue skies
The countenance of the east
glow with the smiling light
The sun will shine,
The golden radiance
A new day will be dawning
What was promised will come
It is the new tomorrow.

To the 85 percent of the almost 87 million Filipinos, this is the hope of the resurrection. The dark reality of suffering and death is palpable, but the hope for liberation is a powerful, energizing vision. This hope for a new day has even made lovers change their arcane love songs and dreams of happiness. In "Awit ng Pag-ibig" (song of love) sung by women, lovers were invited to weave dreams with them and to sing songs of love not just for themselves but for the people as well:

Nayon iba na ang ating awit, Mahal	Now our song is different, my dear
Di lamang sa atin ang kaligayahan	Happiness is not only for us
Dako pa roon ang ating hangganan	Ours is beyond that limit
Puso'y may tungkulin. . . .	The heart has a duty. . . .
May ibayong damdamin.	It brings a special feeling
Halina, tumayo ka't ating awitin	Come, arise, and let us sing
Awit ng pag-ibig na siyang awit natin	The song of love that is our song
Pag-ibig sa bayan, pag-ibig sa kapwa.	Love of country, love of fellow beings
Ito ang dalisay; ito ang dakila.[68]	This is the pure, this is the sublime love.

A love song that celebrates the resurrection is a song that embraces the lover in the bosom of the Motherland. Then it becomes a love song for the land that has cradled and nourished the singers and their songs in her womb. This love song is also for other creatures to which the earth has given birth. The song tells of a vision that points to a resurrection experience. In a country where the sociopolitical system smothers human dignity and snuffs out lives in their prime upon the altar of Mammon, one cannot simply speak of resurrection in terms of an ethereal, spiritualized notion. The resurrection is about life lived in its fullness. It is not a postmortem reward for suffering. It is not something reserved for a certain privileged class. Fabella strongly stresses that resurrection is life lived on earth, and lived according to the will and purpose of God. She seems to echo the new song that lovers sing in the context of struggle when she says that "true life is the message of the resurrection—life that has meaning, life that endures."[69] To take Jesus' resurrection seriously, one must not only speak of resurrection as the restoration of dignity and honor for which people have been struggling on the personal and societal level.[70] One must also take in its ecological implications, so that the earth can continue to sustain life.[71]

Encompassing the *lakbayan* of struggle, the *pasyon* is an image of suffering, but it also points to a new way of life. The image of a woman in labor is another metaphor for it. The *pasyon* gives birth to a new embodiment of a new Christ, a Christ born in each woman who, in the words of the third-world women theologians, has "passion and compassion" for life.[72] This view is anchored in the Filipino feminist theologians' understanding of Jesus as a historical figure. Jesus is viewed as one who is fully human in the sense that he is fully free, one who knows what it means to be liberated, and who therefore works to liberate those who are shackled by forces that dehumanize them.

JESUS–FULLY LIBERATED HUMAN BEING AND LIBERATOR

Recurrent in the writings of Virginia Fabella and Mary John Mananzan is the image of Jesus as the fully liberated human being and as the liberator. He is the Paschal Lamb, both a revolutionary and a political martyr. His teachings and ministry led him to the cross. Fabella and Mananzan do not glorify the suffering that oppressive social structures impose on people. They recognize, however, that suffering endured for the sake of the realization of God's reign can be redemptive. Mananzan makes it clear that, in a context of struggle, Christ is the liberating figure, the one "whose mission, actions, words were focused on the poor and the oppressed, and who continues to work out with struggling people as a total and concrete salvation from structural evil towards concrete blessings that have already begun but are still to be perfected."[73]

Jesus and the New Christ: The Fully Liberated and Liberating Human Being

The longing for fullness of life among the Filipino people pervades the stage plays that have emerged from the people's *pasyon*. A poignant but powerful example that Mananzan cites is the play "Bagong Kristo" (new Christ). This play has inspired ordinary people during different epochs of Philippine history. People have appropriated it to proclaim their message. The theme that runs through the play is the purpose of the main character, a Jesus figure, which is to lead and liberate the oppressed and embrace them in unity and love. In appropriating the play, the workers have portrayed Jesus as a "union leader who struggled for his companions, was betrayed by one of them, and was killed in the picket line."[74] To dramatize the resurrection, the workers carry "the assassinated Christ on their shoulders in a procession across the stage and an actor stepped forward saying, 'They may kill a revolutionary, but they cannot kill the revolution.'"[75] In her reflection upon this play Mananzan develops the image of the new Christ as a fully liberated person who risks his life to usher in the liberation of the victims of injustices and oppression. Mananzan's Christology stands on the ground of her trinitarian understanding of God. The coming of the Holy Spirit uncovers the liberated Christ in the fully liberated person. Jesus' fearful apostles came out from hiding when the Holy Spirit emboldens them to continue the tasks of Jesus the Christ. To drive home her point, Mananzan says, "It has become clear to me that the experience of the resurrection is the experience of the fully liberated Christ, which is in itself liberating."[76]

In another instance Mananzan speaks of her own empowerment in light of her understanding of the resurrection: "My experience of liberation in Christ's resurrection urges me to continue with courage to struggle with the poor and the oppressed in the midst of insecurity."[77]

Time and context have shaped Mananzan's Christology. As a young novice she held onto a gentle Jesus and meek Christ who inspired her traditional, quiet novitiate life. Her image of Jesus changed when she joined the 1975 La Tondeña workers, who went on a landmark strike during the martial-law years.[78] This event initiated her into the people's struggle for justice. On the picket line Mananzan saw an angry Jesus who chased the corrupt entrepreneurs out of the temple. As her involvement with the people's struggle went deeper, her understanding of Jesus as a "fully liberated and liberating human being" also widened. Mananzan recalls:

> As I got more and more involved in the struggle of the people, I began reflecting on Jesus as the fully liberated, and liberating human being. When I read the Gospels, I noticed how Christ was imbued with so much inner freedom that made him free from the slavery of material things, free from the oppressive yoke of the law, and from the undue influence of human respect. He did not shun material things, but used them to facilitate life.[79]

Ironically, when Mananzan claimed the stance of Jesus toward the poor as her own, she began experiencing the "red scare," a smear campaign the government officials, the privileged, and the conservative church hierarchy employs to threaten those who stand with the struggling poor. "If Christ would be living in the Philippines today, people who were considered outstanding Christians, even recipients of papal awards, would certainly also condemn Him as 'subversive.'"[80]

In the Philippines today the practice of one's profession in the service of truth and justice is a dangerous business. In the same manner, doing theology that seriously follows the steps of Jesus of Nazareth is hazardous to one's life. As in many third-world countries, people who try to be true theologians run the risk of harsh critique and cruel treatment by people who are in positions of power inside and outside the church. Assassins may even get promotions for snuffing out the lives of nonconformists in the name of national security. In most cases those in power use their religion and orthodoxy to dominate. People who begin to articulate a Christology that seeks to liberate people from dogmatism and from unjust situations are anathema to them. Thus, people who through their actions and speech articulate a liberating Christology from the perspective of the oppressed, though not in systematic and academic ways, have been harassed, summarily executed, or simply disappeared.[81] Yet, even though these cruel realities continue until the present, the challenge to follow Jesus remains. Women are challenged to understand Jesus as the expression of God's love that takes risks.

The Incarnation: Expression of God's Love That Takes Risks

Like Mananzan, Teresa Dagdag, a Maryknoll missioner, came to view Jesus as a fully liberated person. Her method was to "re-root the Gospel message in the genuine and enduring Filipino values."[82] She retrieved native wisdom and followed the clue of Catholic lay theologian José de Mesa.[83] To articulate her theocentric Christology, she appropriated the native concept of *bahala na* (come what may).[84] *Bahala na* in both Cebuano and Tagalog expresses one's willingness to take risks, as in "so-what?-I-will-do-it-anyway" in the positive sense, of trusting and hoping for the best outcome of an act done with the best of intentions. Along with the concept of *bahala na*, Dagdag has also drawn out from the Filipino value of *malasakit* (empathy), that kind of concern for the other that "exerts painful efforts to achieve its purpose" without expecting a reward or payback. To her, the creation of human beings and giving them freedom was God's great act of *bahala na*, of a love that takes a risk. Moreover, God took a risk by becoming human in Jesus the Christ. The incarnation is a story of God taking a risk. Dagdag writes: "*Bahala na* with *malasakit* becomes a Christian *bahala na*. God must have said '*bahala na*' when God created human beings out of love. . . . The incarnation of Jesus was a big venture for God."[85]

Dagdag's *bahala na* Christology brings to mind Jesus' parable of the vineyard. In this parable the owner sends servants to collect the owner's share from the tenants. However, the tenants seize and beat some of the servants, and even kill others. Thinking that the tenants will respect him, the vineyard owner sends his own beloved son. Instead of welcoming the son, the tenants kill him (Mk 12:1–8).

Dagdag reflects upon Jesus' life in a fresh way. She makes us see a fully liberated Jesus, whose actions stem from his deep understanding of human life and not from a prepared script. The theme of risk taking runs through the stories of Jesus' life and ministry. The gospel deepens our appreciation of Jesus as the good shepherd who goes out of his way, and even lays down his life, for the sheep out of *malasakit* (empathy). Only a fully liberated person could practice such *malasakit* and risk his life in the sense of saying "*Bahala na*!" ("Come what may!") This risk is taken to make people liberate themselves from misery and injustices, from a state of "nonbeing" to becoming "somebody." To Dagdag, the historical Jesus is a model of a fully liberated person who acts out of the sense of *bahala na* and *malasakit* even at the risk of death. To be sure, Jesus was not without fear. Even so, he shows that human beings have the capacity to live boldly as God's image, to love fiercely, to know the truth, and to experience the fullness of life: "Jesus becomes for us the *bahala na* servant of Yahweh. This is why Christ crucified and risen can become our driving force to take risks for the sake of the well-being of others filled as we are with hope that our efforts shall not be in vain."[86]

Having in mind the exhortation of Jesus to his audience to be perfect (Mt 5:48) and to be merciful (Mk 6:36), Dagdag challenges Filipinos to apply this in the Philippine context: "The message of Jesus, *the Bahala Na* servant of Yahweh for the Filipinos of the angry 70's is 'have *malasakit* for your brothers and sisters and be risk takers as your Father in heaven is a risk taker.'"[87]

The concept of *bahala na* can be used in a negative sense to express an uncaring and fatalistic view of life. It can be used to express complacency and indifference, as in, "So what? I don't care." It can come close to Cain's rhetorical question, "Am I my brother's keeper?" (Gn 4:8). Dagdag, however, reclaims and lifts up its positive meaning and uses it to drive home the challenge that a relevant Christology must go beyond the pages of books or academic discourses. Instead, Christology must take the risk of immersion in ordinary people's daily struggles and embody the principles of Jesus, the risk taker. As a risk taker, Jesus is an advocate for human rights and for the realization of God's reign on earth.

Jesus, Human Rights, and the Reign of God

To Filipino feminist theologians, the main agenda of Jesus' risk taking is clearly the realization of the reign of God. As a Maryknoll missioner, Virginia Fabella's Christology takes into account the concern of mission that intertwines with ecclesiology, ethics, anthropology, and culture. She anchors her Christology upon the significance of the historical Jesus, for "to bypass history is to make an abstraction of Jesus, and thus to distort his person, mission and message of love and salvation."[88] She stresses that Jesus did not preach about himself but rather proclaimed the reign of God as the core message of his teachings and preaching. The kingdom of God is inclusive, and Jesus demonstrated inclusivity in his relationship with the excluded ones, with those who were regarded as the "other" in his society. In this light Fabella asserts that Christology must engage in dialogue with life and with other religions and recognize that Jesus' ministry points to the kingdom of God, not to Jesus himself. Echoing an Asian/Buddhist proverb, Fabella says, "Let us not take the finger pointing at the moon to be the moon itself," and hints that Jesus is a finger pointing to God and the reign of God.[89] Like the rest of the Filipino feminists, she does not turn her gaze away from the situation of Filipino women or of other Asian women. She insists that Christology will only be meaningful for her if it is "liberational, hope-filled, love-inspired, and praxis-oriented." Like Mananzan, she strongly claims the image of Jesus as the liberator, and she makes it clear that her concern is to make her Christology as "liberating and empowering for other women" as it is liberating for her.[90]

In the same vein Lydia Lascano claims Jesus the Christ as liberated and liberating, so much so that Jesus passes on the "task of continuing the process . . . towards genuine democracy and Reign of God" to everyone, to all of those who stand "in a chain of active waiting while hastening its coming fulfillment."[91] Affirming the same spirit, Ruiz-Duremdes, once a political detainee, amplifies the challenge to pursue the task of realizing the reign of God that Jesus articulated in his life and teachings. She asserts that human rights advocacy is a Christian imperative, because Jesus himself was a human rights advocate in his time and context. She challenges every "sensible Bible-reading Christian" not to gloss over the call of God for people "to be advocates for those whose rights are trampled upon." Working for a just social condition and struggling for economic and political self-determination are important ministries of the Christian and of the church. She urges Christians not to claim to be faithful believers in God who is incarnate in Jesus if they cannot take seriously the fact that Jesus stood in solidarity with the nobodies of society. Furthermore, Ruiz-Duremdes says, "It is incarnating the liberating power of the good news of Jesus Christ into the economic processes in society which translates in opposing the unjust distribution of wealth, inequitable trade agreements, and the stranglehold of imperialist globalization."[92]

At this point one senses that Filipino feminist theologians speak of Christology only in relation to the social, political, and economic realities and injustices in the country, and in the Third World overall. One must understand that a theologian who takes the historical Jesus seriously cannot ignore the glaring realities of Philippine society. As women share the concerns of male Filipino theologians, they realize that any Christology will be inadequate if it ignores women's experiences of oppression, specifically because of their being women. Does it matter to Filipino feminist theologians that the historical Jesus is male?

Jesus' Maleness: "Accidental" to the Salvific Process

Feminist debates on the issue of gender give us some understanding of the shape of feminist Christologies. Moderate feminists take Jesus' gender as not crucial to his liberating acts. Those who go beyond the traditional view that only Jesus reveals the Christ and proceed to explore the feminine embodiments of the christic and the divine may be called radical feminists. To most Filipino feminist theologians the vision and action of the fully liberated human Jesus are all encompassing. Thus, they have no problem with Jesus' maleness and affirm the moderate view that Jesus the Christ is a feminist male savior who liberates women from patriarchy. After all, what is important for one to be a feminist is to answer positively these two basic questions: "Are you aware of the women question? Are you committed to do something about it?"[93] Jesus the Christ, according to Mananzan, would have answered these questions positively. She states: "I am amazed at the inner freedom with which Christ broke through the customs and prejudices of the patriarchal Hebrew society."[94] Similarly, Fabella considers Jesus a liberated male Jew. She reasons that Jesus showed a "most uncommon" attitude and treatment of women that could not have been expected "even for a 'good' Jew of his day."[95] Jesus, she notes, did not conform to the norms of his society. This view of Jesus is indeed liberating for many women in the church. Indeed, the Gospels show evidence of patriarchy in the Jewish society in Jesus' time. However, the text needs to be liberated also from androcentrism, and so feminists must be keen in discerning their method of reading the text. Thus, like their Asian sisters, Filipino feminist theologians must take measures to avoid the pitfall of an unconscious endorsement of anti-Semitism.

On the question of Jesus' gender, Mananzan and Fabella agree that the maleness of Jesus is not important; it is only functional in his becoming human. They acknowledge, however, that feminist concern regarding the issue of Jesus' maleness still stands because historically patriarchy has distorted Christology and has used Jesus' maleness as a basis for the treatment of women as inferior and less human than men. This distorted view of the female gender is still strong in the churches that block the move for women's ordination. According to Fabella:

> Among Asian women, the maleness of Jesus has not been a problem for we see it as "accidental" to the salvific process. His maleness was not essential but functional. By being male, Jesus could repudiate more effectively the male definition of humanity and show the way to a right and just male-female relationship, challenging both men and women to change their life patterns.[96]

Considering her work for women's empowerment and emancipation, Mananzan affirms Fabella and notes that she was able to transcend "Christ's maleness, realizing that his maleness is not essential but rather functional." Yet, Mananzan does not dismiss the issue of Jesus' gender and continues to wrestle with the implication of a male Savior and with the idea of "being one with the suffering Christ." She is certainly aware that the male-dominated church has used both notions as tools to perpetuate the victimization of women as well as to instill a victim mentality in women. Some women have internalized the idea of being a victim to the extent that they have used these notions as a religious justification to remain in abusive relationships and to make sacramental their victimization. There are instances of women who internalize the role of victim and want to remain in the situation as the only way they can get attention. Mananzan is critical of concepts commonly held by women who join or who belong to the religious orders. Mananzan points to the possibility that some women hold the idea of having a "personal relation with Christ" as an unconscious projection of the long-held view that "a woman cannot be happy without a man."[97] Mananzan's suspicion opens the door for women to explore further the erotic and sexual discourse among women in their reference to Jesus, including the idea of the novices' entry into the nunnery as taking vows in marriage with Jesus as their "husband." This discussion opens further the question of the methodology women use in doing theology.

SOME ISSUES ON METHODOLOGY

Social Class, Gender, and Storytelling

Filipino women theologians generally do not articulate explicitly their methodology in doing theology. Yet it is obvious in the above discussions that Filipino women take experience as their starting point and that they affirm the approach of women who are not trained in theology. For instance, Lascano has observed that among urban poor women, one cannot speak of liberation from male domination as if it were separate from the community's liberation from social problems. She asserts that urban poor women's inclination for storytelling is a potent factor for the proclamation of the gospel. Women who have experienced Jesus' liberating and empowering presence have a great role to play in ushering in the realization of a transformed society. This liberation is happening, and will continue to happen, as women arise and tell in many ways the gospel story that they have claimed as their own. Anointed by their own liberation experience, the women tell their story of their healing and deliverance: "How their broken hearts were healed by building community; their liberation from the captivity and discrimination and second-rate citizens status; their process of freeing themselves from the prison of male domination towards becoming equal partners to transforming society."[98]

Race and Ethnicity

Filipino feminist theologians recognize that race must also have a place in doing Christology. The issue of race is already embedded within the struggle against imperialism, and thus, it is assumed to be included in the discourse. However, so far, like the male theologians, they have not addressed the issue with intentionality. While the image of the Black Nazarene is present in some Roman Catholic churches, the image that is predominant and ubiquitous in the Philippines is still the colonial, white Jesus. A blond, blue-eyed Jesus is still present in the visual materials for church schools, especially among Protestant churches. This reinforces the internalization of a notion of beauty that is associated with a fair complexion, which is still considered the norm of beauty among the brown-skinned people. The mail-order bride phenomenon among Filipinos is triggered not only by the longing among the women for economic uplifting, but also marrying a white person is a path to the fulfillment of the desire, conscious or unconscious, to have children whose looks are "upgraded" into the *mestizaje* category.

Moreover, the issue of ethnicity needs to be addressed in connection with the retrieval of the indigenous traditions. To say the Philippines is the only Christian country in Asia is almost equivalent to saying that it is the most colonized country in Asia. Its theological training centers follow a Western approach and curriculum. Thus, the theologies produced here hardly take notice of the reality that Filipinos come from different tribal groups and that ethnocentrism exists. Somehow, theological reflections tend to ignore the vilification of indigenous spiritualities as an effect of the homogenization effort of the colonizers to consolidate their power over the country.

Gender and Sexuality

Feminist theologians in the Philippines have made an important contribution by bringing into the discourse gender as an important ingredient in doing Christology. However, they have avoided the matter of sexuality and sexual orientation or the preference of some women to relate to other women. They have not addressed in their writings the problem of homophobia within the church and in society.[99] Needless to say, the issue of sexual orientation, along with gender issues, must be included in the agenda for doing Christology in the future.

At this point one can only say that feminist Christology in the Philippines is still a project in progress, and there is yet much work to do in this area.

Religion and Culture

Thus far, we have seen that feminist theologians in the Philippines have argued for a relevant and holistic Christology. Christology must consciously address also the issue of religion and culture. Mananzan acknowledges that her encounter with people from different religious traditions has broadened her perspective on Christology and has helped her to distinguish the historical Jesus from the Christ. She understands that Asian religions also have their saviors or Christ-figures. She stresses that her deep respect for the Christ-figures of Asian religions has enriched rather than diminished her Christian faith:

> It is the Christness that is important and not the fact that Jesus was a Nazarean. I began to appreciate Buddha, Mohammed, the Hindu Gurus, and all the "Christs" of all times, ages, and places who made God visible to people. Nevertheless, Jesus of Nazareth remains for me the Christ of my own history of salvation. His life and teachings remain an inspiration to me, especially the liberating experience of His resurrection.[100]

In the process of colonization, and in the midst of ongoing neocolonization, the European-American Christian consciousness has almost succeeded in wiping out the memories of indigenous religions from the official theology of the church. This is especially true among the Protestants. Some Protestant and Catholic theologians have observed that among Filipinos who practice folk Catholicism, conversion was only a "change of garments"; that is, they "replaced their *anitos* with the images of the Christian saints."[101] However, the church, Catholic and Protestant, officially has dismissed as superstition what remains of the indigenous religions' beliefs and practices, such as ancestor worship and beliefs in *anitos*/spirits, and d*iwata*s/goddesses/gods. Thailand-based Protestant theologian Salvador Martinez does not see any liberating dimension in popular piety or indigenous religiosity. In categorically saying that these priestesses are "actually witches and sorcerers,"[102] he implies that women who carry on the tradition of the indigenous priestess through their folk Christianity are also witches. Martinez simply affirms the colonizers' view that demonized the priestesses.

Dipping into the Springs of Indigenous Spiritualities

Some women, however, insist that there are other sources and ways of doing theology. Without romanticizing the indigenous traditions, Filipino feminist theologians realize that rural people, especially the tribal peoples, have much to teach, as their indigenous consciousness of the Sacred has remained intact. Because of their experience of poverty and the evident destruction of the earth around them, the indigenous peoples have stood at the forefront of the struggle against the life-destroying forces of Mammon. With their continued affinity for the feminine principle of the Sacred, the indigenous peoples have given a clue to the feminist and ecofeminist theologians of the positive value of reclaiming earth-based spiritualities.

Today, more and more Filipino women are beginning to identify and to appreciate the liberating elements in the Filipino traditions and indigenous spiritualities, elements that have enriched the articulation of their theologies.[103] In spite of this, Filipino women theologians remain hesitant to explore the feminine principle of the Sacred as the image of the Christ. They are hesitant to stretch, if not transgress, the boundaries set by traditional Christologies. One could logically surmise that their claim to have no problem with the maleness of Jesus has something to do with such timidity. The women may be restrained by the chauvinistic view that Christians have nothing to draw from indigenous and Asian religions, especially prophetic-political resources.[104] Christian theology taught converts that the Christ is located only in the person of Jesus. Besides, Christianity has also inculcated deep in the Filipino convert's consciousness that Christ is "the" family name of Jesus, and consequently, they conclude that if Jesus is male, then Christ must be male, too. Some Filipino feminist theologians, however, have begun to see the new Christ embodied by struggling women and by some liberated and liberating human beings. How far will Filipino feminist theologians go in appropriating indigenous traditions as a resource in their christological construction? Some Filipino women's emerging christological reflections associate Jesus the Christ with the feminine principle of God.

FEMINIST IMAGES OF CHRIST

Woman as Christ Disfigured, Christ as Mother

Immersed in the liberationist tradition of EATWOT and the theology of struggle, Virginia Fabella easily sees Jesus as the liberated and liberating person. Understandably, Fabella has had difficulty shaking off the image of the male Jesus and the subsequent implication that the Christ is male. Even so, she has begun to look at Christ through a new lens. This perspective allows her to see the Christ in the lives of struggling mothers like Digna. Digna was pregnant. Her husband lost his job due to illness. Desperate, Digna attempted to poison her family by feeding them fertilizer to end their suffering in abject poverty. In looking at the plight of many women who are caught in the dark pit of despair, Fabella states that they "are today the Christ disfigured in his passion."[105] Yet, Fabella moves beyond the disfigured Christ. She looks at the resurrection as the event that not only confirmed the Christness of Jesus but also freed Jesus from the limitation of "the particularities of his maleness and Jewishness. . . . Jesus is alive and we encounter him in our sisters and brothers."[106]

The image of the disfigured Christ is seen in the life of Visminda Pangilinan-Gran. Frail and small, Pangilinan-Gran has worked as pastor, human rights advocate, evangelist, and friend of the poor. When inundated with threats upon her life, Pangilinan-Gran uttered these words, reflecting on her possible death: "It would be good to die seeing the dawn and brightness of the morning. But if my life is needed in the night to usher in the morning, then, I have nothing else to give, because I am poor, but this life of mine."[107]

Her work and her preaching against the abuses and human rights violations perpetrated by the military and powerful politicians led to her death. On May 1, 1989, she and her husband were murdered in their home. People who knew her considered her an embodiment of Christ; she was "Christ-centered, life-giving."[108] She is, for the youth, a *nanay* (mother), but more specifically, a Christ-mother, as expressed in the poem "Nanay Minda":

> During our suffering you helped us,
> We were hungry and you gave us food;
> Thirsty and you gave us drink,
> We were astray and you led us and sheltered us.

They called you communist—
We call you God's gift to us.

They hated and brutally killed you
Because of your kind heart and great mind,
They took you away from us;
Enemies of change, woe to them!

You left us with open eyes, minds, hearts
to the realities in life,
Your death strengthens us to follow
The pursuit of attaining God's Kingdom
That we may all have abundant life.

Nanay Minda—
In you we know what real service to
The people is—it is death!
How can we follow the way you offer
Your life for God's people?

We cherish you.[109]

The artwork printed with the poem portrays a figure of a slain woman lying on the ground, arms stretched to the side. Over the body four high-powered rifles form a cross. Emerging from the body is a dove, flapping its wings, rising. Thus, an anonymous artist has expressed an understanding of the woman-Christ seen not only in the life of Visminda Pangilinan-Gran, but also in many others whose lives have been snuffed out before their time by those who wield the power of the gun. A poster that shows a burning candle captures the story of these women. Its caption reads, "Those who give light must endure burning."

Another image of a mother as a disfigured Christ comes from the reflection of Rebecca Asedillo, a Protestant and the first national coordinator of the Association of Women in Theology. She discerns the Christ in mothers who do everything to enable their beloved children to survive and live. She recalls a story shared by a sugar-plantation worker at a time when the collapse of the sugar industry brought much hunger to Negros and hundreds of children starved. "I saw a mother with three starving children in the cane field. The children were crying because they were hungry, but the mother had nothing to feed them. So, with her bare hands, she started to squeeze the juice out of the sugar cane and gave it to her children. I discovered Christ in that life-giving act."[110]

Asedillo affirms the sugar-plantation worker's discovery that Christ was in the life-giving act of that distressed mother. Asedillo's reflection points to the basic meaning of the word *Christ:* life giving. Like most Filipino feminist theologians, she does not distinguish the gender of the historical Jesus from the gender-neutral Christ when she says, "Christ himself, 'though he was a man,' expressed himself in images that connote mothering qualities."[111]

Asedillo recognizes that Christ has expressed himself in terms of motherhood. She has referred to Jesus' analogy of himself as a mother hen who longed to gather her brood under her wings but wept over stubborn Jerusalem's preferred path (Mt 23:37; Lk 13:34). Jesus knew the pain and anguish of a mother who sees her children treading the path to destruction rather than choosing the way to life. Jesus the Christ showed the nature of motherhood, standing up "for everything that affirms life and oppose everything that brings death."[112] Filipino feminists do not romanticize motherhood, nor do they downplay the thorny issue of gender roles in raising children. Yet, the mothering practices in the Philippines allow women across class boundaries to enjoy, in varying degrees, the material and moral support of relatives. In the rural areas mothering is still a community responsibility. Thus, in spite of the material and emotional pressures of raising children, to many Filipino women "the work of mothering is at once burdensome and an unequaled source of joy."[113] The song "Awit ng Isang Ina" (song of a mother) expresses the depth of a mother's love and concern for her child in the midst of a difficult situation:

Dugo at pawis ang puhunan	Blood and sweat I offered
Nang iluwal ang sanggol	To give birth to my child
Kaya't di tutugot	That is why I would never stop
Hanggang maidulot	Until I can give you
Ang bukas na ligtas sa salot.	A future free from the beasts.
Tahan na anak ko, tahan na	Stop crying my child, stop crying
Nagsisikip and dibdib ng iyong ina	Your mother's heart (chest) is heavy
Mga kamay ko'y masdan	Look at my hands
Para sa iyo ay sugatan	For you, they are wounded
Paglilinis ng marumi ng ilan.	Cleaning the mess of the privileged few.

Pakinggan mo ang daing ng bayan	Listen to the cry of the people
Sinisiil ng sakim na iilan	Oppressed by the greedy few
Kalayaa'y ginapos	Freedom is shackled
Mamamaya'y nagpupuyos	The people are suffering
Ang sigaw, pagbabagong lubos.	Their cry, genuine transformation.
Dugo at pawis ang puhunan	Blood and sweat I shed
Upang ipagtanggol ang sanggol	To keep, protect my child from harm
Mga kamay na laan	The hands that are ready
Umaloy sa duyan	To swing the hammock
Matututong lumaban para sa bayan.[114]	Will learn to fight for the people.

Imaging Christ as the Feminine Face of God

Catholic theologians Rosario Battung, Arche Ligo, and Agnes Miclat-Cacayan admit that their encounters with the indigenous peoples have deepened their understanding of the Sacred. Many indigenous peoples who have converted to Christianity continue to carry within them their primal religiosity. They use this perspective as a lens to understand the God that the Bible speaks about. Indigenous traditions understand the Sacred as the source of life, the tender mother who breastfeeds her children with mother's milk. God's breasts are the land and the forests that give the people the things they need. These theologians consider indigenous spirituality an important resource in rethinking the meaning of atonement. Healing is the central theme in indigenous spirituality. In light of this understanding, "at-one-ment" could mean "making whole again and returning to the original harmony and blessing nature is [as well as] being one with oneself and with others, and with the nurturing God of the cosmos."[115]

Seeing the Christ through the Mirror of the Goddess Traditions

In her early writings Mary John Mananzan denied the existence of a goddess tradition, saying, "In Philippine history, there are no traditions of women goddesses."[116] On the contrary, the roots of Filipino belief of God as Mother trace their roots back to the goddess traditions among the indigenous peoples. The need for the feminine image of God surfaces in the veneration of Mary in the Roman Catholic Church. The Manobo tribes in Mindanao have Dagau, the rice goddess, and Ibo, the goddess of the underworld and afterworld. The Mandaya tribe has Manamoan, the earth goddess who presides over childbirth, and on Panay Island, the natives have Alunsina, the creator of the earth, the forests, the lakes, and everything in them. The Tagbanuas have Diwata, their tribal goddess.[117] In the Cordilleras people have rice gods and goddesses *(bulol)*. Among the Bagobo tribe the concept of God breastfeeding the people comes from their belief in the goddess Mebuyan, the many-breasted Mother. There are several variations of the Mebuyan myth. A common strand maintains that Mebuyan is the daughter and embodiment of Tuglibong, the Great Mother, who at the same time created and personified the earth. The indigenous peoples consider Tuglibong and Mebuyan as one. As the source of rice, the goddess Mebuyan is depicted holding her symbols, namely, the pestle and mortar. Represented by the pestle, the tree symbolizes the Great Mother upon whom all that lives grows and hangs. Mebuyan is a symbol of fertility. With her body covered with milk glands, Mebuyan is also a symbol of the One who is life giving and life sustaining. Through her many breasts she feeds the creatures on earth. In many pre-patriarchal societies, breasts are symbolic of the "divine source of life giving moisture" and therefore are associated with the goddess.[118]

The Visayas-based anthropologist priest Pieter Jan Raats has observed that the image of the many-breasted Goddess suggests that all motherhood is rooted in Mebuyan. Mebuyan rides on her mortar, swirls down into the earth to open up a path to the underworld/afterworld in order to prepare the dwelling place for those who die, and guides them to her city in the Beyond. She dies during her journey. Her death is a trip to the underworld/afterworld, and, as she goes down, she drops rice along the way. This act of dropping rice makes her the giver of both life and death. Just as she drops rice, some people die like fallen grains of rice. Yet, she also drops rice that grows and sustains those who are left behind for a while. Mebuyan is the "lasting source of all partial and temporary fertility on earth."[119] Rice, life, and death are interconnected in this goddess tradition. Life and death are not opposites; they are part of the whole of life. Along this line, Miclat-Cacayan views Mebuyan as one of the feminine faces of God.[120] Her view finds support from sociologist Teresita Infante, who holds that the indigenous priestesses have a subterranean connection with the goddesses and female deities, and thus they draw power from these deities.[121] Battung and Ligo hold that indigenous peoples' cosmic spirituality for the wholeness of life connects God, women, and the earth as "sources and roots of life."[122]

The works of these few women are seminal for Filipino Christology. They open a new frontier that not only explores but also reclaims the Filipino goddess traditions in order to understand the feminine face of the Sacred, of God. The image of the many-breasted Mother is a powerful one. Yet, these theologians are not explicit in connecting their reflections on the goddess tradition with Christology. Certainly, they hold the fundamental notion that Jesus the Christ reveals God. If they see the goddess as the feminine image of God, what will the Christ look like as the revelation of the Goddess? One can sense the tension between the women's inclination to dip their fingers into the waters of the goddess tradition and their reluctance to draw and drink from it. One can only hope that these women will gain the audacity to explore the christic characteristics and liberating acts of these goddesses. After a time Mananzan seemed to change her mind and began to acknowledge the tradition of the spirits *(diwatas)*. *Diwata* may also mean deity, gods, and goddesses. Mananzan regards Mariang Makiling as a *diwata* who "brought peace, calm, order, and well-being in the community."[123]

The hesitance of Filipino feminist theologians to explore the connection of the goddess tradition with Christian theology is understandable. It is not easy to shake off the negative and condescending pagan label that Christianity has given to indigenous traditions. This condemnation has been entrenched deep within the colonized consciousness of Filipinos. But if Jesus the Christ reveals the God who carried the people in her womb, who gave them birth (Is 46:3–4), who nursed them as her child (Is 49:10–15), and "as a mother, comforts her child" (Is 66:13), is it so difficult to explore the view that the Christ is a many-breasted Nanay or Ina (mother)? It would be helpful for theologians to lift up the concepts of some early church fathers who understood the close connection of flesh, body, and blood when it comes to nourishing an infant. Clement of Alexandria associates milk with Christ, and Ambrose calls Christ the Virgin who "fed us with her own milk."[124]

In Filipino communities many mothers have nursed and breastfed babies who are not their own because the mothers were unable to do so. Where mothering in some places is a community responsibility, is it not possible to see Christ metaphorically as the many-breasted Mother? If women are part of the body of Christ, are they not the embodiment of Christ's breasts? And can it not be said that in the context of a mothering community, Christ is present as the many-breasted

Mother? Although one cannot romanticize the Goddess, one should also not dismiss the tradition, because it makes us conscious of the "full implication of archetypal female power."[125] Perhaps one need not take the Goddess anthropomorphically. One may, however, embrace the Goddess as the Spirit-Energy, the Feminine Principle that moves us to feel, to see, and to act to change life-destroying realities, and to reflect and to celebrate life. Futher, one need not limit the exploration of Christ as the breastfeeding Mother to the image of the many-breasted Goddess Mebuyan. One can probe deeper into the scriptures to find the image of Christ as the Wisdom-Mother who nurses and nurtures her children. As an echo of the Wisdom tradition in the Hebrew scriptures, in the Gospel according to John, one can see Jesus as a reflection of the image of the breastfeeding mother (Jn 6—7). In the eucharistic discourse in John 6, the Christ is imaged as incarnate Wisdom, breastfeeding her children.[126]

THE WALK WITH JESUS GOES ON– THE JOURNEY TO REIMAGE THE CHRIST MUST CONTINUE

Like a new plant, Filipino feminist theology is still in the process of growing new buds. Even at this stage we can see that the women's Christologies show the potential to deconstruct traditional images of Christ that prop up patriarchal, rigid, and hierarchical patterns in women's lives. The image of Christ as Mother Ina/Nanay/Inay "builds the maternal, compassionate, sensitive, bearing, and up bearing relationship among people."[127] Filipino women need to take bolder steps in exploring and lifting up the feminine image of the Christ by seeing through the lens of the Filipino indigenous traditions. If the prophetess Prisca (Quintilla) in the third century had the courage to proclaim her dream-vision that Christ "in the form of a woman in a white garment"[128] came to her to put wisdom inside her, I have no doubt that Filipino theologians have the courage to discern new, meaningful images of Jesus the Christ in their context today. The image of Jesus as the fully liberated human being who labors to liberate others, of the Christ as the woman-mother who does everything to sustain the life of her child, and of the Christ as the many-breasted Mother who nurtures all life on earth, when taken together, will be empowering and liberating. At this moment globalization takes the offensive to impose a new "religion" marked by the doctrine of free market and consumerist values.

Imperialism is obsessed with going to war and sucking the earth into its machinery. At this crucial time women must gain wisdom from the risk-taking, many-breasted Christ who has passion for life and the power to help us wage peace. Filipino women must face the challenge to keep going, to embody the Christ in accompanying the people in their journey out of the bondage of evil. Her prophetic ministry, her dances, her songs and rituals, must provide healing and inspiration to the wounded spirits out there.[129]

> Women, you *babaylans*
> keep on going, keep on dreaming
> hone poems of resistance
> sing prophetic stories
> kindle fires to cleanse
> kiss the Earth to heal
> dance to celebrate life
> walk with Jesus, friend, *kauban* [companion].
>
> Hold her hands, she, the Christ Mother
> who breathes in us, her milk sustains us
> breathe in, breathe out
> Energy, Wisdom, vast Mystery
> give life—kiss fear goodbye
> embrace the suffering earth
> in the long journey
> in the struggle
> in the fullness of time
> for the fullness of life.

Chapter 5

Gazing at the Postcolonial Jesus

The Multiple Identity of Christ in Hong Kong

There is more possibility to produce an efficacious Christology with our creative imagination, nurtured by our own historical experiences.

—Marcella Althaus-Reid, *Indecent Theology*

DEMOLISHING THE BOUNDARY BETWEEN EAST AND WEST

A huge marketplace. That is how I imagined Hong Kong to be in my childhood days. My image of it took shape from the stories I overheard from a wealthy Chinese Protestant woman who would regularly visit Hong Kong to see relatives and to shop. Indeed, a tourist map introduces Hong Kong as "the destination for entertainment, shopping, dining, culture, heritage, arts and business." It is a beautiful place marked by a seemingly indelible British influence. Recently, Asia's upper-middle class found Hong Kong Disneyland as an alternative to faraway California and Florida. Yet to thousands of Filipino children Hong Kong is the city where their mothers, aunts, and teachers go to work as DHs (domestic helpers). Many of these women leave low-paying professional jobs in the Philippines to work in Hong Kong. For Filipinos and other Asians, Hong Kong is a huge market—a job market.[1]

Hong Kong is located in eastern Asia, bordering China and the South China Sea. In 1842 China ceded Hong Kong to Britain in the Treaty of Nanking, which ended the Opium War, and later ceded Kowloon in the Convention of Peking after another defeat in 1860. In 1898 China was forced to lease the New Territories to Britain for ninety-nine years.[2] Inclusive of Kowloon, the New Territories, and Hong Kong Island, this world city has an area of eleven hundred square kilometers with a population of almost seven million. On July 1, 1997, Hong Kong became the Special Administrative Region (SAR) of China, ending its status as a British colony and fulfilling the provisions of the 1984 Sino-British Joint Declaration. Acquiring a postcolonial status evoked different responses from various segments of Hong Kong society. The idea of being governed, though indirectly, by socialist China kindled insecurity among those who were used to the capitalist system of Hong Kong. Some think that China's socialism has yet to prove its economic success, while Hong Kong's capitalism has "no convincing critics to check its excesses."[3] The early writings of Rose Wu, general secretary of the Hong Kong Women's Christian Council, reflect the people's anxiety. That anxiety stems from the common view that China's concern for human rights is limited to the socioeconomic dimensions of life and does not include civil liberties.[4] In 1997, as the changeover grew nearer, emigration increased. People left Hong Kong, mostly for North America, Europe, and Australia. With a tinge of sadness, Shum Yun Shan asked, "Who are the true Hong Kong people?" She answered her own question by pointing to those who chose to remain "out of sense of belonging to Hong Kong . . . and those in the lower class without any favorable condition to emigrate."[5]

Now, under the "one country, two systems" principle, Hong Kong maintains autonomy in terms of retaining its capitalist economic system. Over the next fifty years it will also maintain an independent system of governance except in matters of defense and foreign affairs.[6] Hong Kong bustles with the characteristic energy of the First World, marked especially by its free-market economy. In this part of Asia the capitalist economy and technology have blurred the boundary between the East and West, or so it seems, on the surface level.[7] Dependent on international trade, Hong Kong had enjoyed a high growth rate as one of Asia's tiger economies. In 2000 it managed to recover from the 1997–98 Asian financial crisis. Although the outbreak of SARS battered its economy, Hong Kong was able to bounce back and claim strong economic growth by late 2003.

The Other Side of Hong Kong's Prosperity

Hong Kong is proud of its strong growth, courtesy of its free market and entrepot economy, which is highly dependent on international trade. One may applaud Hong Kong for its economic prosperity. But one needs to look carefully at this image of prosperity. Two decades ago the World Council of Churches reported that one-third of the suicides in Hong Kong were related to problems of poverty, unemployment, debts, and sickness.[8] Although statistics register a low of 6.7 percent unemployment rate in 2004, official reports tend to show that none of Hong Kong's 6.9 million people lives on or below the poverty line, in contrast to South Korea's 4 percent, or India's 25 percent.[9] These reports gain the affirmation of some economists, while refuting the result of the joint study by the Hong Kong Council of Social Service and Oxfam Hong Kong.[10] In 1996 this joint study pointed out the rising poverty and income disparity in Hong Kong. In 1998 Fok Tin-man of the Society for Community Organisation, a social concern group in Hong Kong, exposed "the hidden poverty in a city of plenty."[11] She pointed out that women, especially the elderly, and children are the most affected. Acknowledging the effects of neoliberal economic schemes, Hong Kong's former chief executive Tung Chee-hwa said in his 2004 policy address that "globalization has aggravated poverty generally in many places around the world and we are no exception."[12] Indeed, not all citizens of Hong Kong have benefited from its economic boom. Its rapid urbanization has even caused serious environmental problems.

Indonesian feminist theologian Marianne Katoppo and Filipino economist Walden Bello point out, however, that in general the Hong Kong labor force gets relatively higher pay than its counterparts in other Asian countries.[13] It is curious to note that while feminist theologian Rose Wu asserts that women are often the poorest of the poor in the Asian context, she does not cite Hong Kong women's experience of poverty and economic oppression.[14] While women in the labor force have definitely contributed to the economic boom in Hong Kong, they remain at the bottom of the salary scale.[15]

The phenomenon of DHs made it possible for Hong Kong women to have the freedom to participate in the economic industry of Hong Kong.[16] These women have absorbed the burden of household work. Anthropologist Nicole Constable discovered that DHs in Hong Kong are "imported" mostly from the Philippines, but also from India, Sri Lanka and other Asian countries. They have to endure discrimination, unjust labor practices, and strict rules in Hong Kong.[17] Constable further points out that some Hong Kong women's social status increases when they are able to employ a live-in *banmui*, especially when these maids are required to wear a uniform.[18]

The Challenges of Plurality and Postcoloniality

In this former British Crown Colony approximately 10 percent of the population is Christian. The rest practice a mixture of local religions. The Chinese population of Hong Kong is mostly Buddhist, but there are also practicing Taoists, Hindus, Muslims, and Jews. Hong Kong's religious plurality and its postcolonial context pose challenges to theology and give shape to its postcolonial discourse. Given such a context, one may ask how Hong Kong Chinese Christian women look at Jesus. Before I proceed to discuss the Christologies of Hong Kong women, a brief statement on postcolonial theory should help us appreciate their postcolonial christological discourse.

Postcolonial critic Arif Dirlik explains that the term *postcolonial* carries a multiplicity of meanings. The term is used in three ways:

> (a) as a literal description of conditions in formerly colonial societies, in which case the term has concrete referents, as in postcolonial societies or postcolonial intellectuals; (b) as a description of a global condition after the period of colonialism, in which case the usage is somewhat more abstract and less concrete in reference, comparable in its vagueness to the earlier term *Third World*, for which it is intended as a substitute; and (c) as a description of a discourse on the above-named conditions that is informed by the epistemological and psychic orientations that are products of those conditions.[19]

The third category of usage largely influenced the theological articulation of Hong Kong women. Postcolonial theory emerged from the criticism of the construction of the "Orient" as the "other," as exotic but stagnant and inferior to whatever is Western.[20] This theory articulates discomfort with the modernist thought that extremely privileges reason, spuriously insists on the possibility of an objective truth, wantonly dominates nature, and espouses nationalist ideals.[21] As cultural criticism, postcolonial theory encourages the examination of travel writings, biography, literary works, aesthetics, and other texts produced by the colonizers and the colonized in order to identify inscribing and reinscribing cultural hegemonies.

Birmingham-based Sri Lankan theologian R. S. Sugirtharajah states that while postcolonialism shares practically all the concerns of postmodernism, it also criticizes the detached attitude of postmodernism. That attitude encourages fragmentation to such an extent that postmodernists hardly offer a theory of resistance or a transformative agenda. Postcolonial theorists also refuse to employ Western master narratives as nationalists/Marxists theorists do in their critique of colonialism.[22] They contend that using Western intellectual tools to dismantle Western colonialism merely reinscribes the centrality of the West.[23] However, considering the condition of the intelligentsia in the world of global capitalism, Arif Dirlik warns that postcolonial theorists must also face the challenge of generating a solid ideological self-criticism and "formulate practices of resistance against the system of which it is a product."[24]

Hong Kong feminist theologians speak about women's varying experiences and are breaking away from the bonds of patriarchal Christologies. They are creatively constructing Christologies that are distinctive to their postcolonial experiences and location. They articulate Christologies that have emerged from their postcolonial gaze at Jesus the Christ. Aware of the colonizing impact of texts, they have become critical of universalizing discourses. Some of them have begun to appropriate the "otherness" of the wisdom tradition of the Chinese culture in constructing their Christologies. They have found ways of using the language of the erotic in their christological project. The voices of the women from Hong Kong, indeed, demonstrate the diversity of christological interpretations in Asia.

FINDING THE MEANING OF JESUS IN THE POSTCOLONIAL WORLD

God in Human Form Suffers and Weeps with Us

Anglican Kwok Pui-lan emerged as a theological voice to be reckoned with when she carried on her task as a university professor in Hong Kong. Her earlier writings reflected her understanding of the concrete struggles of women in Asia. Kwok's past involvement with the ecumenical movements in Asia and with EATWOT has deepened her understanding of the concrete struggles and theologies of third-world women. This engagement also gave her a vantage point from which she could see the strengths and weaknesses of liberation theologies.[25] She was already conscious of the multiple identities of women that results from the multiple oppressions they experience under the patriarchal systems that cut across all segments of society, regardless of class, ethnicity, race, or cultural and religious diversity.[26] The reality that the majority of Asian women live in poverty and suffer gender-specific as well as political oppression led Kwok Pui-lan to see Jesus as the embodiment of a God "who weeps with our pain."[27]

As a Chinese woman, she saw the implications of China's one child per family policy for women. The Chinese government implemented this policy as a convenient response to the burden of an ever-growing population. The policy only reinforced the existing prejudices and discriminatory treatment of girl children. In her impassioned narration of a true story about little Ah Ching, Kwok draws our attention to girls and women not only as victims of patriarchy but also as persons who have moral agency and who have refused to give the oppressive ideology and structure the last word about their lives. Having escaped from her father's attempt to kill her, Ah Ching sought refuge with her grandmother, who cried upon hearing her story. Yet when night came, the grandmother smothered Ah Ching. She did it to save Ah Ching from further suffering in a patriarchal society.[28] This occurred after the Cultural Revolution.

Ah Ching's story finds a parallel in the experience of black slave mothers in antebellum America who said, "We'd rather set our children free in death than have them sold into slavery."[29] In black novelist Toni Morrison's *Beloved*, Seethe killed her daughter before the white master could take the child away. Seethe explained: "How if I hadn't killed her, she would have died and that is something I couldn't bear to happen."[30] Ah Ching's mother wept for herself, for her daughter, and for many women of China. The mother's lament provided Kwok Pui-lan with a lens through which to understand the Gospel writer's feminine metaphor for Jesus—Jesus as the one who wept in deep sorrow over Jerusalem, as the one who longed to embrace "as a hen gathers her brood under her wings" (Mt 23:37). It is not difficult to think that Jesus shares women's experiences of "nobodyness" because Jesus himself experienced the suffering of a nobody on the cross.

It is clear to Kwok, however, that not all women remain victims. She senses that a woman whose suffering touches the core of her being is also capable of feeling "the pain of the suffering God . . . who cried from the cross."[31] She saw this in the lives of the Chinese revolutionary artist Zhang Zhi-Xin and Korean student leader Suk Wah. For women like Zhang Zhi-Xin, resistance means taking the risk of being arrested and executed for criticizing the weaknesses of the Chinese revolution, even though she believes in its basic principles. As moral agents, women like Suk Wah have generated courage from the depths of their pain and have converted that pain into the power that propelled them to choose the path of resistance to the enormity of dictatorial regimes. These women's stories reveal their passion for justice, a passion from the womb that gives birth to hope.

To speak of hope is not an easy task, Kwok admits, but she points to the resurrected Jesus as one who empowers women to have hope in the midst of despair.[32] Not all Asian women caught in oppressive situations take the revolutionary option that Zang Zhi-Xin and Suk Wah have chosen. Depending on their specific contexts, women have many options for resistance. I agree with Kwok, however, that a Christology that sees Jesus "as the God who takes human form and suffers and weeps with us" speaks to many Asian women at a gut level.[33] They endure numerous kinds of unspeakable suffering.

Intercultural Approach to Christology

As a Chinese woman, Kwok questions the traditional image of Jesus portrayed in Western Christianity. She notes that the Christian concept of Jesus as God incarnate is unbelievable and absurd for many Chinese. The Christian missionaries tried to use the Chinese concept of *taiji (tai chi)* to explain the notion of God's incarnation. Confucianists, however, find it impossible to relate the *taiji*, the Cosmic Origin, to demanding obedience from people. The idea that the Cosmic Origin decided to be born on earth as a human being is even more unthinkable for them. Kwok observes that Buddhists resonate with the Christian idea of the resurrection or transformation of the body without much difficulty. This is because they hold that the Buddha also exists in the form of a spiritual body. However, Buddhists do not accept the Christian notion that God was manifest in one unique person in history. A nondualistic religion, Buddhism believes that the body of the transformed Buddha manifests in thousands of people. Buddhist thought holds the "one" and the "many" together.[34]

Among the Chinese, the image of Jesus as healer is nothing special because Chinese healers abound in Chinese communities. Moreover, in a tradition that gives importance to a person's family lineage, the

Chinese reject the idea of the virgin birth as strange and unconvincing. Understandably, the notion of Jesus as redeemer is controversial among the Chinese because it harps on the idea of human depravity in a religious sense. Such an idea is absent from most Asian traditions. What is common among Asians, including the Chinese, is the notion of shame and guilt.[35] The humanist Confucian tradition and Mahayana Buddhism resolve this condition of shame and guilt by stressing the potentialities of human nature to be good and the possibility for individuals to achieve sagehood or Buddhahood through the practice and discipline of self-cultivation and the development of their moral faculty.[36]

Conscious of the colonizing tendencies of both text and interpretation, Kwok takes the multiplicity of biblical narratives as a reminder that there is no single human narrative but rather a diversity of human beliefs and experiences. Applying this concept to Christology, she sees multiple identities of Jesus in the biblical accounts. Thus, she has no problem holding on to Jesus as the image of God weeping with our pain, while at the same time paying attention to the Chinese perception of Christ based on a world view that stresses balance and harmony of elements.[37] Kwok insists that Chinese tradition sees elements such as the yin/yang, female/male, mother/father, heaven/earth, and so on as complementary parts of the whole and not as binary opposites.[38] Kwok observes that because the Chinese Buddhist tradition offers salvific figures that are both male and female, such as Guanyin (Kuan-yin) and Mazu, the maleness of Jesus does not seem to be an issue for Chinese Christian women.[39] Contrary to Hong Kong–based theologian Wong Wai-Ching's critique that Kwok ignores the issue of Jesus' maleness and ignores this factor in women's oppression,[40] Kwok asserts that in the goddess Kuan-yin many Chinese women affirm both the maleness and femaleness of a deity. Refusing to problematize the maleness of Jesus does not mean that Chinese women gloss over Jesus' gender and sexuality.

Yet, far from romanticizing the Chinese tradition, Kwok sees the necessity of challenging the androcentric images of the Christ through the retrieval of a Chinese view about religion and the world: "A Chinese religious worldview requires symbolizations of Christ using both feminine and masculine metaphors, images and concepts, such that women and men can find their experiences reflected in the divine."[41]

To be able to reflect on the significance of Christ in a religiously pluralistic world, then, Kwok urges theologians to consider an intercultural approach. At the same time she points to the fact that the

New Testament unmistakably displays "highly pluralistic and hybridized" images of Jesus/Christ. This evidence only points to the reality that Christology is an open-ended enterprise.

Jesus/Christ: A Hybridized Identity

Now an exile by choice, Kwok's vision of Jesus has evolved over time as her context has changed, but she has not abandoned her earlier view of Jesus. Postcolonial criticism propels Kwok's theological thought and writings. Some Asian women theologians became uneasy when they detected this shift.[42] They echoed the postcolonial critics' doubt about the transformative capacity of postcolonialism. Postcolonial critics suspect that postcolonialism may only collude with global capitalism by obscuring its capitulation to the imperialist agenda and by subtly hiding racism and exploitation.[43] Kwok acknowledges this danger and moves on by taking "postcolonial imagination" as a framework in constructing her Christology.[44] She defines postcolonial imagination as the resolve and the practice of breaking free from the "colonial syndrome" created by the colonizing process that encompasses the social, political, cultural and the discursive.[45] With such awareness she expands her hermeneutical tools without losing sight of the concrete conditions of oppression and marginality of women and Asian communities. Indeed, Kwok's vision has flourished as she has sought to make her Christology responsive to the lived situation of women. With postcolonial imagination she pushes the limits of conventional theological thought and pays attention to "the emergent voices that are shaping the christological debate at the beginning of the millennium."[46]

Kwok rereads the biblical text through the lens of her diasporic experience. She explores the meaning and applicability of "hybridity" in biblico-theological interpretation in the face of multiple ways people use their own language and cultural images to speak about the Christ. To postcolonial theorists, hybridity is not only about the colonized imitating the colonizer's culture, or transgressing established social norms and categories, or mixing local and non-local influences.[47] Taking a cue from postcolonial critic Homi Babha, Kwok asserts that hybridity is about "colonial authority and power of representation," in that the presence of the suppressed knowledge threatens the dominant discourse and destabilizes its power.[48] Lifting up the contribution of liberation theologies that highlight the epistemological privilege of the margins, Kwok declares that one can no longer speak of a universal view about Jesus the Christ. She writes, "The most hybridized concept in Christianity is that of Jesus/Christ."[49]

I find very compelling Kwok's discovery of the space between Jesus and the Christ not only as the meeting point between humanity and the Divine, but also as the fluid and troubling location of resistance to "easy categorization and closure."[50] If in the past this space became the field where the powerful won their doctrinal as well as their political battles, today this space jolts us to the excitement of liberating Christology from the clutches of the powerful propagators of the dominant discourse. Kwok's construction of an organic Christology demonstrates how the fluid space between Jesus and the Christ becomes a location of resistance.

Jesus and an Organic Christology

The encompassing destruction of the bio-network of the planet is an urgent challenge to which theology must respond. Given this context, Kwok offers four principles for what she calls organic Christology.[51] First, Christology must be accountable to history. Thus, her approach aims to expose the falseness of christological formulations that endorse images of the militaristic crusader-Christ, of the king-Christ who has warranted Western political domination, and of the myth of Jesus' uniqueness, which has debased other Asian religions. These christological images have justified cultural hegemony, conquest, and genocide.[52]

Second, Christology must be accountable to nature. She sees the need for an approach that lays bare the anthropocentric bias of the concept that Jesus is the Logos and the Son of God.[53] Third, Kwok considers it imperative to bridge the gap between the Chinese religious world view and the biblical tradition. An ecological model of Christology, asserts Kwok, recovers the nonhuman metaphors Jesus used to describe himself in the Bible.[54] The organic model makes use of a plurality of images drawn from the Bible in reconstructing Christologies that are feminist and are responsive to the vision of eco-justice for both humans and nature. Kwok finds the Fourth Gospel replete with organic images of Jesus. She considers these images of Jesus—the vine, the bread of life, the living water, the shepherd, the door, the hen protecting her brood, among others—to be sources that Asian women need to explore in constructing their Christology. An organic Christology offers a "hybridized" Jesus in a positive sense.[55] As a fourth principle, an organic model of Christology also seeks to discuss the relationship of woman and nature in terms of political struggles for justice, rather than as the subject of metaphysical and essentialist debates.[56]

Kwok considers feminist theology as an intercultural discourse, thus we can be certain that she also envisions organic Christology as an intercultural discourse.[57] Considering that "sin is more than the disobedience and egotism of human beings, but has a cosmological dimension as well," Kwok suggests that Christology must rethink the notion of sin and salvation.[58] She gives credit to the indigenous peoples and to those who have continued to uphold and to live their traditional cultures for their challenge of dominant christological constructs. Following their lead she has been able to discern that salvation is both for human beings and for nature. Kwok recognizes the reality of sin in a profound, down-to-earth sense. Sin is the collapse of interconnectedness of all things that threatens the web of life and chokes Mother Earth. Kwok recognizes it as structural and systematic evil that privileges the minority of the human race that gobbles up the resources and thus prevents the majority from enjoying the fullness of life. In short, Kwok defines sin as the "absence of love and compassion."[59] With such an understanding of sin, one could think of salvation only in terms of making right relationships among human beings, as well as between human beings and nature. One must be ever mindful that human beings are not the center of the creation but are part of nature and its processes.[60]

POSTCOLONIAL CRITIQUE OF ASIAN FEMINIST THEOLOGY

Trained at the University of Chicago Divinity School, Wong Wai-Ching is currently a professor of religion in a university in Hong Kong. Wong employs postcolonial theory as a cultural criticism in reading Asian feminists' writings. She reads them with a particular eye for discourses that she considers to have reinscribed cultural hegemonies. Wong also uses the lenses of postmodern theory. Wong has delved particularly into the works of Ahn Sang Nim, Lee Oo Chung, and Chung Hyun Kyung of Korea; Swarnalatha Devi of India; Virginia

Fabella and Mary John Mananzan of the Philippines; and Kwok Pui-lan of Hong Kong.

The Issue of Theological Methodology

Wong Wai-Ching strongly criticizes Asian feminists' methodology in doing theology as a capitulation to a Western framework. She observes the strong influence of white feminist thought on the works of these Asian feminist theologians. She points out that white feminists, such as Rosemary Radford Ruether and Elisabeth Schüssler Fiorenza, take on the "universal humanist ideals of the Enlightenment" as a framework in their construction of a fully integrated historical subject. Wong argues that the "liberationist" Christologies of Ruether, Schüssler Fiorenza, and even of Asian feminists have failed to deal with the relation between women's "femaleness" and the notion of the divine. Consequently, they are caught up with "the notion of the 'degendered' oppressed victims or 'wo/men.'"[61]

Wong charges that Asian feminists not only followed the framework used by white feminists but are even worse than white feminist theologians because they also use the discourse of male liberation theologians and have surrendered theology to the political agenda of the nationalists. To Wong, Asian women's identification with the nationalistic agenda is troubling because she sees this as an "uncritical appropriation of an almost equally 'orientalist' representation of women in the Third World."[62] By sticking to the binary pairing of victim-hero, these theologians create a monolithic third-world woman and end up closing the space in between for the average Asian woman who is neither a victim nor a hero. This line of thought, Wong contends, is reflected in the Christologies of Asian women. Moreover, she finds the "nationalist-versus-imperialist discourse" in Asian feminist theology and Asian women's methodology restrictive for the growth of a theology "of and about women in Asia."[63]

Wong offers a corrective to the Asian feminist theologians' method of making women's experience of oppression a starting point for constructing their Christologies. She considers a good starting point the notion of women's multifaceted agency and their being a not fully autonomous subject. She asserts that this two-pronged starting point is important for the exploration of a "dynamic and culturally informed theology of women in Asia."[64]

The Nexus of the Poor Woman and Jesus the Liberator

Wong Wai-Ching submits that Asian women's way of universalizing the Asian woman as "the poor woman" and linking this with the idea of Jesus as liberator could be problematic. She argues that this theoretical, rhetorical construction of "the poor woman in Asia"[65] led the theologians to take "suffering" as an across-the-board experience of Asian women, thus misrepresenting the Asian woman as "poor." These tendencies to essentialize the Asian woman as "the poor woman," according to Wong, have a bearing on Asian women's understanding of God and of Jesus.

Wong cites Kwok Pui-lan's early work as representative of Asian feminist theologies that essentialize God "as a suffering God incarnate in the person of Jesus."[66] Asian feminists' idea that Jesus must not be a Western-style colonial master as the bottom line of Asian women's Christology makes feminist Christology an easy prey of nationalistic politics defined by hegemonic masculine discourse.

Wong finds the presentation of a "uniform construction of Jesus as a political historical liberator" to be a limiting factor in the works of Virginia Fabella of the Philippines and the New York-based Korean Chung Hyun Kyung.[67] Wong thinks this construct is consistent with an overarching view that "Asian women's theology, like Asian theology in general, must be a liberation theology."[68] Wong finds this unsettling. She insists that a Christology that views Jesus "as a political and historical liberator" is problematic because Asian feminist theologians see women as nothing more than victims whose only way to salvation is to become revolutionaries and combatants.[69] Wong writes:

> One of the problems of this postcolonial construction of Jesus Christ as a political and historical liberator is that it is confined to a regional, anti-imperialistic agenda and does not take into account women's interests as they may define them. The immediate consequence is the normalization and routinization of women's one type of experience—as victim of foreign and local exploitation—and one form of agency—as national liberation combatants.[70]

Wong worries that the "normalization and routinization" of one kind of women's experience and of "one form of woman's agency" may make women sever ties with the West and retreat to a limited "space" called the indigenous and the political—spaces that, according to Wong, are always defined by men.[71]

Obviously, Wong is wary of discourse that may fall into a blind nationalism that stifles creativity and freedom. However, Wong could have taken more effort to understand the context of struggle from which these Asian feminist theologians come. Instead, she quickly affirms Korean Kang Nam-Soon's claim that liberationist Asian feminists are merely taking up the masculinist nationalist agenda in their theology.[72] Kang has described Asian women as having no memory of freedom and resistance in history other than the memory of suffering.[73] But women struggle to resist domination and to rise precisely because they want to keep the memory of freedom a reality. This is true in many places in South and Southeast Asia. Even if patriarchy is a reality in Asia, men do not define all indigenous and political spaces. Moreover, women struggle to claim or reclaim their place in spaces that are occupied by men.

Asian Feminist Christology and Its Anti-West Discourse

Wong Wai-Ching seeks a Christology that is not embedded in a discourse around oppression and liberation. She does not want Christology to get stuck in the liberator image of Jesus, as she thinks Asian feminist theologians are doing. Wong contends that Asian feminist theologians not only reinscribe the Asian woman as "the Other to Western colonialism," but they also construct Asia as consistently anti-West.[74]

Wong finds "postcolonial/nationalistic construction of Jesus in Asian feminist discourse." She concludes that Asian feminist theology has "collapsed" Christology into the box of "postcolonial/nationalistic politics," and has simply reinforced the victim-hero image of women. As a result, Asian women's Christology creates an image of Jesus who suffers the same fate as the women: a victim or a hero, one who "suffers and dies as a political martyr, only to rise again as the Christ in the midst of the continued historical struggle for liberation." The only accomplishment of this kind of Christology, according to Wong, is the differentiation of Asian theology from that of the Western imperialistic missionary churches. This sort of Christology merely positions Asian theologians to contest the authority of West-defined tradition and Western theological discourse. Ultimately, Wong states, this problem restricts women from being "free and responsible" in exploring a theology that speaks to contradictory experiences and multiple agencies of women from different cultures and backgrounds, races, locations, gender. In her view, Asian women failed to do Christology that reflects "in actuality, a hybridity of all forms." Wong believes that a "totalizing" discourse of women as oppressed-who-must-become-combatants obscures women's need to resist the "multifaceted economic and cultural dynamics" that women face every day.[75]

Woman as Subjects-in-Process

Having criticized Asian feminist theology, what does Wong Wai-Ching offer as an alternative Asian feminist Christology? Wong offers a Christology that seeks first to understand the hybridity of women's identity and speaks to a variety of experiences and agencies of Asian women. The multiplicity of Asian women's experience is pertinent in the construction of Asian Christology. Concerned that Asian feminist theologians shied away from using fiction as an alternative resource for doing Christology, Wong demonstrates that it can be done; she uses the works of two Hong Kong fiction writers, Xi Xi and Wu Xubin. Contrary to Asian feminist theologians' view of Asian women, these Hong Kong writers do not present them as suffering victims, poor, or as indomitable and strong.[76] The marginalized "Hongkongese"[77] women are the "happy-going ordinary guys of Xi Xi's stories of the city, and the confused, frustrated and yet never fully resigned personae and mountain searchers in Wu's narrative 'silences.'"[78] Wong reads Xi Xi and Wu Xubin using the theory of Bulgaria-born French linguist Julia Kristeva that female subjectivity and sexuality are unfixed and, thus, a woman is a subject-in-process. Consequently, Wong argues that the identity of the Asian woman is also "in process," fluid, and chaotic.[79] With this model Wong argues for a theological discourse that creates "a space for a self-critical understanding of the 'imaginary' structure of a postcolonial Asian identity, including its strength and limitations to a theology formulated out of a reactionary position of a formerly suppressed people and culture."[80]

Creating a space for difference in the sense of defying sameness is, to Wong, a position of resistance. Difference, not in the sense of otherness but in the sense of being in between, is important for theology's self-criticism. I agree with Wong that sameness is boring, but indecisiveness is also frustrating. Although Wong does not seem to use the term *reactionary* as a synonym for ultra-conservatism, her desire for the "reactionary position" is troubling and contrary to her notion of woman as subject-in-process. Wong seems to ignore that as a product of historical dialectical processes, a subject is capable not only of transgressing boundaries[81] but of cutting through a unity, both in positive and negative senses. Being in process, subjectivities may also face the risk of deterioration or cooptation by the extreme, such as fascism, and can be rechanneled into selfish idolization of an alluring personality or ideology or structure. A discourse that lacks accountability and an Asian subjectivity that is too fluid and too messy fall into the pit of complacency and rootlessness. A proverb aptly comments on this kind of subjectivity: A rolling stone gathers no moss.

Wong's assertion that women have multifaceted identities is true, but one must also consider that their contexts of survival call for responsible subjectivity. The image of Hong Kong women as happy-go-lucky evokes the image of an excessive fluidity that is incapable of forging solidarity with other human beings and other creatures on earth. The attention span of this kind of person tends to be short. Thus, this subjectivity is suspect of being unable to forge and sustain a commitment toward a transformative and emancipatory project with the marginalized communities. How can an unstable subject resist an empire's complex network that seeks to secure its hegemony over the world and to suck the world's lifeblood in order to feed its own political and economic machineries?

The Variegated Jesus, a Subject-in-Process

When Wong speaks of Hong Kong women as subjects-in-process, she inevitably constructs a Christology that reflects her context. The Hong Kong fiction writers and her environment gave her the lenses to recognize the resonance between the variety of Jesus images in the Gospels and Jesus as a subject-in-process. This "variegated Jesus" opens to women a new space and a new way of "being-in-the-world."[82] Situated in a city-state that represents the economic tigers, or the First World within third-world Asia, Wong does not want to meet a Jesus trapped in the static image of the suffering. She proposes to explore a new and open space where a plurality of women's experiences and multiplicities of women's agency may find their way to a meaningful correlation with the person and symbols of Jesus the Christ. Unfortunately, Wong does not show us a full picture or model of such christological exploration. She merely offers a clue in the fragmented identities and images of Xi Xi's and Wu Xubin's "non-heroic little guys" who attain "down-to-earth happiness" by going along with the rhythm and flow of life in the "simple materiality of Hong Kong."[83] In this way they resist the nationalistic grand narrative. These various fictional representations of women in the writings of Xi Xi and Wu Xubin as subjects-in-process lead us to recognize women's subjectivity in relation to the "variegated Jesus in-process-on-trial" in the New Testament writings.[84] Like the women's subjectivity, Jesus is also a subject "in-process-on-trial" and opposes binary schemes of thought. This fractured, flexible, and decentered Jesus opens up new spaces that, Wong thinks, other Asian feminists fear to enter.

One must note that Wong also recognizes some resonance of liberationist Christologies with her postcolonial Jesus in-process-on-trial. Wong sees the potential of Chung Hyun Kyung's Jesus as shaman priestess in developing a women's incarnational theology. Wong affirms Japanese feminist Hisako Kinukawa's evaluation of the Markan Jesus who learned from the women, not from the rabbis, lessons toward liberating himself from social and cultural boundaries of his time in order to become truly a savior.[85] Understandably, Wong tries to move away from the "heroification" of one historical figure. To Wong, Jesus is neither a hero nor a liberator. Wong insists that Jesus is simply one who strove to work out his vision and beliefs in the midst of rejection, betrayal, misunderstanding, brokenness, frustration, and feelings of isolation and vulnerability on the cross.[86] Wong speaks of this down-to-earth human experience of Jesus without referring to any notion of failure or success. In effect, she tells her readers that it is not impossible to follow the path that Jesus took.

Looking through the Glass: Whose Lenses?

The liberationist discourse of the first-generation Asian feminist theologians disturbs Wong Wai-Ching. This discomfort stems from Wong's view that the context of Asian feminist theologians is more of a postcolonial rather than as a neocolonial condition. Wong reads the works of Asian feminists using the lens of postcolonial theory as a discourse in cultural and literary criticism. In Dirlik's words, such discourse "seeks to constitute the world in the self-image of intellectuals who view themselves (or have come to view themselves) as postcolonial intellectuals."[87] On the contrary, liberationist Asian women do theology as they describe their concrete historical conditions.

THE IMPACT OF CONTEXT ON CHRISTOLOGY

Context remains crucial in doing Christology. Christology in Asia must face the challenges posed by Asian contexts. The Christian minority must face the challenge of living its faith in an Asian world of religious plurality. Moreover, except for the few tiger economies, people in Asian countries are still facing the reality of poverty. Wong's Jesus, the subject "in-process-on-trial," must address these Asian realities. Yet Wong is silent about the context that brought Jesus to the cross. She speaks about Jesus' suffering in a very indirect manner, if at all. Perhaps reflecting Hong Kong's fear of reintegration with China, Wong gives the impression that her Christology is more concerned with the good times and that it could not imagine facing bad times. Consequently, her Christology strikes one as a variant of a "theology of glory."[88]

We need an image of Jesus who dances and offers wine to celebrate weddings, banquets, and feasts. Yet, the scriptures also offer an image of a Jesus who, from infancy, shared the lot of the poor. Are the Gospel writers guilty of "essentializing" a Jesus who is biased for the poor? It is Christology's task to help the suffering people make sense of their pain. Thus, it is the task of Christology to make the non-victim, non-suffering Christian ask why the variegated Jesus, a subject-in-process, ends up on the cross. How will this type of postcolonial Christology make sense of a crucified Christ? Will it simply ask the "non-heroic little guys" of Hong Kong fiction to look away or to gaze stoically at the betrayed, broken, and hanging contemporary Jesuses—male and female, young and old—on the crosses erected by patriarchy and globalized capitalism in postmodern times? Does this Jesus, the subject-on-trial, offer some sense of salvation to people who do not have a chance to savor the prosperity the Hongkongese are experiencing? What will this Jesus, the subject-in-process, say to the exploited DHs in Hong Kong and Singapore, to overseas workers in Saudi Arabia, to mail-order brides and sex workers, and to the malnourished children all over the world? Will a subject-in-process Jesus have anything to say in the face of ecological degradation? What is the relevance of the postcolonial Jesus who refuses to be a liberator to people who need liberation from poverty and oppression? What is the meaning of a postcolonial Jesus who cannot be a mother to the motherless child or bread, rice, and milk to those who are hungry and malnourished or a healer to the sick? What is the use of talking about God's love if Jesus cannot be a lover to the unloved, forsaken, and lonely, if Jesus cannot be a companion to those who must walk the long journey in pain and suffering?

Filipino postcolonial critic E. San Juan, Jr., compellingly argues that the "urgent-life-or-death questions are simply ignored by postcolonial theory outside the multiculturalism debate."[89] Thus, Asian feminist Christology must continue to raise these questions, even as it shares with Wong a vision of a stage for Asian theological discussion that can give space to the multiple interests and identities of women and other minority groups.[90]

To be sure, Wong offers a new way of gazing at a Jesus who refuses to be frozen in the creeds of Nicea-Chalcedon and in patriarchal discourses. However, a Christology that depends solely on postcolonial theory is in danger of falling into the trap that it seeks to demolish. When it serves only the interest of a few privileged academicians who are cozy in the shelter of first-world universities, it may run the risk of "mystification and moralism,"[91] the very thing it claims to repudiate. An Asian feminist Christology cannot be neutral, vacillate, or play safe behind the veil of discourses in vogue that blur our vision of making God's reign on earth a reality. Just as Jesus explicitly took on the bias of God for the disenfranchised, marginalized, and poor—which include women, men, gays, lesbians, children, and the earth itself—so must Asian feminist Christology be accountable to marginalized persons and communities.

Social Location: A Crucial Factor in Doing Christology

Wong's critique of the Christologies of Asian feminist theologians give Asian women something to think about. However, such critique would have been more helpful, as Kwok notes, had Wong done justice to Asian women's theological writings.[92] Wong needed to gain an embodied knowledge of the struggle of many women in Asia in order to survive. Like the dalit women of Swarnalatha Devi, many women in Asia fight the daily battle of finding potable water, firewood for cooking, and something to cook for themselves and for their families. Wong needs to be sensitive to Devi's call for solidarity. Asian feminist Christology is concerned with the cry of the people like the dalits, but it is also a commitment to protect life and make it flourish abundantly for the local communities.[93] It means navigating in a complex context where systems and structures have reinforced patriarchal norms. Wong must not turn her gaze away from the experience of tribal and Muslim women, along with other rural women, who are in constant fear of ethnic cleansing and militarization.[94] Indeed, some women have opted to become combatants in the resistance movements against repressive governments. More Asian women, however, have invented ways of subverting oppressive power and overcoming phallocratic violence creatively to keep their sanity and to support their families in the midst of grinding poverty that privileged Hong Kong women may not have experienced. In Hong Kong, Filipino DHs resist the oppressive treatment of their employers in a variety of ways, even with the knowledge that these forms of resistance are inadequate.[95] Kwok is right in pointing out that Wong has stretched too far the generalization that Asian feminist theologians "reinscribe the masculinist discourse."[96] As with many Asian feminist women, my feminist consciousness emerged out of my own experience of marginalization in the church and in the resistance movement, both dominated by patriarchal leaders. My feminist perspective surfaced precisely because women's issues and experiences of oppression as women received mere token attention within the nationalist space. Thus, in the Philippines, AWIT, and its umbrella organization, GABRIELA, attend to issues that affect women bodily, spiritually, politically, and economically.

Considering the notion of theology as an imaginative construction, a postcolonial Christology offers a space where we may explore ways to express life realities and texts of different worlds that are made closer to each other through the technologies of a postmodern world. Postcolonial Christology further explores Wisdom Christology, drawing from the scriptural image of God as Lady Wisdom/Sophia/Hokmah. Although white feminist theologians, such as Elisabeth Schüssler Fiorenza and Elizabeth Johnson, have explored Wisdom Christology, Asian feminist theologians offer a nuanced understanding of this image. They bring the particularity of their culture and location as they negotiate for a postcolonial identity.

EXPLORING WISDOM CHRISTOLOGY, FINDING AN EPIPHANY OF GOD

Concern for ecological issues brings Kwok's organic Christology within the embrace of the Wisdom tradition that recovers the cosmological dimension of theology. Christology cannot afford to lag behind the ecological movement to save the earth. "God so loved the world . . . God did not send the Son into the world to condemn the world, but in order that the world might be saved through him" (Jn 3:16–17). Historian Lynn White, Jr., in his ground-breaking essay in 1967, claimed that Christian theology serves as the matrix of modern Western science and that "Christianity bears a huge burden of guilt" for the ecological crisis the earth faces.[97] The responses from theology and the churches came slowly, only speeding up during the last two decades of the second millennium.

The ecofeminist movements and the indigenous peoples' wisdom prompted feminist theologians like Kwok Pui-lan to reflect on the connections among ecology, theology, and patriarchy. Ecofeminist studies have identified the partnership of theology and Enlightenment philosophy, an alliance that has masked greed and reinforced patriarchal and ecocidal/biocidal views. For so long theology has bought into the notion that nature is not the mother that indigenous peoples have revered but a female body that is subject to exploration and control by masculine power.[98]

In response to this prevailing view, Kwok suggests that we abandon the dualistic, hierarchical Christianity that ceased to instill respect for life and the Earth.[99] Kwok examines the doctrine of Christology in relation to the ecological problem in light of her organic Christology. She asserts that our assumptions about nature shape our images of Jesus.[100] An organic model of Christology highlights the interrelationship of human beings with nature and reclaims the potential of Wisdom Christology. Scholars who have sifted the biblical traditions have directed our gaze to Jesus as a wisdom teacher or as "Sophia's prophet."[101] Toward the end of the first century, according to some biblical scholars, early Christian communities considered Jesus as the embodiment or incarnation of Sophia herself. This early Christian view opens a space for women today in the sense that "the wisdom tradition in the Hebrew Bible highlights Wisdom's creative agency, providential power, redeeming capacity, immanence and the promise of shalom, salvation and justice."[102] Indeed, a Sophia Christology resonates with those who are looking for a women-friendly Christology. Along with some other Asian feminist theologians, Kwok identifies and turns our attention to various images of Jesus in the scriptures. Among them are the images of Jesus as the sage, the prophet of Sophia, and the incarnation of Wisdom. Various Wisdom figures have made their home in Asian traditions for centuries.

Jesus as a Sage, the Prophet of Sophia

The image of Jesus as sage or teacher has received diverse responses, given that the Confucian tradition has high esteem for teachers like Mencius and Confucius.[103] Kwok affirms that a Christology that views Jesus as wisdom teacher and a prophet of Sophia is not difficult for Chinese people to comprehend. This is because the image of the teacher and sage is a respected one in the Chinese tradition. The sage teaches subversive wisdom through parables, stories, proverbs, and maxims. Kwok observes that this view resonates with an Asian mind more than the notion of Jesus as priest or messiah. The notion of Jesus as a sage and prophet, according to Elisabeth Schüssler Fiorenza, provides the christological image of Jesus as a wise teacher whose life touches our longing for God. This is so because Jesus' Sophia-God loves humanity and is greatly concerned with human liberation and empowerment. Thus, Sophia-God calls believers to put into action the teachings of Jesus. In this regard, Wisdom Christology paves a way for Christians to respond to religious plurality.[104]

Although the image of the sage is usually associated with a male person, Kwok asserts that in some Taoist and Buddhist traditions women are not prohibited from becoming teachers and passing wisdom to generations of learners.[105] There are many Asian traditions of wise old women from whom the community seeks counsel. Hong Kong feminists' Wisdom Christology makes sense to other Asian women. Korean-Canadian theologian Grace Kim notes that the relevant teachings in Confucianism on sageliness or sagehood are about practicing the Tao (the Way) of a practical and moral life, of simplicity, tranquility, and benevolence.[106] These virtues are congruent with the teachings of Jesus as a sage, the prophet of Sophia.

Jesus as Sophia Incarnated

The image of Jesus as sage certainly opens up the path for dialogue with Asian religions. However, Kwok thinks that the concept of Jesus as the embodiment or incarnation of Sophia presses for a deeper dialogue with the ancient wisdom traditions in Asia. One can juxtapose the nature sayings of Jesus in the Gospels with the etchings in Confucianism that employ symbols related to nature, such as the plant and the gardener, the cycle of the seasons, the stream and the water, among others.[107] Jesus not only teaches the Tao, but Jesus as incarnate Wisdom also shows us the way of a life of goodness and truth.[108]

One needs only to listen to the Wisdom literature and the New Testament to get the sense that Jesus is the Wisdom of God. Jesus as Wisdom Incarnate invites everyone to a banquet around the table of love. Wong Wai-Ching cites this table as the new space for women's creation, which Wisdom literature pictures as "the divine Wisdom's table" or the "table of the Divine Sophia" (Prv 9:1–6). Jesus as Wisdom Incarnate will not be a strange view to Hong Kong and Chinese women. This is because the object of many Chinese women's devotion, Kuan-yin or Guanyin (Kannon in Japan), the Goddess of Mercy and Compassion, is connected with Wisdom *(prajna)*. In Buddhism, Prajna Paramita is supreme Wisdom. She not only protects women and looks after them in childbirth, but she heals children from illnesses. Kuan-yin's compassion as the embodiment of Prajna Paramita goes beyond concern for human beings. She listens to the cries of the earth, of the animals, and of the plants, mountains, wind, rivers, and skies. Grace Kim finds that the image of Sophia-Prajna as Kuan-yin is more powerful than the male notion of Logos. To her, the grace of Sophia-Prajna in Kuan-yin brings liberation and empowerment to women who have suffered oppression and domination in a sexist, patriarchal, and racist society.[109]

Kwok affirms that a Sophia Christology is an antidote to the patriarchal concept of Jesus as the Son of God and the Logos. The view that Jesus is Sophia lays bare the anthropocentric bias of these christological constructs.[110] The Heart Sutra of the Buddhist tradition hails Prajna Paramita as the greatest mantra that Avalokitesvara/Kuan-yin Bodhisattva embodies and practices. She is one who relieves all suffering. This view opens up a completely new space of understanding, since it means that Sophia-Spirit has been embodied in many forms and ways throughout the centuries. This idea makes Asian feminist theologians see Jesus as the Wisdom Incarnate in the image of Kuan-yin, the Prajna Paramita, the Supreme Wisdom who cannot be imprisoned in one form.

The idea of Jesus as the embodiment of Sophia/Wisdom Incarnate is not foreign to the Gospels, especially the Fourth Gospel. The insight of Schüssler Fiorenza on the Fourth Gospel's presentation of Jesus as "making Sophia present in his/her works" is thought provoking.[111] Certainly, the "I-am" sayings of Jesus in the Fourth Gospel indicate this idea. Jesus the Wisdom Incarnate challenges believers to reinterpret the meaning of the Logos Christology that has been appropriated mostly by male's interpretations. It calls women to reclaim the word *Logos* and to understand it as "story" or "message."[112] As Wisdom clearly concerns herself with the wellness and fullness of life, liberation from suffering and oppression is inherent in her works.[113] "Wisdom is vindicated by her deeds," and among those deeds that Jesus enumerates are "the blind receive their sight, the lame walk, the lepers are cleansed, the deaf hear, the dead are raised, and the poor have good news brought to them" [Mt 11:2–6]. Asian women's idea of Jesus as Wisdom Incarnate finds a parallel in the reflections of Elizabeth Johnson, who asserts that Sophia-Jesus, when understood as the Christ, is the point of encounter between human beings and the incomprehensible God. Sophia is Spirit, the power that vivifies and renews the world. As an agent of Sophia, Jesus embodies and becomes Sophia herself.[114] One cannot capture the mystery of the Spirit. The Spirit continues to manifest in nature and in human beings even two millennia after the flesh-and-blood existence of the Palestinian Jew Jesus the Wisdom Incarnate. This Christology leads us to another dimension of Wisdom Christology, one that views Jesus as the epiphany of God.

Jesus as the Epiphany of God

Ecological/organic and Wisdom Christologies, according to Hong Kong women's postcolonial imagination, dismantles Christianity's "grand narrative," which claims the monopoly of understanding and interpretation of the divine revelation. Undoubtedly, organic and Wisdom Christologies do not negate, in any way, that Jesus reveals God. What these Christologies contest and relativize is the notion that fixes God's revelation in the "finite, historically specific human form" of Jesus of Nazareth.[115] These Christologies view Jesus as the epiphany of God but also assert that Jesus is not the *sole* revelation of the Divine. Kwok writes:

> The notion of an epiphanic Christ allows us to entertain the possibility of encountering Christ in many other ways: in other human beings, in nature, and in God's whole universe. This does not minimize the importance of the revelation of God in Jesus, because his life and ministry is paradigmatic for many Christians. But the incarnation of God can also be seen both in male and female salvific figures in other people's histories, who displays great

> wisdom and compassion, and in forms of existence other than human, exceeding our shallow anthropocentrism.[116]

The Divine reveals itself in many ways in the universe. Kwok points out that we encounter Christ, as the revelation of God, in a multiplicity of forms and ways. Even the reformer John Calvin, in a rarely mentioned position, admitted that

> Wherever you cast your eyes, there is no spot in the universe wherein you cannot discern at least some sparks of his [God's] glory. . . . There are innumerable evidences both in heaven and on earth that declare his wonderful wisdom. . . .
>
> I confess, of course, that it can be said reverently, provided that it proceeds from a reverent mind, that nature is God.[117]

Calvin points out that even as we have "enjoyed a slight taste of the divine from contemplation of the universe," we become arrogant and fail to attribute to the true source "the praise of righteousness, wisdom, goodness, and power."[118] Kwok's position is that the human Jesus, as epiphany of God, is certainly the manifestation of God's Wisdom at a certain point in time and space. She also urges Christians to rethink the assertion that Christ appeared once and for all. Rather than following the Pauline totalizing statement, Kwok says, in effect, that Jesus appeared once and for all in flesh and blood. In this sense Jesus is a prototype of humanity that points to the signs that God is truly with us. From a different perspective, one may understand that, for Kwok, Christ as the liberating Spirit-Wisdom did not appear once and for all, but instead, manifest in many ways through time and space. In the Buddhist tradition the Buddha, the Enlightened, is one and many. Therefore, the story of salvation lies in the incarnation of many Buddhas and bodhisattvas to save all sentient beings.[119] In Kim's reflection the grace of Christ as Wisdom/Sophia/Prajna is manifest in the grace of Kuan-yin. Thus, from the perspective of the Asian traditions, Kwok finds support for her view that Christ is one and many.

Wisdom Christology paves the way for the Christian perspective to move away from a stance of superiority and arrogance and to engage in a genuine dialogue with other living faith traditions in Asia. Although Wong did not speak about Christology in her Niles lecture during the Christian Conference of Asia in Indonesia, she said something that is relevant to the above discussion:

> One of the weaknesses of our established traditions today is trying to depend very much on our rational mind and seek for logical consistency. . . . [Thus] we are losing the ability to discern God's presence and losing the interests in pursuing vision and myth. We are afraid to admit conflicts and contradictions between our belief and cultural values and practices, we are scared to share "strange" ideas which come out from the synthesis of the two.[120]

Unquestionably, since she is speaking from the perspective of postcolonial theory, but obviously more mindful of the Asian world outside academia in her later writings, Wong seems to have mellowed as seen in her Sophia discourse as compared to the obstinate language characteristic of her earlier work on "the poor woman." Wong makes it clear, though, that she does not find the goddess tradition useful as a resource for her theology, and she does not see the goddess devotion as a panacea. Yet, in her reflection on her grandmother's devotion to Guanyin/Kuan-yin, and in her encounter with a paralyzed Christian woman who keeps her devotion to Kuan-yin, she acknowledges that some Chinese women find meaning, peace, and, redemption in Kuan-yin.[121] The conclusion to her address to the Christian Conference of Asia assembly is heartwarming:

> In the end, what we need is the courage to pursue vision, the power to share myths, and wisdom to walk the path of God. Digging deep into our experiences and our faith, I believe, will help to bring out a web of multiple traditions of Asian Christianity which only will provide a helpful counterbalance to the totalistic aspect of globalization and be able to shape true unity of humanity for a new generation.[122]

WOMEN'S SUFFERING AND THE LANGUAGE OF THE EROTIC

Hong Kong's Story

Suffering, a theme feminist theologians from other parts of Asia discuss passionately, does not generate the same intensity in the discourse of Hong Kong women. Hong Kong's location inspires the discourse of postcolonial literary criticism that marks Wong's writings as a kind of criticism that distinctly avoids the issue of suffering. Hong Kong is a first-world city in the midst of poverty-stricken Asia. True, Asia has changed, but that does not mean the countries' economies permit a better life for the majority of Asians. Kwok Pui-lan noticed that "the issues addressed by the Hong Kong authors are so different from that [*sic*] of others."[123] This does not mean, however, that no Hong Kong feminist theologian discusses the issue. Rose Wu follows Kwok Pui-lan in keeping in balance the liberationist and postcolonial perspectives. And Wong Wai-Ching describes Hong Kong from a postcolonial point of view:

> Hong Kong is not about self-pitying nor self-devaluing: nor is it about political correctness, i.e. anti-imperialism (against Britain) or anti-chauvinism (against China). On the contrary, it is about a people who turn their fate into a new beginning of creation in its given limitations. Over the years, Hong Kong has extended its extraordinary uniqueness and vitality by its creative negotiation and appropriation of the contradictions of East and West, tradition and modern: it has explored and developed its own space of survival by building itself into a city of opportunities.[124]

Although Wong suggests that the fiction stories written by Xi Xi and Wu Xubin create a space of respite for the ordinary people of Hong Kong, Kwok points out that many people from other parts of Asia cannot afford the "dream world" that these fictional stories offer.[125] Nor does Hong Kong's story move postcolonial theology, at least the type that Wong appropriates, to wrestle with environmental problems, the suffering of the earth in Hong Kong.[126]

The negotiation and appropriation of the contradictions of East and West and of tradition and modernity that Hong Kong is making have affected the women who live in Hong Kong. In spite of their better economic status, Hong Kong Chinese women have had their share of experiences of gender oppression. Rose Wu points out the economic implications of the cultural practice of sacrificing women on the altar of the family, where they are expected to do all the housework, serve as caregivers for children and the elderly, with little if any recognition, salary, or respite. Furthermore, Confucian cultures hold as a virtue the prohibition of education for women; education is reserved for men. In Hong Kong, men continue to regard women as inferior. A Hong Kong male legislator demonstrated this patriarchal ideology by remarking that "all women are chickens. . . . They are either for public or private consumption."[127] Wu indignantly points out that such a statement shows how patriarchy negates the humanity of women. Chinese misogyny actualized in the form of girl-child infanticide in China results in an imbalance of the male-female population ratio. According to a demographic projection, in the year 2003 more than seventy million Chinese men would not be able to find female partners within China.[128]

Indeed, Hong Kong bills itself as a city of opportunities, but it must acknowledge that it is able to do so only because there are women who, as cheap labor, take care of Hong Kong people's homes and children. These DHs suffer employers' common practices of verbal abuse, threats of termination and deportation, as well as physical abuse when they do not sign documents that are disadvantageous to them.[129] While some Hong Kong feminist theologians, such as Wu and Cheung, give some space in their writings to the issues of DHs in Hong Kong, no one has done an extensive theological reflection on these women's plight or on their identity within Hong Kong society. Perhaps the issue is too thorny. An examination of the multiple identities of Hong Kong women reveals that they are not just contributors to Hong Kong's flourishing economy (notwithstanding their being in the lowest rung of the salary scale), but they also enjoy freedom from the humdrum of household chores and babysitting. Many are mistresses who exercise power over low-paid foreign female labor.

Prostitution and Women's Suffering

Most of Rose Wu's and Cheung Choi-wan's writings focus on the suffering of women in relation to the related issues of prostitution, sexuality, and morality.[130] Wu asserts that globalization is bringing disaster to the lives of millions of women: "I want to point out that the rush toward globalization not only widens the gap between the rich and the poor but turns millions of peasants into landless refugees and forces masses of people to cross borders to seek non-existent urban jobs. Among these people, women are usually the most vulnerable."[131] Wu cites statistics that one out of seven men has admitted to having paid a prostitute for sex; Wu sees this as an indicator of the prevalence of prostitution in Hong Kong. She identifies various ways of trafficking women into Hong Kong for its sex industry. This includes kidnapping or abduction of women from other countries and luring them by the promise of nonexistent jobs:

> Trafficking [is] the process in which migrant women enter prostitution through coercion, deceit, abuse, or violence and in which they are denied their human rights and freedoms. This includes the rights to decide to work as a prostitute, to decide on the conditions to work, to enter and leave the sex industry, to refuse certain customers, to refuse certain sexual acts, to freedom of movement, to a safe working environment, and so forth.[132]

Wu makes it clear that one should not consider the sex trade as a mere personal moral issue. It is connected with the unequal structures of power, as well as the social constructions of gender, sexuality, class, and race. Structures of power create systems that exploit and oppress the weak and vulnerable, among them the poor, the young, people of color, and socially outcast women.[133] Wu points out that most women who leave the rural areas of China to find jobs in the cities, including Hong Kong, find very few options for survival in the cities other than selling their bodies for sex. Traditional Christian theology's response to prostitution is to blame the women as sinners, in effect suppressing the voices of these suffering women.[134] To Wu, this suppression is sin, and she takes the liberationist understanding of sin: "Sin is about oppression as a social system or structure that causes suffering. In the case of prostitution, sin is in the form of militarism, multinational capitalism, patriarchalism, sex tourism, law and the criminal justice systems."[135]

Based on her study, Wu has challenged Christian theology to rethink its notion of sin and sexuality, which only serves the interest of patriarchy. The prostituted women should be the ones to interpret their own experiences, individually and as a group. People need to see the multiplicity of the oppressive structures that give rise to prostitution. Wu stresses that a theology that seeks the liberation of prostituted women must be tested in praxis, allowing the women to "reclaim, redefine, rename, and recreate their sacredness and wholeness that is the gift of God to everyone."[136] In other words, Wu challenges the Christian community to listen hard to the gospel according to the prostituted women. How do Hong Kong women connect the issue of prostitution and suffering to Christology and the language of the erotic?

The Language of the Erotic and Christology

The word *erotic* comes from the Greek noun *eros*, which means "ardor, fondness, desire, and yearning for the other." The term is also used to describe sexual attraction. Its verb form, *erao*, means "to feel passionately about, to have a longing for, and to feel fervently about someone or something." In a wider sense *erotic* means the passion and attraction to something different. Patristic discourses use the word to describe the new Christian converts' fondness and ardor for the prophets and for Christ.[137] The erotic, therefore, is the power that drives human beings to love and to be in touch, bodily and spiritually, with other human beings and other living beings. It is the longing to be connected and to be one with another, just as it is the longing to embrace one's self fully. Those who are detached from the power of the erotic do not know how to love themselves. Consequently, they may have difficulty in loving others fully for they are incapable of savoring what feminist ethicist Iris Marion Young describes as "the pleasure and excitement of being drawn out of one's secure routine to encounter the novel, strange, and surprising."[138] In short, the erotic is the passion for life in relationship and mutuality.

The erotic is the inner sense of satisfaction, according to the late black writer/poet Audre Lorde. It gives the knowledge that one can aspire to be and to become. To Lorde, the erotic is "the nurturer or nursemaid of our deepest knowledge."[139] A problem arose when male cultures abused and devalued the erotic. Men denied the power of *eros* by confusing it with pornography. Lorde reclaims the erotic as

> an assertion of the life force of women, of that creative energy empowered, the knowledge and use of which we are now reclaiming in our language, our history, our dancing, our loving, our work, our lives. . . . Erotic knowledge becomes a lens through which we scrutinize all aspects of our existence forcing us to evaluate those aspects honestly in terms of their relative meaning in our lives.[140]

Feminist theologians have explored the theological meaning of the erotic in their search for a language that empowers. American feminist theologian and Episcopal priest Carter Heyward appropriates the erotic as the "sacred/godly basis of our capacity to participate in mutually empowering relationships."[141] In exploring the meaning of the erotic within the sphere of christological discourse, Rita Nakashima Brock, an Asian-American feminist theologian, finds *eros* to be "sensuous, transformative, whole-making wisdom that emerges with the subjective engagement of the whole heart in relationship."[142] As primal interrelatedness, Nakashima Brock's Christology sees Christ as the erotic power who cannot be imprisoned in the individual figure of the historical Jesus. Christ, as erotic power, is experienced in communities that embody and live out the power of interrelatedness, of caring and openness, of forgiveness and healing, and of making whole broken bodies and spirits. Such passion can only emerge from the heart. Nakashima Brock specifically identifies erotic power with "the feminist eros."[143]

Toward a Theology of Body and Sexuality: Resisting Violence against Women

Among Hong Kong feminist theologians the discourse on the erotic is located in the continuing debate about Jesus and the issue of female sexuality. Wong Wai-Ching charges Asian feminist theologians with avoiding the issue. She argues that feminist Christologies hinge on the issue of Jesus' maleness. Glossing over the issue of Jesus' sexuality, or not recognizing his maleness as a problem, hinders Asian feminist theologians from accessing the language of the erotic. She thinks that the issue of Jesus' maleness is a misplaced question and points out that her interest is not so much in the man Jesus and his divine nature but rather in the identity of women and their divine nature. With a penchant for fluidity, difference, and hybridity of identities in contexts where the gaps and silences are deemed to be "fractured sites of resistance," Wong asserts that Christology must be reformulated into "Christology that can be about a relational or erotic power, a messianic social and cosmic struggle against evil, a collective utopian experiment in faith and praxis, a mystical secret discipleship of Spirit-Sophia-God, which are all present in the gospels for those with ears to hear."[144]

Although not the first Asian theologian to suggest it, Wong's invitation to employ the language of the erotic continues to give fresh insight that is applicable to Asian feminist Christology. Wong's suggestion is informed by the thoughts of French theorists Luce Irigaray and Hélène Cixous, as well as the theologies of feminist Julie Hopkins and Japanese biblical scholar Hisako Kinukawa.[145] Wong thinks that Kinukawa's appreciation of the "embodied man-Jesus" and "women's bodily experiences" is a "good start" toward the exploration of the erotic power in Asian christological construction. To Wong, Kinukawa's contention that women take "an essential part in God's salvific act," as well as her understanding that a mutual transformation in the encounter between Jesus and women "leaves much room for a further exploration of women's experience of the Divine."[146] Wong builds on Hopkins's contention that women's bodies and selves reflect the image of God, and are a potential source of divine presence. From there, Wong suggests that women theologians explore a theology based on women's bodily experience. A "theology of female flesh becoming Logos is natural to women,"[147] she asserts, because women have all the rights to name the divine presence in their own space and time.

Wong takes the epistemological cue from the French post-feminists for her position. Both Irigaray and Cixous advance the notion that women are able to write with difference because they are connected and deeply in touch with the power of the erotic.[148] Drawing from these post-feminist views, Wong contends that the language of the erotic will contribute to the development of an incarnational theology in Asia. She criticizes Asian feminist theologians for not taking the issue of sexuality seriously. She thinks this weakness is a result of "postcolonial politics" that imposed the idea that discourse on sexuality reflects the individualistic and bourgeois values of the First World. Wong cites and charges Kwok Pui-lan with advancing the idea that the "concern over the tragic magnitude of prostitution takes priority attention over the issue of the pleasure of female sexuality, the power of the erotic and the woman's right to control her body."[149]

Unfortunately, Wong misreads Kwok. Kwok was excited about the rediscovery of the power of the erotic in the works of Rita Nakashima Brock and Carter Heyward. Kwok even directs our attention to the strange absence of the language of the erotic in the theological construction of black and feminist theologians from other parts of the world. Yet she also shows deep understanding of why Womanists and Asian women have difficulty speaking about the power of female sexuality. Kwok points to Delores Williams who speaks of the language of the erotic being stolen from African American women when their bodies were defiled and used by the white oppressors.[150] Kwok further observes that Asian women find it painful to use the language of the erotic, given that their sisters go through the travails of sexual violence and are trapped in sex slavery and the sex trade. Asian societies have also prohibited women from talking about the erotic in public.[151] Religion and society have successfully used the discourse of decency as a tool to instill the burden of shame and guilt in women. The discourse of decency, or in Cixous's phrase, "the stupidity of sexual modesty,"[152] inhibited women from getting in touch with their power and stopped them from speaking out against the violations done to their bodies. Having seen the struggle that women's organizations in Asia face as they attempt to help rape victims and prostituted women reclaim their lives and live fully, Kwok writes: "The magnitude of the international flesh trade and the courageous action of these women's groups challenge us to rethink the connection between the language of the erotic, the control of the female body, and power over women in its naked and symbolic forms."[153]

What Kwok wants to highlight is the reality that women in Asia still need to free themselves from the discourse of decency that has made women turn away from their bodies, from their true selves, and from the power of the erotic. Kwok finds the value of the language of the erotic in identifying the christic images in the communities of women and men in Asia, but she is also pragmatic:

> While the French feminists are talking about *jouissance*, and some lesbians are trying to break the taboo to talk about passionate love and relationships among women, many women have yet to find a language to speak about pleasure of the body, female sexuality and the power of the erotic because the yoke of "compulsory heterosexuality" is still heavy upon us. . . . Many of the metaphors of Christianity come out of the familial context and sexual relationships between persons, such as the Father and the Son, the Church as the bride of Christ, and Adam and Eve as the first couple. The experiences of women, whose sexuality has been controlled and who suffer violence to their bodies, challenge some of these "beloved" images and should be taken up as a serious theological issue in our feminist reconstruction.[154]

Kwok is correct. In Asia few people have the courage to imagine what a gospel of prostituted women would be. This is a result of people's being disconnected from the power of the erotic. Christians are afraid of it. Many Asian Christians claim to be communitarian, but, under the shadow of phallocentric hegemony, they are afraid to acknowledge their longing to be connected with the other.

CLAIMING A DIFFERENT SPACE FOR CREATIVE CHRISTOLOGIES

In Asia, the task of reclaiming and putting the language of the erotic at the service of Christology has just begun. Kwok and Wong have challenged theologians to explore the discourse of the erotic as a potential resource for the empowerment of women in Asia. The two women have a basic commonality in their understanding that postcolonial theory, as cultural/intercultural criticism, can enrich the creation of an empowering Christology for women. Both seek to push Asian feminist theology's discourse beyond the bounds of discourses that veil masculinist hegemony and resist essentialism. Hong Kong feminist theologians have demonstrated their solid capabilities in engaging Asian Christology with the critical theories. Wong may not have offered a fully developed Christology, but she posted a sign that urges Asian feminist Christologies to move forward. She offers a "different space" for christological conversation to occur, although one may not agree with her position that prohibits the entry of "radical liberational politics." To Wong, her separatist posture aims to let women "venture into their own journey" free from dominating masculinist discourse.[155] Ironically, Wong hesitates to acknowledge that a healthy Christology needs to hold together in balance and harmony the dialectical relationship of diversity and unity, of the universal and the particular, of women and men, even as she speaks of hybridity.

Kwok straddles the two camps of essentialism and constructivism,[156] the latter represented by Wong. Kwok demonstrates this in her hybridized, organic Jesus as well as in her vision for the future of feminist theology, especially in the Third World:

> Feminist theology will continue to have a future if the kind of work that we are doing stimulates, encourages, and motivates women and men to struggle against all forms of oppression, to seek justice, and to love ourselves and others. . . . If feminist theologians of all colors continue to articulate the voice of the oppressed, to integrate theory with practice, and to be more sympathetic to women's needs in different faith communities, there will be a bright future for feminist theology.[157]

Straddling the two camps of the essentialist/constructivist debate is true to Kwok's postcolonial approach, that of negotiating one's identity among different realities and views. Hers is the "strategic essentialist" position, one that determines what is emancipatory and formulates strong normative judgments without losing sight of the baggage of universalism.[158] One can sense that, for Kwok, strategic essentialism is not merely a survival strategy in writing theology;[159] it is making a commitment by "offering pragmatically useful answers" to one's community of accountability. According to Yale-based theology professor Serene Jones, a strategic essentialist is one who believes that people need a view of human nature that includes "essentials" or "universals." Indeed, constructivism alone—characterized by postmodern and postcolonial views that the self is fluid and chaotic—cannot sustain collective actions and movements that need a normative idea of human nature and human good. Constructivism, characterized by the postmodern and postcolonial discourse, sees the self, like everything else, as dynamic and fluid.[160]

In view of the differences, the Hong Kong feminist theologians who construct their Christologies from the perspective of postcolonial theory have invited the Asian feminist theologians to take a critical look at the existing masculine images of Jesus the Christ. They have shown different ways of looking at Jesus' multiple identity with the use of the postcolonial lens, and in their case, as one who is organic and a subject-in-process. Kwok's contribution stresses a holistic christological view that responds to environmental issues. The language of the erotic gives a clue as to how to affirm female sexuality in constructing Christology. Wong's view of Jesus as a subject-in-process has affirmed the practices and the writings of many Asian feminist theologians. From the beginning the nascent Asian feminist Christologies have claimed the multiplicity of Jesus' images and identities. That Jesus is a prototype of the sign of God's presence and that Christ is the power of the erotic drive home the reality that God reveals the divine self and speaks to Asian women in multiple ways. Indeed, Jesus the Christ is many things to many women. Most important for them is Jesus' life-giving, life-enhancing image, which empowers them in their life journeys.

Epilogue

Who Is This Jesus Who Comes to My House?

Once, when I was desperately in need of liberation, someone came to my house: a white baby Jesus garbed in a red satin cape with golden trimmings. He stood at my door, the Señor Sto. Niño. He was like a miniature king, wearing a crown, with a scepter in one hand. Though familiar with this ubiquitous replica of the icon that the Spanish friars gave to their first converts, I must admit his presence made me uneasy. As I pondered the strangeness of my feelings toward the image, I began to realize it was not my Protestant sensibilities that evoked the discomfort but rather the image of white royalty. The image gave me the impression that the conqueror's Jesus, even in infancy, already wielded the power to dominate. The image neither stirred up any motherly instinct in me nor spoke to my predicament and struggle against patriarchy. I longed to meet the Jesus the Gospel writers speak about. I wanted to meet the one who embodies the Christ, who practices the ethics of love and compassion, and who provokes women to be in touch with their inner power to rise up and to resist patriarchy. Then the Asian feminist theologians beckoned to me and shared with me their passion. They led me to the world where they met Jesus the Christ—to the banks of Ma Ganga, to the foot of the salt mountain, to Xi Xi's bustling city, and to the foot of Mt. Talinis. After "walking" through Asia with women theologians of India, Korea, the Philippines, and Hong Kong, one may ask if Asian women meet Jesus in the land of the spirits, gods, goddesses, and tears. I say yes. They meet Jesus the Christ in many faces and in different shapes.

ASIAN WOMEN'S JESUS, THE ASIAN CHRIST

I have pointed out that Asian women, when freed from patriarchal blinders, are able to articulate their own understanding about Jesus the Christ creatively. Asian women's social locations and cultures have marked the similarities and differences in their Christologies. Overall, the Jesus of Asian women is the Asian Christ who accompanies them in their daily struggles for liberation from all forms of oppression and suffering. This Christ seeks to engage with religions, cultures, and indigenous spiritualities to make life flourish for every living being. This resurrected Christ transcends gender as the Beauty and Wisdom of God. Shakti and Wisdom Christologies enable Asian women to connect with their concern for ecology and the degradation of the earth. Indeed, Jesus takes multiple and variegated identities. Organic Christology liberates Jesus the Christ from patriarchy. The images of the vine, bread, and water, for instance, show the life-giving character of Jesus and negate the traditional social, political, and economic hierarchies. Christ is the way to the fullness of life for individuals and communities. This is so because Christ is the embodiment of the passion for life in relationship and mutuality.

I welcome to my house Jesus the Christ who in multiple identities reveals the Divine, the God of many names. Indeed, I met this Jesus at the foot of Mt. Talinis. This Christ welcomed me and my children to the inn, for this Christ was embodied in a community of caring women and men. Yet, even as I met Jesus among the Christians, I also found the Christ among women and men who live out a loving, life-giving, and life-sustaining praxis. This liberated Christ continues to call everyone to follow the way that leads to the fullness of life for all.

"Do You Love Me?" The Call to Carry On the Christic Task of Jesus

The Christhood of Jesus is defined by his liberating, loving, and life-giving acts. The term *Christ* comes from the Greek rendering of the Hebrew word *mashiah*, "the anointed."[1] The Greek verb *chrio* ("to anoint") is used in the phrase *echrisen me* in Luke 4:18, which is translated "he has anointed me."[2] This phrase could be rendered "he has *christed* me," that is, the Spirit of the Lord "has made me Christ." This is the strength of the phrase when Jesus succinctly declared his christic task:

"The Spirit of the Lord is upon me,
because he has anointed me
to bring good news to the poor,
He has sent me to proclaim release to the captives
and the recovery of sight to the blind,
to let the oppressed go free,
to proclaim the year of the Lord's favor." (Lk 4:18)

Christians need to understand the roots of the word *Christ* in order to appreciate the challenge Jesus posed to his followers. Remembering and reclaiming the meaning of Christhood to signify the blessing and dedication of a person to carry out loving, liberating, and life-nurturing acts liberates the Christ from the shackles of patriarchal and sexist definitions. This understanding dismantles "christolatry" and sets Christ free from spiritualization, pacification, and abstractions invented by the dominating systems that perpetuate the culture of "othering."[3] Reading the Gospels from my location makes me understand that Jesus' Christhood begins with the recognition of the gift of anointing by the Holy Spirit. Jesus' christic acts are intertwined with the vision and mission of God and the Holy Spirit. The Gospels point out that Christology cannot be understood apart from the work of God the Creator and the Holy Spirit. The christic character of the prophetic tradition that Jesus honored was a gift of the Holy Spirit. Jesus' Christhood is known through his praxis of love (Jn 14:11; Lk 7:22). And so, the Christ finds embodiment in different times and spaces, as the Christ responds to people's yearning for salvation and fullness of life. Jesus is indeed one manifestation or revelation of the Divine, a prototype of a sign that points to the reality that God is with us and that, in Asia, Christ is one and many.[4]

"Do You Love Me? Feed My Lambs. Feed My Sheep."

Jesus called on his disciples to continue his work through the empowerment of the Holy Spirit. While the Holy Spirit endows the christic gift of God to Christians, the Holy Spirit also gives the christic gift to Jesus' "sheep outside the fold" (Jn 10:16–17). Thus, the gift of embodiment of the christic is given to all of humanity. No individual or group has a monopoly on the gift of the Spirit. For Christians, Jesus is the paradigm of the embodied Christ. Yet, the christic task continues with the challenge Jesus left for communities of believers, that is, to make the gift manifest through the prophetic and liberating acts outlined in the Gospels. The language that carries this challenge is the language of love, for the word love encompasses the meaning of *agapao* and *erao*.[5] Thus, a community that embodies the power of the erotic is known only through its christic practice. It is known through its new way of living out the mandate of loving one another; of embodying God's love (Jn 14:10–11), of feeding the little sheep (Jn 21), of being friends with one another rather than enslaving others (Jn 15:14–15), and of laying down one's life for one's friends (Jn 10:17–18).

Biblical scholar Gail R. O'Day suggests that at the heart of the Gospel of John is his vision of the beloved community's fulfillment of the new interpretation of the commandment to love. The language of love in the Gospel of John that highlights the image of fullness and abundance balances the language of discipleship in the Synoptic Gospels that focuses on the concept of self-emptying.[6] The Johannine notion of fullness and love that characterizes discipleship and faith is important for women because it focuses on one's capacity to give out of an abundance of love. The language of emptying and self-denial drains life out of women, for it adheres "to an ethos of perpetual self-sacrifice and the meaninglessness of self."[7]

ENCOUNTERING AND REIMAGINING CHRIST

The Christ is not imprisoned in one single person in history; we meet the Christ in many faces and forms. Rita Nakashima Brock locates Christ in christa/community, the "church's imaginative witness to its experiences of brokenness and sacredness of erotic power in human existence."[8] To Catholic Mai Thành of North Vietnam, Christ is an intimate friend, a partner, a spouse, a brother.[9] Womanist theologian Kelly Brown Douglas sees Christ in the face of her grandmother, "as she struggled to sustain herself and her family."[10] Black people's experience makes black theologian James H. Cone to see Christ as black, asserting that the title Christ is universal when it "points to God's universal will to liberate particular oppressed people from inhumanity."[11] In the same vein Womanist theologian Jacquelyn Grant encounters Christ within the community of black women as a black female.[12] Native Americans see Jesus as the Corn Mother but also as the Trickster, a transgressor of boundaries and limits and disrupter of social norms.[13]

Indeed, the Christ is not imprisoned in a single person or in a single experience of a particular group of people in history. Escaping from patriarchal space, Asian women transgress the boundaries of the Nicea-Chalcedonian formulas to meaningfully meet Jesus, the subject-in-process, the Christ who confronts us in many ways wearing many faces. All these manifestations and the embodiment of the Christ in individuals and communities signal and point to the power of the christic, a gift from God given through the Holy Spirit that ushers in the hope for a new life.

Thus, Christology must be holistic and should not separate liberation and salvation.[14] It demands praxis of love, compassion, and risk taking. Jesus as the prototype symbol of God's presence is the norm for this praxis. Risk taking is about loving fiercely to fight injustice and to resist the culture of violence. It is about embarking into the concrete but dangerous work of compassion, to resist the violence of crucifixions, and to bring down the crosses erected by patriarchy and imperialistic political and economic structures that the sociocultural infrastructures of the dominant nations prop up. A holistic Christology affirms Brazilian Ivone Gebara's assertion that "through acts of love and justice we . . . proclaim the scandal of all the crosses represented by the many forms of violence throughout society."[15] Christology seeks to nurture the seed of life, allowing it to flourish even in the harshest conditions and to bear fruit.

Inang Bayan as an Embodiment of the Christ

Resonating with the Asian feminist theologians' variegated images of Jesus as the Christ, I lift up the image of the Inang Bayan as an embodiment of the Christ. *Ina* means "mother," and *Bayan* means "land and people." The Sacred that Christians call God reveals itself in the land and in the life of the struggling people. The common thread that runs across the indigenous peoples' spirituality is the ecological wisdom that connects them to the primal memory of the Breastfeeding Goddess.[16] The image of Inang Bayan is woven from the ancient memory of the many-breasted Mother, she who has many names.[17] She is the one who gives us birth, breastfeeds us, and provides us with the resources for sustenance. Inang Bayan is the manifestation of the

Wisdom of God. She is the embodiment of the Christ and the many-breasted Mother who embraces and nurses her many children–Christian, tribals and indigenous peoples, Muslims, female and male, gay and straight, young and old, the trees, the birds, and the fishes. Inang Bayan does not discriminate in giving her life-sustaining love.

The historical Jesus has, indeed, embodied the Christ and revealed in his life the love of the Divine. For the early Christian communities Jesus was a sign pointing to God's presence. Jesus as Sophia invited his friends, especially the poor, to a banquet to celebrate life. It is in this spirit that Clement of Alexandria conceived of Christ as the "milk of Wisdom from the breast of the Bride."[18] Along the same vein, Ambrose of Milan imagined Christ as the "Virgin Who bore us, Who fed us with Her own milk."[19]

However, one must not forget that the Christ is larger than the historical Jesus. Drawing wisdom from the wellsprings of indigenous Filipinos, Christ is discerned in Inang Bayan, the life-giving and sustaining principle, evident in land that supports the life of the people. Caring communities that continually struggle for their well being also embody Inang Bayan's Christhood. Inang Bayan wept and died at the death of her children, slain in their struggles for justice, liberty, and dignity. She has been abused by some of her children and subjugated by strangers. She is crucified by those who constantly seek to "grab her hair,"[20] scour the depths of her womb for wealth, and steal her milk for her children. Yet, this mother rises again and again in the communities that continue to struggle for the fullness of life. Inang Bayan is the Christ who rises over death and continues to defy evil powers (Jn 7:7b), who empowers the powerless (Lk 7:22), who accompanies us on our journey, who is manifest in growing rice, corn and *kolò* (breadfruit), and who makes the waters teem with fish to feed the hungry and to celebrate new life (Lk 24:13–49). The Christ increases in those who value the gift of life in the christic. This Christ is indeed the many-breasted Mother.

WHAT IS THE FUTURE TASK FOR ASIAN WOMEN'S CHRISTOLOGY?

Asian feminist theologians have proven that they are able to articulate their Christologies creatively, standing firmly upon their Asian heritage, social location, and circumstances. This nascent freedom must continue to flourish. Yet, Asian feminist theologians must also reach out not only to women in the pew but also to women who could not even enter the church's doors because the church's norms through written and unwritten codes forbid them to do so. Because the ultimate goal of Christology is the realization that God's will for all is to live the fullness of life, an overarching theme that Asian women's Christologies must engage with is the cross. Asian feminist theologians need to wrestle with the meaning of the cross because the violence that brought Jesus to his death on the cross continues to be a reality in women's lives not only in Asia but all over the world.[21] The task of liberating women from imposed suffering continues to be a challenge. Helping violated people make sense of their pains and empowering them to overcome the evils of violence is a task the followers of Christ must do. To struggle for the fullness of life is to abolish suffering and to wrestle with the reality and meaning of the cross. This struggle encompasses the issues of patriarchy, sexism, homophobia, classism, ethnocentrism, racism, xenophobia, and all the "isms" that dehumanize and denigrate life.

While the struggle against patriarchy and sexism is the strongest thread that binds Asian women, Asian feminist Christology still needs to address the issue of homophobia. Asian Christian feminists need to forge and strengthen their solidarity with feminists from other Asian faith traditions and cultures to uproot patriarchy, sexism, and homophobia from all areas of life. Furthermore, the retrieval of the power of the erotic will help women to be constantly vigilant and to avoid having their "self" and their faith co-opted by a patriarchal ethos. Women who are sensitive to the stirrings of the christic power of the erotic may also help men to see how patriarchy dehumanizes them. Men need redemption from a culture of evil and greed, where abuse of power in whatever form dominates.

Asian feminist Christology also needs to continue to draw wisdom from the deep wells of Asia's culture and traditions. Women must push further the boundaries that traditional Christianity has set and explore the christic in the nontraditional. Asian culture and indigenous traditions are great resources for christological constructions. Asian women must not be afraid to drink from our own wells, to use the words of Gustavo Gutiérrez, in doing Christology. They need to continue to lift up the liberating and life-sustaining elements of their indigenous religions and their sacred texts, the goddess traditions, myths, stories, dances, art, and the experiences of the people.

Asian feminist Christology also needs to engage with critical theories. Some Asian feminist theologians have already started doing this. Engaging Christology in dialogue with feminist social, cultural, and literary theories will help women see things from different angles and allow them to take bolder steps in creating a women-liberating Christology. Moreover, the insights gained from feminist critical theories could help Asian feminist theologians create a space and offer an invitation for dialogue with the Christologies of the marginalized groups. It will be a space where mutual respect is genuinely upheld; a space where men who are committed to leaving behind their patriarchal and phallocentric arrogance may learn to listen to women's voices. Conversations help Asian feminist Christologies facilitate the building of communities of peace, communities that embody the Christ who embraces both the lovely and the unlovable. Engaging with critical theories also will help Asian feminist Christology to unveil and resist the impoverishing grip of any nation aspiring to be an empire. Asian feminist Christology must address neoliberal globalization that hampers the globalization of justice. Women need to be conscious that critical theories can help them in the construction of life-giving and life-enhancing Christologies. Such theories should not veer away from the ethics of accountability. Debates over issues of identity, difference, subjectivity, and sexuality need not be detached from the concrete realities of women in Asia. Christ-talk is Christology half done. It has to be practiced. Jesus has shown us how.

Finally, Asian feminist Christology prods us to continue the journey of reimagining and reinterpreting Jesus the Christ. At the same time, it opens us up to the signs of God's revelation and christic gifts in other traditions, communities, and locations. Then, communities of various traditions will journey together in their search for the fullness of life for all. Christ is God-with-us who weeps with our pain, dances with us to celebrate our little triumphs over the many crosses in our lives, and leads us toward the fullness of life at the breast of the ultimate Mystery we call God.

Notes

PROLOGUE

1. The second biggest island located in the southern part of the Philippine archipelago.

2. Ferdinand Marcos declared martial law on September 21, 1972.

3. Niall O'Brian, *Island of Tears, Island of Hope: Living the Gospel in a Revolutionary Situation* (Maryknoll, NY: Orbis Books, 1993), 4, 24–30.

4. Gregorio F. Zaide, *Political and Cultural History of the Philippines*, 2 vols. (Manila: Garcia Book Store, 1957). See also Richard L. Deats, *Nationalism and Christianity in the Philippines* (Dallas: Southern Methodist Univ. Press, 1967). Zaide and Deats highlight the contributions of the colonizers to the advancement of Philippine civilization, but they do not point out the negative effects of colonization.

5. Renato Constantino, *The Philippines: A Past Revisited (Pre-Spanish-1941)* (Quezon City: by the author, 1975), 16–25. See also M. D. David, "Introduction: The Nature of Western Colonialism—A Handicap to the Growth of Christianity in Asia," in *Western Colonialism in Asia and Christianity*, ed. M. D. David (Delhi: Himalaya Publishing House, 1988), 1–19. Jean-Marc Éla of Cameroon and Native American George E. Tinker share the same observation. See Jean-Marc Éla, *African Cry* (Maryknoll, NY: Orbis Books, 1986); George E. Tinker, *Missionary Conquest: The Gospel and Native American Cultural Genocide* (Minneapolis: Fortress Press, 1993).

6. Constantino, *The Philippines*, 219. The treaty was signed on December 19, 1898. Under the Treaty of Paris, Spain also ceded Puerto Rico to the United States and relinquished sovereignty over Cuba.

7. Ibid., 249. Brig. Gen. Jacob Smith ordered the Balangiga massacre in Samar: "I want no prisoners. I wish you to kill and burn, the more you kill and burn the better you will please me." He and Gen. Franklin Bell were together in Batangas. Smith was promoted later, becoming governor general of the Philippines.

8. Davianna Pomaika'i-McGregor, "1989–1998: Rethinking the US in Paradise," *Rethinking the US in Paradise Newsletter* 1, no. 1 (July 1998): 1, 3. *Argonaut* was the name of the newsletter dated 1902.

9. Eusebius of Caesarea, *Ecclesiastical History, Complete and Unabridged*, trans. C. F. Cruse, rev. ed. (Peabody, MA.: Hendrickson Publishers, 1998), 343–45, 379. Eusebius interpreted the cross as a signal to conquer, for the expansion of the Roman Empire's territory would mean the expansion of God's kingdom on earth. See 9.9.10–11.

10. Gerald H. Anderson, "Providence and Politics behind Protestant Missionary Beginnings in the Philippines," in *Studies in Philippine Church History*, ed. Gerald H. Anderson (Ithaca, NY: Cornell Univ. Press, 1969), 299–300.

11. Ibid., 285. Anderson quotes extensively the euphoric words of Methodist Bishop James M. Thoburn.

12. Ibid., 286. The statement comes from the Baptist Union.

13. Ibid., 296.

14. United States Information Service, "The American Contribution to the Philippine Education: 1898–1998" (Manila: U.S.I.S., 1998). These scholars were identified as Thomasites, or the six hundred schoolteachers who came to the Philippines on August 21, 1901, aboard the US Army ship *Thomas.*

15. Deats, *Nationalism and Christianity in the Philippines;* see also Zaide, *Political and Cultural History of the Philippines.*

16. Mark Twain, *Mark Twain's Weapons of Satire: Anti-Imperialist Writings on the Philippine-American War*, ed. Jim Zwick (Syracuse, NY: Syracuse Univ. Press, 1992). A notable writer under the pen name Mark Twain, Samuel Langhorn Clemens was one of the leaders of the Anti-Imperialist League of America. He argued that the American imperialist ventures were "un-American" and violated the principles of the American Constitution. He started to write articles against American and European imperialism in the Pacific and in Africa in 1900, but his publishers and newspapers rejected and suppressed his serious political writings. Among his staunch critics were the Christian missionaries and the leaders of the army.

17. Of the debt, 58 percent is owed to the United States and 22 percent is owed to Japan. The debt in 2004 was US$56.718 billion. Considering internal and external debts, RP national debt reached US$69.7 billion in 2004.

18. Migrante International, *The Progressive Movement of Overseas Compatriots* (Quezon City: Migrante International, 1999), 37.

19. Christian V. Esguerra, "6,000 Doctors Studying to Be Nurses; DOH Alarmed," in *Philippine Daily Inquirer* (August 4, 2005), 1, 4.

20. Nicole Constable, *Maid to Order in Hong Kong: Stories of Filipina Workers* (Ithaca, NY: Cornell Univ. Press, 1997).

21. Migrante International, *The Progressive Movement of Overseas Compatriots*, 39.

22. Epifanio San Juan, Jr., *Beyond Postcolonial Theory* (New York: St. Martin's Press, 1998), 220–26.

23. Carol P. Christ, *Diving Deep and Surfacing: Women Writers on Spiritual Quests* (Boston: Beacon Press, 1980), 1. Christ uses the word *story* in a broad sense to include all media of expression that articulate women's experiences.

24. Karen Morin, "Autobiography," in *A Feminist Glossary of Human Geography*, ed. Linda McDowell and Joanne P. Sharp (New York: Arnold, 1999), 10.

1 LOOKING AT JESUS THROUGH ASIAN EYES

1. K. M. Kostyal, ed., *National Geographic: Peoples of the World* (Washington, DC: National Geographic Society, 2001), 14–15.

2. Ibid.

3. Aloysius Pieris, "Towards an Asian Theology of Liberation: Some Religio-Cultural Guidelines," in *Asia's Struggle for Full Humanity*, ed. Virginia Fabella (Maryknoll, NY: Orbis Books, 1988), 80.

4. Victoria Tauli-Corpus, "Reclaiming Earth-Based Spirituality: Indigenous Women in the Cordillera," in *Women Healing Earth*, ed. Rosemary Radford Ruether (Maryknoll, NY: Orbis Books, 1996), 100–101.

5. Aloysius Pieris, *Fire and Water: Basic Issues in Asian Buddhism and Christianity* (Maryknoll, NY: Orbis Books, 1996), 66.

6. Ibid.

7. Tauli-Corpus, "Reclaiming Earth-Based Spirituality," 100–101.

8. Pieris, *Fire and Water*, 66.

9. Roy C. Amore and Julia Ching, "The Buddhist Tradition," in *World Religions: Eastern Traditions*, ed. Willard G. Oxtoby (New York: Oxford Univ. Press, 1996), 302.

10. M. D. David, ed., *Asia and Christianity* (Bombay: Himalaya Publishing House, 1985), vii–viii.

11. Amore and Ching, "The Buddhist Tradition," 301–2; see also Pieris, *Fire and Water*, 66. Pieris takes the cue from Stanley Samartha, who argued that a "helicopter christology" kicks a lot of dust and creates so much noise as it descends that people could not hear or find meaning in what it says. See Stanley J. Samartha, *One Christ—Many Religions: Toward a Revised Christology* (Maryknoll, NY: Orbis Books, 1991), 115–17.

12. Aloysius Pieris, *An Asian Theology of Liberation* (Maryknoll, NY: Orbis Books, 1988), 39.

13. Not all Christian traditions share the history of the Western church—Roman Catholic or Protestant. Their questions were different from those raised by the Christians in the West. See Timothy Ware, *The Orthodox Church*, new ed. (London: Penguin Books, 1963).

14. Ken Curtis et al., *Glimpses #43: Time for Reorientation*, Part 1 of a 6–part series on the History of the Church in the Orient (Asia) (Worcester, PA: Christian History Institute, 2003). Available online. See also Philip Jenkins, *The Next Christendom: The Coming of Global Christianity* (Oxford: Oxford Univ. Press, 2002), 3. In Asia, Christians represent "a mere 3.5% of the population," and Asian Christians make up only 10 percent of the world's Christian population.

15. David, "Introduction," 9.

16. Pieris, *Fire and Water*, 66; see also Samartha, *One Christ—Many Religions*, 115–17.

17. Pieris, *An Asian Theology of Liberation*, 39.

18. *Balikbayan* is a Filipino term coined from two words: *balik*, "come back," and *bayan*, "homeland or country."

19. Pieris, *Fire and Water*, 65–66.

20. Anscar J. Chupungco, *Liturgies of the Future: The Process and Methods of Inculturation* (New York: Paulist Press, 1989), 23–25.

21. Ibid., 23.

22. Ibid., 17, 24.

23. Russell J. Chandran, "Development of Christian Theology in India: A Critical Survey," in *Readings in Indian Christian Theology*, ed. R. S. Sugirtharajah and Cecil Hargreaves (London: SPCK, 1993), 4–13.

24. Denis L. Edwards, *Christianity: The First Two Thousand Years* (Maryknoll, NY: Orbis Books, 1998), 347.

25. John W. Witek, "Ricci, Matteo," in *Biographical Dictionary of Christian Missions*, ed. Gerald H. Anderson (Grand Rapids, MI: Eerdmans, 1998), 566–67. A bull from Rome issued in 1742 banned any participation by Chinese Catholics in ancestral or Confucian rituals.

26. Sugirtharajah and Hargreaves, *Readings in Indian Christian Theology*, 247.

27. David L. Edwards, *Christianity: The First Two Thousand Years* (Maryknoll, NY: Orbis Books, 1998), 347–48.

28. Michael Amaladoss, "Nobili, Robert de," in Anderson, *Biographical Dictionary of Christian Missions*, 498–99.

29. Pieris, *An Asian Theology of Liberation*, 54.

30. Chandran, "Development of Christian Theology in India"; see also M. M. Thomas, *The Acknowledged Christ of the Indian Renaissance* (London: SCM Press, 1969).

31. Stanley J. Samartha, *The Hindu Response to the Unbound Christ* (Madras: The Christian Literature Society, 1974).

32. Thomas, *The Acknowledged Christ of the Indian Renaissance*, 333.

33. Vasudha Naranayan, "The Hindu Tradition," in *World Religions: Eastern Traditions*, ed. Willard G. Oxtoby (New York: Oxford Univ. Press, 1996), 76.

34. Thomas, *The Acknowledged Christ of the Indian Renaissance*, 1, 16–28. Drawn toward the Synoptic Gospels' account of Jesus' life, Thomas points out that Roy criticized Christians who tended to forget the teachings of Jesus and gave more attention to inquiries into Jesus' nature.

35. Naranayan, "The Hindu Tradition," 75.

36. Thomas, *The Acknowledged Christ of the Indian Renaissance*, 56–82, 102.

37. Sugirtharajah and Hargreaves, *Readings in Indian Christian Theology*, 245. The Sanskrit term *advaita* expresses the notion that there is no separation between God and the created world. This principle was expounded by Sankara.

38. Ibid., 248. The word *yoga* means "union."

39. Thomas, *The Acknowledged Christ of the Indian Renaissance*, 122, 331.

40. Ibid., 155.

41. Mahatma Gandhi, *All Men Are Brothers*, ed. Krishna Kripalani (New York: Continuum, 2000), 65.

42. Thomas, *The Acknowledged Christ of the Indian Renaissance*, 195–205. Gandhi believes that *satya* (truth) must always be coupled with *ahimsa* (non-violence) and *swadeshi* (service to people). *Satyagraha* means resistance to evil through voluntary suffering. This is the opposite of *himsa*, which means body force, that is, inflicting suffering on others.

43. Gandhi, *All Men Are Brothers*, 166.

44. Teruo Kuribayashi, "*Burakumin* Liberation Theology," in *Dictionary of Third World Theologies*, ed. Virginia Fabella and R. S. Sugirtharajah (Maryknoll, NY: Orbis Books, 2000), 33.

45. Sundar Clarke, "Dalit Movement–Need for a Theology," in *Towards a Dalit Theology*, ed. M. E. Prabhakar (Delhi: ISPCK, 1988), 32.

46. Anthony Raj, "Disobedience: A Legitimate Act for Dalit Liberation," in *Towards a Common Dalit Theology*, ed. Arvind P. Nirmal (Madras: Gurukul Lutheran Theological College and Research Institute, 1989), 40–41.

47. Arvind P. Nirmal, "Towards a Christian Dalit Theology," in *A Reader in Dalit Theology*, ed. Arvind P. Nirmal (Madras: Department of Dalit Theology Gurukul Lutheran Theological College and Research Institute), 59. Nirmal presented a valedictory address entitled "Towards a Christian Dalit Theology" at United Theological College, Bangalore, in April 1981.

48. Ibid., 58–59.

49. Ibid., 69.

50. Ibid., 65.

51. Ibid., 63.

52. M. E. Prabhakar, "The Search for a Dalit Theology," in Nirmal, *A Reader in Dalit Theology*, 50.

53. James Massey, *Roots of Dalit History, Christianity, Theology, and Spirituality* (Delhi: ISPCK, 1996), 76–79.

54. M. Azariah, "The Church's Healing Ministry to Dalits," in Prabhakar, *Towards a Dalit Theology*, 113–21.

55. Prabhakar, "The Search for a Dalit Theology," 43.

56. Elizabeth Joy, "The Meaning and Origin of Dalit Theology" (M.Th. thesis, South Asia Theological Research Institute, 1998).

57. Raj, "Disobedience."

58. Suh Nam-Dong, "Towards a Theology of Han," in *Minjung Theology: People as the Subjects of History*, ed. Commission on Theological Concerns of CCA (London: Zed; Maryknoll, NY: Orbis Books; Singapore: CCA, 1981), 64.

59. David Kwang-sun Suh, *Korean Minjung in Christ* (Hong Kong: Christian Conference of Asia, 1991), 170–73.

60. David Kwang-sun Suh, "Asian Theology in a Changing Asia: Towards an Asian Theological Agenda for the 21st Century," *CTC Bulletin*, Special Supplement 1 (November 1997), 27.

61. Ibid.

62. Suh, *Korean Minjung in Christ*, 174.

63. C. S. Song, "Christ behind the Mask Dance: Christology of People and Their Culture," *CTC Bulletin* 3, no. 3 (December 1982): 39–42.

64. C. S. Song, *Theology from the Womb of Asia* (Maryknoll, NY: Orbis Books, 1986), 221–24.

65. C. S. Song, "Oh, Jesus, Here with Us!" in *Asian Faces of Jesus*, ed. R. S. Sugirtharajah (Maryknoll, NY: Orbis Books, 1993), 146.

66. Song, "Christ behind the Mask Dance."

67. Ibid., 41–42.

68. Pieris, *Fire and Water*, 68.

69. Ibid., 68–69.

70. K. M. Panikkar, *Asia and Western Dominance: A Survery of the Vasco Da Gama Epoch of Asian History 1498–1945* (London: George Allen and Unwin, 1959), 322. Panikkar points out that the notion of "one Asia" was first articulated at the beginning of the twentieth century by Japanese artist Okakura Kakuzo in *Asia Is One*.

71. David, *Asia and Christianity*, xi. See also Amore and Ching, "The Buddhist Tradition," 245. One can observe the Indian influence in East Asia and Southeast Asia through syncretistic Hindu civilization. The Chinese influence also began to spread with the trade efforts of the Tang Dynasty.

72. David, "Introduction," 1.

73. T. R. de'Souza, "The Portuguese in Asia and Their Church Patronage," in David, *Western Colonialism in Asia and Christianity*, 14. Portugal's and Spain's search for another trade route to the East resulted from the blocking of the Mediterranean route by Venetian and Genoan merchants.

74. Renato Constantino, *The Philippines: A Past Revisited (Pre-Spanish-1941)* (Quezon City: by the author, 1975), 19–22. Meanwhile, in colonies like the Philippines, the friars and Spanish administrators squabbled over the control of lands.

75. De'Souza, "The Portuguese in Asia and Their Church Patronage," 13. Portugal and Spain secured the rights over Eastern Asia.

76. Carolyn Merchant, *The Death of Nature: Women, Ecology, and the Scientific Revolution* (San Francisco: HarperSan Francisco, 1989), 164–90.

77. Linda McDowell, "Enlightenment/Enlightenment Theory," in *A Feminist Glossary of Human Geography*, ed. Linda McDowell and Joanne P. Sharp (New York: Arnold, 1999), 71.

78. James Scherer, "International Missionary Council," in *The Encyclopedia of Christianity*, ed. Geoffrey W. Bromiley (Grand Rapids, MI: Eerdmans, 2001), 726–28. The presence of the "younger non-Euro-American churches" in the 1928 Jerusalem meeting of the International Missionary Council

prompted the IMC missiological statement that "the indigenous churches of Asia, Africa, and Latin America, rather than Western mission societies, were responsible agents for mission in their respective areas."

79. Ibid. The International Missionary Council was organized in October 1921. Composed of seventeen Protestant missionary councils (thirteen Western, the rest from Asia, Africa, and Latin America), the IMC was the "most significant and effective planning organization for international Protestant missionary cooperation of the twentieth century." In 1961 the IMC integrated with the World Council of Churches and the WCC Commission on World Mission and Evangelism.

80. The December 1938 meeting of the International Missionary Council in Madras followed up on the issues raised during the Jerusalem conference in 1928. In Jerusalem the IMC was more introspective and focused on "rethinking missions." Hendrik Kraemer judged the theological position of the Jerusalem meeting to have manifested a "remarkable mixture of sincere devotion to the missionary cause as a Christian obligation with a very weak sense of apostolic consciousness." See Hendrik Kraemer, *The Christian Message in a Non-Christian World* (New York: Harper and Brothers, 1938; reprint, Grand Rapids, MI: Kregel Publications, 1977).

81. Ibid., 118–21, 321–83.

82. In explicating the doctrine of the Word of God, Karl Barth, for instance, wrote that the revelation of God comes to abolish religions. See Karl Barth, *Church Dogmatics*, ed. Geoffrey W. Bromiley and T. F. Torrance, 14 vols. (Edinburgh: T & T Clark, 1956), 1:280.

83. Ibid. Kraemer cites Barth's argument that negates any continuity between nature and grace, between reason and revelation. Kraemer proceeds to give an extensive but pejorative assessment of Asian religions.

84. Barth, *Church Dogmatics*, 1:122–23.

85. Ibid., 1:338.

86. Ibid., 1:444.

87. M. M. Thomas, *Some Theological Dialogues* (Madras: The Christian Literature Society, 1977), 28–30. See also Joachim Wietzke, ed., *Paul D. Devanandan: A Selection* (Madras: The Christian Literature Society, 1983), 92, 123–28. Devanandan and Thomas raise questions about the adequacy and the correctness of Kraemer's theological tools in his assessment of Asian religions and cultures.

88. Thomas, *The Acknowledged Christ of the Indian Renaissance*, 245.

89. The hanging in 1872 of Fathers Gomez, Burgos, and Zamora—the *Tres Martires* of Cavite—was a landmark in the struggle for indigenization of the clergy in the Philippines. The founding of the *Iglesia Filipina Independiente* (Philippine Catholic Church) marked the revolutionary effort to indigenize not only the clergy, but also the rituals and church holdings that the Spanish friars had controlled.

90. Thomas, *The Acknowledged Christ of the Indian Renaissance*, 237–39.

91. Virginia Fabella, "Inculturation," in Fabella and Sugirtharajah, *Dictionary of Third World Theologies*, 104–6.
92. Chupungco, *Liturgies of the Future*, 28.
93. K. P. Aleaz, "Indigenization," in Fabella and Sugirtharajah, *Dictionary of Third World Theologies*, 106–8.
94. Chupungco, *Liturgies of the Future*, 14.
95. Pieris, *Fire and Water*, 67–68.
96. Aloys Grillmeier, *Christ in Christian Tradition: From the Apostolic Age to Chalcedon (451)*, rev. ed. (Atlanta, GA: John Knox Press, 1975), 1:443–72.
97. Samuel Hugh Moffet, *A History of Christianity in Asia* (Maryknoll, NY: Orbis Books, 1998), 1:306.
98. Ibid., 1:310–14.
99. Ibid., 1:304.
100. Ibid., 1:305–14.
101. Chandran, "Development of Christian Theology in India," 7–8.
102. Thomas, *The Acknowledged Christ of the Indian Renaissance*, 108.
103. Charles W. Foreman, "Upadhyaya, Brahmabandav," in Anderson, *Biographical Dictionary of Christian Missions*, 689.
104. Thomas, *The Acknowledged Christ of the Indian Renaissance*, 109.
105. Ibid., 109–10.
106. Ibid., 99, 111.
107. Vengal Chakkarai, "The Historical Jesus and the Christ of Experience," in Sugirtharajah and Hargreaves, *Readings in Indian Christian Theology*, 78–82.
108. Ibid.
109. Ibid.
110. Albert Schweitzer, *The Quest of the Historical Jesus: A Critical Study of Its Progress from Reimarus to Wrede* (New York: Macmillan, 1968), 398.
111. Elie Humbert, *C. G. Jung: The Fundamentals of Theory and Practice* (Wilmette, IL: Chiron Publications, 1988), 33–34, 65.
112. James Massey, "Ingredients for a Dalit Theology," in Prabhakar, *Towards a Dalit Theology*, 320–21.
113. Aiyadurai J. Appasamy, "I and the Father Are One," in Sugirtharajah and Hargreaves, *Readings in Indian Christian Theology*, 195–99.
114. P. Chenchiah, "Where Lies the Uniqueness of Christ? An Indian Christian View," in Sugirtharajah and Hargreaves, *Readings in Indian Christian Theology*, 90.
115. Ibid.
116. Ibid.
117. Ibid., 92.
118. Ibid., 91.
119. Sugirtharajah and Hargreaves, *Readings in Indian Christian Theology*, 248. Chenchiah followed Aurobindo Gosh's concept of integral yoga.

120. Chenchiah, "Where Lies the Uniqueness of Christ?" 91.

121. Hans-Werner Gensichen, "Chenciah, Pandipeddi," in Anderson, *Biographical Dictionary of Christian Missions*, 130.

122. Chenchiah, "Where Lies the Uniqueness of Christ?" 89.

123. Wietzke, *Paul D. Devanandan*, 163–65. Devanandan agreed to adapt religious practices such as *dhyana* for meditation; *sadhana* for religious disciplined life; yoga for the soul to seek communion with God; and *ashrama dharma*, a procedure for religious education.

124. Ibid., 105.

125. Ibid., 106–7.

126. Ibid., 80.

127. Ibid., 107.

128. Ibid.

129. Ibid., 80–81.

130. Ibid., 128–33.

131. Ibid., 147.

132. Ibid., 14, 133.

133. Ibid., 135.

134. K. P. Aleaz, *Jesus in Neo-Vedanta: A Meeting of Hinduism and Christianity* (Delhi: Kant Publications, 1995), 139.

135. Walden Bello, *The Future in the Balance: Essays on Globalization and Resistance* (London: Food First/Institute for Food and Development Policy, 2001), 197. The United States instituted reforms that masked its interest in these countries. The Americans awarded vast tracts of friar lands to the Filipino *ilustrados* to create a "national ruling class that would serve as the base of American colonial rule." *Ilustrado* Emilio Aguinaldo, who stole the leadership of the 1898 revolution, received vast tracts of land. The Americans installed him as first president of the Philippine Republic. Douglas MacArthur condoned the Japanese collaborator Manuel Roxas and installed him as president of the new Philippine Republic after World War II.

136. Ibid., 194–95. The United States pressured reactionary Syngman Rhee of S. Korea to implement land reform to suppress pro-North Korean sentiments in the countryside. In Taiwan, it supported land reform to build up an anti-Mao peasantry. It also supported land distribution to the conservative local Taiwanese landlords and rivals of Chiang Kai-shek's Kuomintang. In Japan, the United States proposed land reform to cripple the gentry that served as the social base of Japanese militarism and its aggressive economic programs (190).

137. Walden Bello, Shea Cunningham, and Bill Rau, *Dark Victory: The United States, Structural Adjustment and Global Poverty* (London: Pluto Press, 1994), 165–69. Robert McNamara, former US defense secretary and advocate of the US occupation of Vietnam, became the president of the World Bank. He instituted the policy of liberal containment by increasing loans to Asia and third-world countries.

138. World Council of Churches, *Lead Us Not Into Temptation . . . Churches' Response to the Policies of International Financial Institutions* (Geneva: WCC, 2001), 1–7. Upon the invitation of the United States, the conference held at Bretton Woods—attended by 144 countries but dominated by the industrialized countries—established a system of financial rules that eventually led to the founding of the International Monetary Fund (IMF) in 1944 and the World Bank in 1945 (Bello, *The Future in the Balance*, 1–34). The World Trade Organization (WTO) was formed as a result of final negotiations of the General Agreement on Tariffs and Trade (GATT) at the Uruguay Round in 1990. Its main concern is global trade and foreign investments, particularly in the Third World.

139. Walden Bello, David Kinley, and Elaine Elinson, *Development Debacle: The World Bank and the Philippines* (San Francisco: Food First/Institute of Food and Development Policy, 1982), 13. This phrase, "colonization without an occupation force," was used by Teodoro Valencia, former propagandist for the dictator Ferdinand Marcos, when he stumbled upon leaks of the World Bank report on the Philippines.

140. Bello, Cunningham, and Rau, *Dark Victory*, 10–17.

141. Bello, *The Future in the Balance*, 17–18; see also David C. Korten, *When Corporations Rule the World* (West Hartford, CT: Kumarian Press; San Francisco: Berrett-Koehler Publishers, 1995).

142. Alvin Y. So and Yok-shiu F. Lee, eds., *Asia's Environmental Movements: Comparative Perspectives* (New York: M. E. Sharpe, 1999), 3; see also Walden Bello and Stephanie Rosenfeld, *Dragons in Distress: Asia's Miracle Economy in Crisis* (San Francisco: Institute for Food and Development Policy, 1992).

143. Bello, Cunningham, and Rau, *Dark Victory*, 72, 138. The United States implemented the unilateral anti-dumping order that imposed punitive duties on imports from the Asian tigers. This unilateral order reserves for the US government the "right to apply sanctions against trading partners believed to be selling their goods below a reasonable rate of return in the United States."

144. Donald Messer, "The Asian Face of the Global HIV/AIDS Scenario," in *Health, Healing and Wholeness: Asian Theological Perspectives on HIV/AIDS*, ed. A. Wati Longchar (Jorhat, Assam: ETE-WCC/CCA, 2005), 9–10.

145. Chupungco, *Liturgies of the Future*, 19–20.

146. Tissa Balasuriya, *Planetary Theology* (Maryknoll, NY: Orbis Books, 1984), 10–12.

147. James H. Cone, *A Black Theology of Liberation* (Maryknoll, NY: Orbis Books, 1970); Gustavo Gutiérrez, *A Theology of Liberation*, trans. Sr. Caridad Inda and John Eagleson (Maryknoll, NY: Orbis Books, 1973).

148. Sugirtharajah and Hargreaves, *Readings in Indian Christian Theology*, 93. See Sugirtharajah's introduction to Thomas's contribution, "Secular Ideologies of India and the Secular Meaning of Christ."

149. Thomas, "Secular Ideologies of India and the Secular Meaning of Christ," 93–101.

150. Ibid., 99, 100.

151. M. M. Thomas, *Risking Christ for Christ's Sake: Towards an Ecumenical Theology of Pluralism* (Geneva: WCC, 1987), 115.

152. Thomas, "Secular Ideologies of India and the Secular Meaning of Christ," 98–99.

153. Thomas, *Some Theological Dialogues*, 44–47.

154. Ibid., 42–65.

155. M. M. Thomas, *Religion and the Revolt of the Oppressed* (Delhi: ISPCK, 1981), 53. See also Thomas, "Secular Ideologies of India and the Secular Meaning of Christ," 99.

156. Thomas, *Some Theological Dialogues*, 107–8. Thomas addressed this letter to theologian Hendrick Berkhof of Leiden, the Netherlands. Thomas proposed that "there is no defined boundary" when it comes to defining the church in relation to the common humanity in Christ.

157. Thomas, *Risking Christ for Christ's Sake*, 119; see also Thomas, *Religion and the Revolt of the Oppressed*, 69.

158. Nirmal, "Towards a Christian Dalit Theology," 55.

159. Song, "Oh, Jesus, Here with Us!" 138.

160. Deane William Ferm, *Profiles in Liberation: Thirty-six Portraits of Third World Theologians* (Mystic, CT: Twenty-Third Publications, 1988), 108–9.

161. C. S. Song, *The Compassionate God* (Maryknoll, NY: Orbis Books, 1982), 81–82, 83, 95, 140.

162. Song, "Christ behind the Mask Dance," 39–42.

163. C. S. Song, *Jesus, the Crucified People* (Minneapolis: Fortress Press, 1996), 214–15, 217.

164. Ibid., 225–27.

165. Song, "Oh, Jesus, Here with Us!" 142.

166. Song, *Jesus, the Crucified People*, 85.

167. Sebastian Kappen, *Jesus and Freedom* (Maryknoll, NY: Orbis Books, 1977), 31–51.

168. Sebastian Kappen, "Towards an Indian Theology of Liberation," in Sugirtharajah and Hargreaves, *Readings in Indian Christian Theology*, 24, 30.

169. Kappen, *Jesus and Freedom*, 60.

170. Kappen, "Towards an Indian Theology of Liberation," 25.

171. Sebastian Kappen, "Jesus and Transculturation," in Sugirtharajah, *Asian Faces of Jesus*, 173–74.

172. Kappen, *Jesus and Freedom*, 130.

173. Kappen, "Jesus and Transculturation," 177–83. To Kappen, the ethos of fear is brought about not only by foreign domination and class, but also by culture's caste system, gender oppression, and by elemental spirits–good or bad. The fear of pollution is lesser in the lower rung of the caste hierarchy, and is absent among tribals in India.

174. Kappen, *Jesus and Freedom*, 185.

175. Kappen, "Jesus and Transculturation," 184, 185, 177–83.

176. Kim Chi Ha, *The Gold-Crowned Jesus and Other Writings*, ed. Chong Sun Kim and Shelly Killen (Maryknoll, NY: Orbis Books, 1978), 124.

177. Ferm, *Profiles in Liberation*, 78–79.

178. Ahn Byung Mu, "Jesus and People (Minjung)," in Sugirtharajah, *Asian Faces of Jesus*, 166.

179. Ahn Byung Mu, "The Body of Jesus-Event Tradition," *East Asia Journal of Theology 3*, no. 2 (1985): 295.

180. Ahn, "Jesus and People (Minjung)," 166.

181. Ahn Byung Mu, "Jesus and the Minjung in the Gospel of Mark," in *Voices from the Margin: Interpreting the Bible in the Third World*, ed. R. S. Sugirtharajah (London: SPCK; Maryknoll, NY: Orbis Books, 1995), 150–51.

182. Ahn, "Jesus and People (Minjung)," 168. Ahn insists that the historical facts gave rise to the passion story and that the *ochlos* told it as it was because the Jesus-event was, and is, their story.

183. Ahn, "Jesus and the Minjung in the Gospel of Mark," 150–51, 70.

184. Ahn, "Jesus and People (Minjung)," 169, 167.

185. See Kim Yong-Bock, "Jesus Christ among Asian Minjung: A Christological Reflection," *Voices from the Third World* 19, no. 2 (1996): 83.

186. David Kwang-sun Suh, "Theology of Story Telling: A Theology by Minjung," *Voices from the Third World* 9, no. 2 (1986): 48.

187. Suh, *Korean Minjung in Christ*, 126–29.

188. Suh, "Asian Theology in a Changing Asia," 29.

189. Ahn Byung Mu, "The Korean Church's Understanding of Jesus," *Voices from the Third World* 8, no. 1 (1985): 54–59.

190. Karl Gaspar, "Doing Theology (in a Situation) of Struggle," in *Religion and Society: Towards a Theology of Struggle*, ed. Mary Rosario Battung et al. (Manila: Forum for Interdisciplinary Endeavors and Studies, 1988), 71.

191. Ibid., 57.

192. Carlos H. Abesamis, *Backpack of a Jesus-Seeker*, Book One (Quezon City: Claretian Publications and Socio-Pastoral Institute, 2004), 11.

193. Carlos H. Abesamis, *The Mission of Jesus and Good News to the Poor* (Quezon City: Claretian Publications, 1987).

194. Carlos H. Abesamis, *The Third Look at Jesus* (Quezon City: Claretian Publications, 1999), 190.

195. Julio X. Labayen, "Cry of the People–Challenge to the Churches," *Voices from the Third World* 10, no. 1 (1987): 3–10.

196. Luna Dingayan, "Towards a Christology of Struggle: A Proposal for Understanding the Christ," *CTC Bulletin* 10, no. 1 (1991): 26–27.

197. Levi Oracion, *God with Us: Reflections on the Theology of Struggle in the Philippines* (Dumaguete City: Silliman Univ. Divinity School, 2001), 116–23.

198. Feliciano Cariño, "What about the Theology of Struggle?" in Battung et al., *Religion and Society*, v–xv.

199. Raimundo Panikkar, *The Unknown Christ of Hinduism: Towards an Ecumenical Christophany* (Maryknoll, NY: Orbis Books, 1981), 165–68. Panikkar

appropriated Aquinas's method of proving the existence of God, his principle of analogy, and the use of reason in articulating religious beliefs.

200. Aleaz, *Jesus in Neo-Vedanta*, 138.

201. Kim Knott, *Hinduism: A Very Short Introduction* (Oxford: Oxford Univ. Press, 1998), 30, 212.

202. Panikkar, *The Unknown Christ of Hinduism*, 20.

203. Ibid., 23.

204. Ibid., 152–62. Isvara is also known as Isa in the Upanishads and Isana in the Rig Vedas.

205. Ibid., 164–65.

206. Ibid., 26–27, 37.

207. Ibid., 49.

208. Raimundo Panikkar, "The Jordan, the Tiber, and the Ganges: Three Kairological Moments of Christic Self-Consciousness," in *The Myth of Christian Uniqueness*, ed. John Hick and Paul Knitter (Maryknoll, NY: Orbis Books, 1987), 113–14.

209. Panikkar, *The Unknown Christ of Hinduism*, 169.

210. Panikkar, "The Jordan, the Tiber and the Ganges," 108–9.

211. Tissa Balasuriya, "Humanity's 'Fall' and Jesus the Savior," *Voices from the Third World* 11, no. 2 (December, 1988): 41–75.

212. Tissa Balasuriya, *Planetary Theology* (Maryknoll, NY: Orbis Books, 1984).

213. Balasuriya, "Humanity's 'Fall' and Jesus the Savior," 56–57.

214. Ibid., 72.

215. Balasuriya, *Planetary Theology*, 185–87.

216. Balasuriya, "Humanity's 'Fall' and Jesus the Savior," 73.

217. Samartha, *The Hindu Response to the Unbound Christ*, 4–10, 14.

218. Balasuriya, "Humanity's 'Fall' and Jesus the Savior," 74; see also Samartha, *The Hindu Response to the Unbound Christ*, 160.

219. Samartha, *One Christ—Many Religions*, 115.

220. Pieris, *Fire and Water*, 65.

221. Pieris, "Towards an Asian Theology of Liberation," 75–95; see also Aloysius Pieris, "The Dynamics of A.T.C.: A Reply to the Editor of Satyodaya," *Voices from the Third World* 2, no. 1 (June 1979): 23–28.

222. Pieris, *Fire and Water*, 69.

223. Ibid., 69–74.

224. Aloysius Pieris, "Christology in Asia," *Voices from the Third World* 11, no. 2 (1988): 162.

225. Aloysius Pieris, "Two Encounters in My Theological Journey," in *Frontiers in Asian Christian Theology: Emerging Trends*, ed. R. S. Sugirtharajah (Maryknoll, NY: Orbis Books, 1994), 143.

226. Pieris, *Asian Theology of Liberation*, 15–23.

227. Aloysius Pieris, *Love Meets Wisdom: A Christian Experience of Buddhism* (Maryknoll, NY: Orbis Books, 1988), 110–35.

228. Ibid., 135.

229. Aloysius Pieris, "Inter-Religious Dialogue and Theology of Religions," *Voices from the Third World* 15, no. 2 (December 1992): 188.

230. Pieris, *Love Meets Wisdom*, 132.

231. Samartha, *The Hindu Response to the Unbound Christ*, 145–47.

232. Pieris, *Love Meets Wisdom*, 134; see also Pieris, *Fire and Water*, 75.

233. Pieris, "Towards an Asian Theology of Liberation," 62.

234. Samartha, *One Christ—Many Religions*, 133.

235. Stanley J. Samartha, "The Cross and the Rainbow," in Hick and Knitter, *The Myth of Christian Uniqueness*, 69–88.

236. Samartha, *One Christ—Many Religions*, 116–17.

237. Balasuriya, *Planetary Theology*, 190–91.

238. Samartha, *The Hindu Response to the Unbound Christ*, 196.

239. Pieris, "Two Encounters," 141–46; see also Pieris, *An Asian Theology of Liberation*, 45–50.

240. Pieris, "Inter-Religious Dialogue and Theology of Religions," 184–87.

241. Tissa Balasuriya, *Mary and the Human Liberation: The Story and the Text* (Harrisburg, PA: Trinity Press International, 1997); Pieris, *Fire and Water*, part 1; Choan-Seng Song, *The Tears of Lady Meng: A Parable of People's Political Theology* (Maryknoll, NY: Orbis Books, 1982); Stanley J. Samartha, *The Search for New Hermeneutics in Asian Christian Theology* (Bangalore: Board of Theological Education of the Senate of Serampore College, 1987); Michael Amaladoss, *Life in Freedom: Liberation Theologies from Asia* (Maryknoll, NY: Orbis Books, 1997).

242. Carlos H. Abesamis, "Ano Po Ang Laman Ng Mangkok? How [Not] to Do Theology in Asia Today," *CTC Bulletin* 15, no. 1 (1998): 22.

243. Rosemary Radford Ruether, *Sexism and God-Talk* (Boston: Beacon Press, 1983), 116.

244. Mary Daly, *Beyond God the Father* (London: Women's Press, 1975), 73–74; see also Leonard Swidler, "Jesus Was a Feminist," *Catholic World* 212 (January 1971): 177–83. Available online.

245. See Delores S. Williams, *Sisters in the Wilderness: The Challenge of Womanist God-Talk* (Maryknoll, New York: Orbis Books, 1993); Ada María Isasi-Díaz, *Mujerista Theology* (Maryknoll, NY: Orbis Books, 1996); Elsa Tamez, ed. *Through Her Eyes: Women's Theology from Latin America* (Maryknoll, NY: Orbis Books, 1989); Mercy Amba Oduyoye, *Hearing and Knowing: Theological Reflections on Christianity in Africa* (Maryknoll, NY: Orbis Books, 1991); Rita Nakashima Brock, *Journeys by Heart: A Christology of Erotic Power* (New York: Crossroad, 1988), 4, 49, 54; and see also Ivone Gebara, *Out of the Depths: Women's Experience of Evil and Salvation* (Minneapolis: Fortress Press, 2002), 48, 88, 103–4, 113.

246. Dulcie Abraham, "Jesus the New Creation: Christology in the Malaysian Context," in *Asian Women Doing Theology: Report from Singapore Conference,*

November 1987, ed. Dulcie Abraham (Hong Kong: AWRC, 1989), 189–94; Hisako Kinukawa, *Women and Jesus in Mark: A Japanese Feminist Perspective* (Maryknoll, NY: Orbis Books, 1994); Chun Kwang-Rye, Yoshiko Isshiki, Hisako Kinukawa, and Satoko Yamaguchi, *Women Moving Mountains: Feminist Theology in Japan*, trans. and ed. Margaret Warren (Malaysia: AWRC, 2000).

2 DO INDIAN WOMEN FIND JESUS IN THE GANGES?

1. Vandana Shiva, *Staying Alive: Women, Ecology and Development* (London: Zed, 1989), 184.

2. R. S. Sugirtharajah and Cecil Hargreaves, eds., *Readings in Indian Christian Theology* (London: SPCK, 1993), 244.

3. Vandana Mataji, "Water Symbolism in the Gospel of St. John in the Light of Indian Spirituality," in Sugirtharajan and Hargreaves, *Readings in Indian Christian Theology*, 208.

4. Ibid., 210.

5. Vandana Mataji, *Jesus the Christ: Who Is He? What Was His Message?* (Anand, India: Gujarat Sahitya Prakash, 1987), i–ii.

6. Ibid.

7. Aruna Gnanadason, "Foreword," in *Towards a Theology of Humanhood: Women's Perspectives*, ed. Aruna Gnanadason (Delhi: ISPCK, 1986), i.

8. Stella Faria, "A Reflection on the National Consultation: Ecumenicity of Women's Theological Reflections," in Gnanadason, *Towards a Theology of Humanhood.*

9. Leelamma Athyal, "Mariology: A Feminist Perspective," in Gnanadason, *Towards a Theology of Humanhood*, 51–52.

10. Ibid., 53.

11. Monica Melanchton, "Christology and Women," in *We Dare to Dream: Doing Theology as Asian Women*, ed. Virginia Fabella and Sun Ai Lee Park (Hong Kong: AWRC/EATWOT Women's Commission in Asia, 1989), 16–18.

12. Ibid., 18–22.

13. Margaret Shanti, "Hinduism: Caste, Gender and Violence," *LILA: Asia-Pacific Women's Studies Journal* 5 (1995):17.

14. Elizabeth Joy, ed., *Lived Realities: Faith Reflections on Gender Justice* (Bangalore: CISRS Publications Trust for Joint Women's Programme, 1999); see also Lalrinawmi Ralte et al., eds., *Envisioning a New Heaven and a New Earth* (Delhi: ISPCK/NCCI, 1999).

15. Rose Paul, "Educated Women in the Marriage Market," in *Dalits and Women: Quest for Humanity*, ed. V. Devasahayam (Madras: Gurukul Lutheran Theological College and Research Institute, 1992). Sr. Rose Paul noted this practice to be prevalent in the area of Kerala.

16. Ibid., 174.

17. Evangeline Anderson-Rajkumar, "Dowry: Destroyer of the Human Values," in *Lived Realities: Faith Reflections on Gender Justice*, ed. Elizabeth Joy (Bangalore: CISRS/JWP, 1999), 113–19.

18. Kumari Jawardena, *Feminism and Nationalism in the Third World* (London: Zed, 1986), 73–107.

19. Esther Rajashekar, "Devadasi System: Sexual Abuse in the Name of God," in Joy, *Lived Realities*, 49–57.

20. Kamal Raja Selvi, "The Dalit Woman—Fourth Class Citizen," in *Frontiers of Dalit Theology*, ed. M. Devasahayam (Madras: ISPCK/Gurukul, 1997), 118.

21. Paul, "Educated Women in the Marriage Market," 174–77.

22. Omana Mathews, "Rape: A Trauma until Death," in Joy, *Lived Realities*, 58–64; see also Evangeline Anderson-Rajkumar, "Asian Feminist Christology," *In God's Image* 22, no. 4 (December 2003): 4–5.

23. Elizabeth Joy, "Divorce: A Last Resort for Survival," in Joy, *Lived Realities*, 130–33.

24. The term *outcaste* is a combination of the words *outcast* and *caste*. Dalits use this term to emphasize that, being outside the ladder of the caste system, they experience double discrimination as outcasts and as untouchables.

25. Sugirtharajah and Hargreaves, *Readings in Indian Christian Theology*, 247.

26. Govindarajan Saraswathy, "Caste, Women and Violence," in Devasahayam, *Dalits and Women*, 150–51.

27. Engelbert Mveng, "Third World Theology—What Theology? What Third World?" in *Irruption of the Third World*, ed. Virginia Fabella and Sergio Torres (Maryknoll, NY: Orbis Books, 1983), 220.

28. S. Faustina, "From Exile to Exodus: Christian Dalit Women and the Role of Religion," in Devasahayam, *Frontiers of Dalit Theology*, 94–96; see also Prasanna K. Samuel, "Church and Women," in Devasahayam, *Dalits and Women*, 190–94.

29. Selvi, "The Dalit Woman—Fourth Class Citizen," 125.

30. Ibid., 113.

31. N. G. Prasuna, "The Dalit Woman," in Devasahayam, *Frontiers of Dalit Theology*, 100–116.

32. Aruna Gnanadason, "Dalit Women—The Dalit of the Dalit," in *Towards a Common Dalit Theology*, ed. Arvind P. Nirmal (Madras: Gurukul Lutheran Theological College and Research Institute, 1989), 109–21.

33. S. Faustina, "Untouchability: Abuse of the Total Person," in Joy, *Lived Realities*, 46.

34. Aruna Gnanadason, "Women's Oppression: A Sinful Situation," in *With Passion and Compassion: Third World Women Doing Theology*, ed. Virginia Fabella and Mercy Amba Oduyoye (Maryknoll, NY: Orbis Books, 1988), 72.

35. Prasuna, "The Dalit Woman," 111.

36. Faustina, "From Exile to Exodus," 96.

37. Beverly Wildung Harrison, *Making Connections: Essays in Feminist Social Ethics*, ed. Carol Robb (Boston: Beacon Press, 1985), 3–21.

38. Ibid., 14–15, 18–20.

39. Faustina, "Untouchability," 40–41, 46.

40. Prasuna, "The Dalit Woman," 111–13.

41. Mary Daly, *Beyond God the Father* (London: Women's Press, 1975), 49.

42. Melanchton, "Christology and Women," 16–18.

43. Pauline Chakkalakal, "Women's Ordination and Priesthood," in Joy, *Lived Realities*, 139.

44. Ibid., 135.

45. Lalrinawmi Ralte, "Doing Tribal Women's Theology," *In God's Image* 19, no. 4 (2000): 2. Northeast India comprises eight states: Arunachal Pradesh, Assam, Manipur, Meghalaya, Mizoram, Nagaland, Sikkim, and Tripura.

46. Lalrinawmi Ralte, "A Silent Cry," *In God's Image* 19, no. 4 (2000): 12–14.

47. Nirala Iswary, "Violation of Human Rights in Bodo Land," *In God's Image* 19, no. 4 (2000): 15–18.

48. Ibid.

49. Ralte, "A Silent Cry," 13.

50. Raimundo Panikkar, *The Unknown Christ of Hinduism: Towards an Ecumenical Christophany* (Maryknoll, NY: Orbis Books, 1981), 45.

51. Ralte, "A Silent Cry," 13.

52. Shiva, *Staying Alive;* see also Vandana Shiva, *Biopiracy: The Plunder of Nature and Knowledge* (Boston, MA: South End Press, 1997).

53. Pauline Chakkalakal, "Asian Women Reshaping Theology: Challenges and Hopes," *Feminist Theology*, no. 27 (2001): 31.

54. Aruna Gnanadason, "What Do These Women Speak Of?" *Voices from the Third World* 16, no. 1 (June, 1993): 44.

55. Ralte, "A Silent Cry," 13.

56. R. L. Hnuni, "Vision for Women in North East India," in *Transforming Theology for Empowering Women*, ed. R. L. Hnuni (Jorhat, Assam: Women's Studies of Eastern Theological College, 1999), 142. *Jhum* cultivation makes use of the land by cutting and burning the undergrowth, leaving the big trees untouched. Usually, after three or four years of cultivation, the land is left to recover its fertility. This is similar to the practice of *kaingin* in the Philippines.

57. Ibid.

58. Ibid., 143–52.

59. Ibid., 148.

60. N. Limatula Longkumer, "Christianity and Naga Women," in Hnuni, *Transforming Theology for Empowering Women*, 57.

61. Ibid. In her email message to the author, Longkumer affirms the case of a male person being elected as secretary of women's fellowship. Cf. R. L. Hnuni, "The Role of Women in the Church," in Hnuni, *Transforming Theology for Empowering Women*, 66.

62. Hnuni, "Vision for Women," 75.

63. R. L. Hnuni, "Biblical Basis for Empowerment of Women," in Hnuni, *Transforming Theology for Empowering Women*, 136–37.

64. Ibid., 138–39.

65. Elisabeth Schüssler Fiorenza, *Jesus and the Politics of Interpretation* (New York: Continuum, 2000), 116–17.

66. Quoted in Park Sun Ai Lee, "Religion and Menstruation," *In God's Image* (December 1982): 4.

67. Gnana Robinson, "Purity and Pollution: A Theological Perspective," in *Feminist Theology: Perspective and Praxis*, ed. Prasanna Kumari (Chennai: Gurukul Lutheran Theological College and Research Institute, 1999), 317–20.

68. Katherine K. Young, "Introduction," in *Religion and Women*, ed. Arvind Sharma (Albany: State Univ. of New York, 1994), 19, 231.

69. Rosalind I. J. Hackett, "Women in African Religions," in Sharma, *Religion and Women*, 82.

70. Ibid., 86.

71. Mercy Amba Oduyoye, *Daughters of Anowa: African Women and Patriarchy* (Maryknoll, NY: Orbis Books, 1995), 194, 118–19, 127.

72. Michiko Yusa, "Women in Shinto: Images Remembered," in Sharma, *Religion and Women*, 115–16.

73. Elizabeth Joy, "The Meaning and Origin of Dalit Theology" (M.Th. thesis, South Asia Theological Research Institute, 1998), 3.2.6. Filipino feminists Sharon Rose Joy Ruiz-Duremdes and Hope Antone connect blood with pathos, especially with women's experiences of violence and oppression. See Sharon Rose Joy Ruiz-Duremdes, "Solidarity and Spirituality: A Theology of Life," in *Dance amid Struggle: Stories and Songs of Hope*, ed. Sharon Rose Joy Ruiz-Duremdes and Wendy Kroeker (Quezon City: AWIT Publications, 1998), 7–8; see also Hope Antone, "Healed by Her Faith," in Ruiz-Duremdes and Kroeker, *Dance amid Struggle*, 67–72.

74. Joy, "The Meaning and Origin of Dalit Theology," 3, 4.

75. Aruna Gnanadason, "Reclaiming Motherhood: In Search of an Eco-Feminist Vision," in *Sustainability and Globalization*, ed. Julio De Santa Ana (Geneva: WCC, 1996), 139.

76. Ajit Mookerjee, *Kali: The Feminine Force* (Bennington, VT: Destiny Books, 1988), 30.

77. Gnanadason, "What Do These Women Speak Of?" 41.

78. JoAnne Marie Terrell, *Power in the Blood? The Cross in the African American Experience* (Maryknoll, NY: Orbis Books, 1998), 125.

79. Gabriele Dietrich, quoted in Chung Hyun Kyung, *Struggle to Be the Sun Again* (Maryknoll, NY: Orbis Books, 1990), 68–69.

80. Ibid., 70.

81. Gabriele Dietrich, *A New Thing on Earth* (Delhi: ISPCK, 2001), 144.

82. Ibid., 145–46.

83. Ibid. See also Renate Rose, "Messianic Economics and Cultures of Hospitality" (Honolulu, HI: n.p., August 1998). Emerging from six years of immersion in Filipino life, Rose reflects on the act of Jesus as a "distribution economy."

84. Dietrich, *A New Thing on Earth*, 147.

85. Janet Morley, *All Desires Known* (Wilton, CT: Morehouse-Barlow Co., 1988), 39.

86. Stella Baltazar, "Domestic Violence in Indian Perspective," in *Women Resisting Violence: Spirituality for Life*, ed. Mary John Mananzan et al. (Maryknoll, NY: Orbis Books, 1996), 64.

87. Ibid., 61–62.

88. Lina Gupta, "Kali the Savior," in *After Patriarchy: Feminist Transformations of the World Religions*, ed. Paula M. Cooey, William R. Eakin, and Jay B. McDaniel (Maryknoll, NY: Orbis Books, 1991), 25–26, 36–37.

89. K. Rajaratnam, "Woman through the Ages: A Brief Survey," in Kumari, *Feminist Theology*, 8–11.

90. Aruna Gnanadason, "Women and Spirituality," in *Feminist Theology from the Third World: A Reader*, ed. Ursula King (London: SPCK; Maryknoll, NY: Orbis Books, 1994), 352–53, 352.

91. Baltazar, "Domestic Violence in Indian Perspective," 64.

92. Ibid.

93. Ibid., 65.

94. Monica Melanchton, "Jesus as Wisdom," in Ralte, *Envisioning a New Heaven and a New Earth*, 240–42.

95. Ibid., 242.

96. Mookerjee, *Kali*, 72.

97. Shiva, *Staying Alive*, 208–9.

98. Gnanadason, "Women and Spirituality," 352.

99. Hans Koester, "The Indian Religion of the Goddess Shakti," *The Journal of the Siam Society* 23, no. 1 (July 1929): 14–15.

100. Kwok Pui-lan, *Introducing Asian Feminist Theology* (Cleveland, OH: Pilgrim Press, 2000), 96.

101. Melanchton, "Jesus as Wisdom," 243.

102. Koester, "The Indian Religion of the Goddess Shakti," 11; see also Mookerje, *Kali.*

103. Aruna Gnanadason, "Women, Economy and Ecology," in *Ecotheology: Voices from South and North*, ed. David G. Hallman (Geneva: WCC, 1994), 184.

104. Gnanadason, "Women and Spirituality," 355.

3 KOREAN WOMEN: MEETING JESUS AT THE FOOT OF SALT MOUNTAIN

1. Chung Hyun Kyung, "'Opium or the Seed for Revolution?' Shamanism: Women-Centered Popular Religiosity in Korea," *Concilium* 199:

Convergences and Differences, ed. Leonardo Boff andVirgil Elizondo (Edinburgh: T & T Clark, 1988), 99–101.

2. Chung Hyun Kyung, "Following Naked Dancing and Long Dreaming," in *Inheriting Our Mothers' Gardens: Feminist Theology in Third World Perspective*, ed. Letty Russell et al. (Louisville, KY: Westminster John Knox Press, 1988), 65, 70.

3. Matsui Yayori, *Women's Asia* (London: Zed, 1989), 138–39.

4. Chung Hyun Kyung, "Han-pu-ri: Doing Theology from Korean Women's Perspective," in *Frontiers in Asian Theology: Emerging Trends*, ed. R. S. Sugirtharajah (Maryknoll, NY: Orbis Books, 1994), 56.

5. Chung Hyun Kyung, "Your Comfort vs. My Death," in *Women Resisting Violence*, ed. Mary John Mananzan et al. (Maryknoll, NY: Orbis Books, 1996), 133. The Japanese government also took women from the Philippines, China, Taiwan, Indonesia, Malaysia, Vietnam, the Netherlands, and Japan to become comfort women for the Japanese military in their bases around the Pacific Rim.

6. Jong Ok-Sun, "Former 'Comfort Woman for the Japanese Army,'" *In God's Image* 15, no. 2 (Summer 1996): 22–23.

7. Korean Women Theologians, "Declaration of Korean Women Theologians on the Peace and Reunification of the Korean People," *In God's Image* (June 1988): 51.

8. Sun Soon-Hwa, "Women Ministers and the Oppressed in Korea," *In God's Image* 2, no. 2 (Summer 1992): 55.

9. David Scofield, "Sex and Denial in South Korea," *Asia Times Online* (May 26, 2004). Scofield notes that nongovernment and civic organizations suggest the number of prostitutes may even be higher "if all informal venues of prostitution, such as the myriad *wonjokyoje*, or younger girls 'dating' older men for cash were factored in." Furthermore, he notes that the Ministry of Gender Equality estimates a yearly profit of more than US$22 billion generated by the sex industry in South Korea.

10. Lee Mi Kung, "U. S. Troops in South Korea and Prostitution," *In God's Image* (March 1990): 9.

11. Lee Oo Chung, *In Search for Our Foremothers' Spirituality* (Seoul: AWRC, 1994), 29.

12. Ibid., 29–30. The *Mingan Kenyusu* provided the basis for women's instruction during the Chosun Dynasty and during the Japanese occupation of Korea.

13. Park Sun Ai Lee, "Confucianism and Women," *In God's Image* (June 1989): 28.

14. Ibid.

15. Lee Oo Chung, *In Search for Our Foremothers' Spirituality*, 30.

16. Ibid., 12.

17. Ibid., 9–10.

18. Park Sun Ai Lee, "Korean Women as the Lamb Bearing the Sins of the World," *In God's Image* (June 1988): 31.

19. Walden Bello and Stephanie Rosenfeld, *Dragon in Distress: Asia's Miracle Economy in Crisis* (San Francisco: Institute for Food and Development Policy, 1992), 397.

20. Park Young-sook, "Justice, Peace, and the Integrity of Creation: Justice and Peace (Life) Movement and Korean Women," *In God's Image* 10, no. 1 (1991): 49. For an extensive treatment of the South Korean model of industrialization and discussion on *chaebols*, agriculture, environment, and the effects of US policies on Korean labor and Korean people in general, see Bello and Rosenfeld, *Dragon in Distress.*

21. Quoted in Yayori, *Women's Asia*, 130.

22. Jennifer Veale, "It's Tough to Be a Working Woman . . . But the Web Is a Bright Spot" *Business Week Online* (2000).

23. Quoted in ibid.

24. Ko Chong-hui, "My Neighbor, Mrs. Ku Cha-Myong," *In God's Image*, no. 28 (June 1988): 28.

25. Lee Oo Chung, *In Search for Our Foremothers' Spirituality*, 22.

26. Ibid., 29.

27. Choi Man Ja, "Feminine Images of God in Korean Traditional Religion," in Sugirtharajah, *Frontiers in Asian Christian Theology*, 84–86.

28. Ibid., 86.

29. Park Soon Kyung, "Unification of Korea and the Task of Feminist Theology," *In God's Image* (June 1988): 17. A basic understanding of these three words helps us appreciate the *minjung* movement as well as what Park calls the Three Min Revolts that occurred in the history of Korea.

30. David Kwang-sun Suh, *Korean Minjung in Christ* (Hong Kong: Christian Conference of Asia, 1991), 24–25.

31. Chung Hyun Kyung, "Han-pu-ri," 56.

32. Quoted in Sun Soon-Hwa, "Women Ministers and the Oppressed in Korea," 48.

33. Chung Hyun Kyung, *Struggle to Be the Sun Again* (Maryknoll, NY: Orbis Books, 1990), 72.

34. Quoted in Sun Soon-Hwa, "Women Ministers and the Oppressed in Korea," 49.

35. Ibid.

36. Quoted in ibid., 54–56.

37. Engelbert Mveng, "Third World Theology–What Theology? What Third World?" in *Irruption of the Third World*, ed. Virginia Fabella and Sergio Torres (Maryknoll, NY: Orbis Books, 1983), 220.

38. Choi Man Ja, "Feminine Images of God in Korean Traditional Religion," 80.

39. Ibid., 82–83.

40. Lee Oo Chung, "Korean Culture and Feminist Theology," *In God's Image* (September 1987): 2–3, 37. Lee Oo Chung also notes that Korean people "are not very conscious about gender in records of history and religion." She further notes that a survey covering thirteen provinces in Korea yields the information that there were 743 gods and goddesses revered in these areas, the majority female deities.

41. Choi, "Feminine Images of God in Korean Traditional Religion," 80–83.

42. Suh, *Korean Minjung in Christ*, 90–93. For a comprehensive yet brief account of Korean Shamanism, see David Kwang-sun Suh, "Shamanism: The Religion of Han," therein.

43. Chung Hyun Kyung, "Han-pu-ri," 59.

44. Choi Man Ja, "Feminine Images of God in Korean Traditional Religions," 82; see also Suh, *Korean Minjung in Christ*, 95.

45. Suh, *Korean Minjung in Christ*, 89–117.

46. Chung Hyun Kyung, "Han-pu-ri," 55.

47. Suh, *Korean Minjung in Christ*, 50.

48. Chung Hyun Kyung, "Han-pu-ri," 60.

49. The *pakkokt* flower blooms at night but becomes "clouded" in sunshine. In Korea, white is the color of mourning.

50. Chang Jung-Nim, "You Are the Crucifix of Korea," *In God's Image* 15, no. 2 (Summer 1996): 35–36.

51. Chung Hyun Kyung, "Han-pu-ri," 59, 61.

52. Suh, *Korean Minjung in Christ*, 108–9.

53. Chung Hyun Kyung, "Han-pu-ri," 59.

54. Quoted in Virginia Fabella, "A Common Methodology for Diverse Christologies?" in *With Passion and Compassion: Third World Women Doing Theology*, ed. Virginia Fabella and Mercy Amba Oduyoye (Maryknoll, NY: Orbis Books, 1988), 112.

55. Chung Hyun Kyung, *Struggle to Be the Sun Again*, 66.

56. Park Sun Ai Lee, "Behold I Make All Things New," *In God's Image* (December 1987–March 1988): 6.

57. Suh, *Korean Minjung in Christ*, 114.

58. Ibid.

59. Grace Ji-Sun Kim, *The Grace of Sophia: A Korean North American Women's Christology* (Cleveland, OH: Pilgrim Press, 2002), 131–61.

60. Lee Oo Chung, *In Search for Our Foremothers' Spirituality*, 63.

61. Chung Hyun Kyung, "Christian Witness amidst Asian Pluralism and the Search for Spirituality from an Asian Feminist Perspective," *Ewha Journal of Feminist Theology* 1 (1996): 36–37.

62. Chung Hyun Kyung, *Goddess-spell according to Hyun Kyung* (Seoul: Yolimwon, 2001), 236–40.

63. Akiko Yamashita, "A Review of Asian Women's Theology: From the Perspective of Women's Life Dialogue in Asia," *In God's Image* 18, no. 1 (1999): 6–7.

64. Harvey Cox, *Fire from Heaven: The Rise of Pentecostal Spirituality and the Reshaping of Religion in the Twenty-First Century* (Reading, MA.: Perseus Books, 1995), 213–18.

65. Aloysius Pieris, *An Asian Theology of Liberation* (Maryknoll, NY: Orbis Books, 1988), 41–42; Andy Smith, "For All Those Who Were Indian in a Former Life," in *Ecofeminism and the Sacred*, ed. Carol Adams (New York: Continuum, 1992), 168–71.

66. Chung Hyun Kyung, "Asian Christologies and People's Religions," *Voices from the Third World* 19, no.1 (June 1996): 217.

67. Chung Hyun Kyung, "Re-Imagining God," *The Witness* 77, no. 7 (July 1994): 26.

68. Rosemary Radford Ruether, *Sexism and God-Talk* (Boston: Beacon Press, 1983), 116–34, 137; see also Rosemary Radford Ruether, "The Liberation of Christology from Patriarchy," in *Feminist Theology: A Reader*, ed. Ann Loades (Louisville, KY: John Knox Westminster Press, 1990), 146–47.

69. Mary Daly, *Beyond God the Father* (London: Women's Press, 1975), 96.

70. Ahn Sang-Nim, "My Understanding of Feminist Theology," *In God's Image* (April 1984):16–19.

71. Lee Hya-Jae, "Celebrating International Women's Day: Korean Women's Perspective," *In God's Image* (April 1986): 22.

72. Lisa Isherwood, *Liberating Christ* (Cleveland, OH: Pilgrim Press, 1999), 114.

73. Ahn Sang-Nim, "Feminist Theology in the Korean Church," in *We Dare to Dream: Doing Theology as Asian Women*, ed. Virginia Fabella and Sun Ai Lee Park (Hong Kong: AWRC/EATWOT Women's Commission in Asia, 1989; Maryknoll, NY: Orbis Books, 1990), 129.

74. Ahn Sang-Nim, "My Understanding of Feminist Theology," 19.

75. Ibid.

76. Ibid.

77. Ahn Sang-Nim, "Feminist Theology in the Korean Church," 134.

78. Park Sun Ai Lee, "Reflections," *In God's Image* (September 1987): 3.

79. Ibid.

80. Ibid. Cf. Gabriele Dietrich. *A New Thing on Earth* (Delhi: ISPCK, 2001), 78. Along Park Sun Ai's thought, Dietrich speaks of Jesus as a model of an integrated personality.

81. Lee Oo Chung, *In Search for Our Foremothers' Spirituality*, 92–93.

82. Chung Hyun Kyung, *Struggle to Be the Sun Again*, 65.

83. Choi Man Ja, "Feminist Christology," in *Asian Women Doing Theology: Report from Singapore Conference, November 1987*, ed. Dulcie Abraham (Hong Kong: AWRC, 1989), 177.

84. Ibid. Cf. Lisa Isherwood, *Introducing Feminist Christologies* (Cleveland, OH: Pilgrim Press, 2001), 87. See the Womanist perspective on suffering and the cross in Delores S. Williams, *Sisters in the Wilderness: The Challenge of Womanist God-Talk* (Maryknoll, NY: Orbis Books, 1993); and the Asian Latina

American and white American women's perspective in Rita Nakashima Brock and Rebecca Ann Parker, *Proverbs of Ashes: Violence, Redemptive Suffering, and the Search for What Saves Us* (Boston: Beacon Press, 2001).

85. Choi Man Ja, "Feminist Christology," 177.

86. Ibid.

87. Ibid., 178.

88. Chung Sook-Ja, Chang Soo-Chul, and Kim Hyun-Sook, "Korean Woman Jesus: Drama Worship," *Journal of Women and Religion* 13 (1995): 45–50.

89. Ibid.

90. Ibid., 45.

91. Chung Sook-Ja, Chang Soo-Chul, and Kim Hyun-Sook, "All Kinds of Women in One Place: Korean Women Church," *Journal of Women and Religion* 13 (1995): 1–2.

92. Chung, Chang, and Kim, "Korean Woman Jesus," 46–50.

93. Park Sun Ai Lee, "Korean Women as the Lamb Bearing the Sins of the World," 32.

94. Park Sun Ai Lee, "A Theological Reflection," in Fabella and Park, *We Dare to Dream*, 77.

95. Choi Man Ja, "Feminist Christology," 177, 179.

96. Park Sun Ai Lee, "Korean Women as the Lamb Bearing the Sins of the World," 31.

97. Chung Hyun Kyung, "Christian Witness amidst Asian Pluralism and the Search for Spirituality from an Asian Feminist Perspective," 37.

98. Kim, *The Grace of Sophia*, 91–96.

99. Kwok Pui-lan, *Introducing Asian Feminist Theology* (Cleveland, OH: Pilgrim Press, 2000), 89.

100. Cox, *Fire from Heaven*, 213–41.

101. Suh, *Korean Minjung in Christ*, 111–17.

102. Chung Hyun Kyung, "Wisdom of Mothers Knows No Boundaries," in *Gospel and Cultures*, Pamphlet 14, *Women's Perspectives: Articulating the Liberating Power of the Gospel* (Geneva: WCC, 1996), 35.

4 WALKING WITH JESUS IN THE PHILIPPINES: SINGING AND DANCING AMID STRUGGLE

1. Ibong Malaya, *Ibong Malaya: Songs of Freedom and Struggle from Philippine Prisons*, vol. 1 (Singapore: Resource Center for Philippine Concerns, 1982), audiocassette. My translation.

2. Ibid.

3. Ma. Corazon Manalo, "Dance: A Woman's Way to Peace," *Religious Studies De La Salle Journal* 19, no. 2 (December 1996): 78.

4. Ibid., 77.

5. Ibid., 79; see also Fe Mangahas, "Are Babaylans Extinct? How the Spanish Colonialist Banished the Native Priestess in the Philippines," *In God's Image* 12, no. 3 (Autumn 1993): 27–33. The Spanish colonizers considered the *babaylans* a stumbling block to the pacification and conversion of the natives in the Philippines, so they wiped them out.

6. Leonor Magtolis-Briones, "Foreword," in *Social Watch Philippines 2005 Report: Race for Survival* (Quezon City: Social Watch Philippines, 2005), iii.

7. Laura Somebang-Ocampo, "A Response to the Paper [Christology in a Changing Church and Society by Melanio Aoanan]," *CTC Bulletin* 8–9, no. 3–4 (October 1995): 44.

8. Mary John Mananzan, *Challenges to the Inner Room: Selected Essays and Speeches on Women* (Manila: Institute of Women's Studies, St. Scholastica's College, 1998), 231.

9. *Social Watch Philippines 2005 Report*, 227. According to Social Watch Philippines, for every peso budgeted, 12 percent goes to basic education and 1.3 percent goes to health. Between 10 and 20 percent is lost to corruption.

10. Agnes Miclat-Cacayan, "The Little Birds of Prey: Two Faces of the Prostituted Girl Child in the Philippines," *In God's Image* 17, no. 2 (1998): 22.

11. Ibid. Girl-child prostitution phenomenon is increasing not only in the Manila area, but also in other regions, especially in tourist destinations like Davao and Cebu.

12. Quoted in ibid., 16.

13. EATWOT Asian Women's Consultation, ed., *Spirituality for Life: Women Struggling against Violence* (Manila: EATWOT, Philippines and Institute of Women's Studies, St. Scholastica's College, 1994), 15.

14. F. Sionil Jose, *Three Filipino Women* (Manila: Solidaridad Publishing House, 1999), 88.

15. Justice, Peace and Creation Team (WCC), *Alternative Globalization Addressing Peoples and Earth (AGAPE): A Background Document* (Geneva: WCC, September 2005), 9–10.

16. May-an Villalba, "Migrant Workers Challenge Globalization," *In God's Image* 19, no. 1 (2000): 34.

17. Joseph E. Stiglitz, *Globalization and Its Discontents* (New York and London: W. W. Norton and Company, 2002), 214–52.

18. Emelina Villegas, "Out of Struggles Comes Hope," *In God's Image* 21, no. 2 (June 2002): 18–19.

19. Eleazar S. Fernandez, *Toward a Theology of Struggle* (Maryknoll, NY: Orbis Books, 1994); see also Levi Oracion, *God with Us: Reflections on the Theology of Struggle in the Philippines* (Dumaguete City: Silliman Univ. Divinity School, 2001).

20. Mananzan, *Challenges to the Inner Room*, 228.

21. Edicio de la Torre, *Touching Ground, Taking Root: Theological and Political Reflections on the Philippine Struggle* (London: Catholic Institute for International Relations and British Council of Churches, 1986), 156.

22. Sharon Rose Joy Ruiz-Duremdes and Wendy Kroeker, eds., *Dance amid Struggle: Stories and Songs of Hope* (Quezon City: AWIT Publications, 1998).

23. Everett Mendoza, *Radical and Evangelical: Portrait of a Filipino Christian* (Quezon City: New Day Publishers, 1999); see also Oscar S. Suarez, *Protestantism and Authoritarian Politics: The Politics of Repression and the Future of Ecumenical Witness in the Philippines* (Quezon City: New Day Publishers, 1999). Mendoza and Suarez, Protestant theologians of struggle, ignore the contribution of women in the church and theology in the Philippines.

24. Karl Barth, *Church Dogmatics*, ed. Geoffrey W. Bromiley and T. F. Torrance, 14 vols. (Edinburgh: T & T Clark, 1956), 1:280; see also Aloysius Pieris, *An Asian Theology of Liberation* (Maryknoll, NY: Orbis Books, 1988), 61.

25. Karl Marx and Friedrich Engels, *On Religion* (New York: Schocken Books, 1964; repr. Atlanta, GA: Scholars Press, 1982); see also Pieris, *An Asian Theology of Liberation*, 61.

26. Mary John Mananzan, "Theological Perspective of a Religious Woman Today," in *The Future of Liberation Theology*, ed. Marc H. Ellis and Otto Maduro (Maryknoll, NY: Orbis Books, 1989), 428.

27. Elizabeth S. Tapia, "Asian Women Doing Theology: The Challenge of Feminism for Theologizing," in Ruiz-Duremdes and Kroeker, *Dance amid Struggle: Stories and Songs of Hope*, 75.

28. Virginia Fabella, "Christology from an Asian Woman's Perspective," in *Asian Faces of Jesus*, ed. R. S. Sugirtharajah (Maryknoll, NY: Orbis Books, 1993), 211.

29. Lydia L. Lascano, "Women and the Christ Event," paper presented at EATWOT meeting, Manila, 1985, 121–29.

30. Kwok Pui-lan, *Introducing Asian Feminist Theology* (Cleveland, OH: Pilgrim Press, 2000), 24.

31. Myrna Francia, Margaret Lacson, and Roy Chiefe, "Asian Women Doing Theology," in *Woman and Religion*, ed. Mary John Mananzan (Manila: Institute of Women's Studies, St. Scholastica's College, 1998), 62.

32. Anscar J. Chupungco, *Liturgical Inculturation: Sacramentals, Religiosity, and Cathechesis* (Collegeville, MN: Liturgical Press, 1992), 104.

33. Ibid., 106–7.

34. Mananzan, *Challenges to the Inner Room*, 225.

35. Reynaldo C. Ileto, *Pasyon and Revolution: Popular Movements in the Philippines, 1840–1910* (Quezon City: Ateneo de Manila Univ. Press, 1979), 15–16.

36. Mananzan, *Challenges to the Inner Room*, 225; see also Mary John Mananzan, "Paschal Mystery from a Philippine Perspective," in *Concilium 2: Any Room for Christ in Asia?* (London: T & T Clark, 1993), 86–94.

37. Ileto, *Pasyon and Revolution*, 15–16, 18–19.

38. Chupungco, *Liturgical Inculturation*, 105: "Altars, which are a ubiquitous Filipino religious phenomenon, are found in homes, shops, grottoes, vehicles, and at street corners."

39. Elizabeth Soriso Padillo-Olesen, "Holy Friday," *In God's Image* 20, no. 1 (March 2001): 48.

40. Elizabeth S. Tapia, "Women Leaders Are Wounded Healers," *In God's Image* 21, no. 1 (March 2002).

41. Quoted in Francia, Lacson, and Chiefe, "Asian Women Doing Theology," 62.

42. Becky Demetillo-Abraham and Karina Constantino-David "Inang Laya" (Philippines: Dyna Products Inc., 1986), audiocassette.

43. Mananazan, *Challenges to the Inner Room*, 231–32.

44. Virginia Fabella, "Asian Women and Christology," *In God's Image* (September 1987): 15.

45. Liberato C. Bautista and Elizabeth Rifareal, eds., *And She Said No!* (Quezon City: National Council of Churches in the Philippines, 1990).

46. Victoria Narciso-Apuan, "In Search of Authentic Discipleship," in Bautista and Rifareal, *And She Said No!*, 117; see also Mary John Mananzan, ed., *Essays on Women*, rev. ed. (Manila: St. Scholastica's College, 1991).

47. Fabella, "Christology from an Asian Woman's Perspective," 211.

48. Lydia L. Lascano, "Signs of New Life," *In God's Image* (March 1989): 7.

49. Corazón Aquino, though the widow of Marcos's archenemy, merely gave a brief "democratic space" during her leadership. Succeeding her were Fidel Ramos, the implementer of martial law in Ferdinand Marcos's regime and the first Protestant president of the Philippines; the movie star Joseph Estrada, a big fan of Ronald Reagan; and Gloria Macapagal-Arroyo, who, without being asked, flaunted her support for US President George W. Bush's foreign policies.

50. PCPR and Kasimbayan, "Lakbayan Ng Mamamayan Laban sa Kahirapan," *Kalinangan* 7, no. 2 (December 1997): 33.

51. Lascano, "Signs of New Life," 7.

52. De la Torre, *Touching Ground, Taking Root*, 157.

53. Villegas, "Out of the Struggles Comes Hope," 21.

54. Teresita B. Obusan, "Foreword," in *Roots of Filipino Spirituality*, ed. Teresita B. Obusan (Philippines: Mamamathala, 1998), 14.

55. Ileto, *Pasyon and Revolution*, 130.

56. Quoted in ibid., 128–29. My translation.

57. Ibid., 130.

58. Isabelo de los Reyes, *La religión del katipunan* (Madrid: Tipolet de J. Corrales, 1900), 23–25.

59. Lascano, "Women and the Christ Event," 127.

60. Roberto S. Goizueta, *Caminemos con Jesús: Toward a Hispanic/Latino Theology of Accompaniment* (Maryknoll, NY: Orbis Books, 1995).

61. Emelina Villegas, "Towards a Culture of Struggle," in *Culture: A Force for Change*, ed. Socio-Pastoral Institute (Manila: SPI, 1988), 6.

62. Philippine Delegates to Asian Theological Conference III, "Philippine Search for a Liberation Spirituality," in *Currents in Philippine Theology*,

ed. Rebecca Asedillo, Liliosa Garibay, and Nonie S. Aviso (Quezon City: Institute of Religion and Culture, Phils., 1992), 49. ATC III met in Suanbo, South Korea, on July 3–8, 1989.

63. Tony Conway, "Christian Signs and Symbols," in SPI, *Culture*, 46–47.

64. Narciso-Apuan, "In Search of Authentic Discipleship," 116.

65. Sharon Rose Joy Ruiz-Duremdes, "Peopling Theology," *In God's Image* 19, no. 1 (2000): 19. Ruiz-Duremdes is the first woman to become head of the National Council of Churches in the Philippines.

66. Elizabeth Soriso Padillo-Olesen, "Easter Morning," *In God's Image* 20, no. 1 (March 2000): 49.

67. Ibong Malaya, "Ibong Malaya." My translation.

68. Ibong Malaya, "Awit ng Pag-ibig." My translation.

69. Virginia Fabella, "Symbols of John's Resurrection Scene," *Voices from the Third World* 10, no. 4 (December 1987): 29.

70. Mananzan, *Challenges to the Inner Room*, 228.

71. Fabella, "Symbols of John's Resurrection Scene," 29.

72. Virginia Fabella and Mercy Amba Oduyoye, eds., *With Passion and Compassion: Third World Women Doing Theology* (Maryknoll, NY: Orbis Books, 1996).

73. Mary John Mananzan, "Who Is Jesus Christ?: Reflection from the Philippines," *Voices from the Third World* 11, no. 2 (December 1988): 11.

74. Mananzan, *Challenges to the Inner Room*, 16.

75. Mananzan, "Who Is Jesus Christ? Reflection from the Philippines," 7–8.

76. Mary John Mananzan, "Who Is Jesus Christ?: Responses from the Philippines," *In God's Image* 12, no. 3 (Autumn 1993): 41.

77. Mananzan, *Challenges to the Inner Room*, 19.

78. As the first to wage a strike during the martial-law years, the workers of La Tondeña not only defied the prohibition of labor unions in 1975, but they also opened the path for the workers to struggle for their sectoral rights.

79. Mananzan, "Who Is Jesus Christ?: Responses from the Philippines," 40.

80. Ibid., 41.

81. PCPR (Promotion of Church People's Rights), *That We May Remember* (Quezon City: PCPR, 1989). This book chronicles the violations of church people's rights, torture, salvaging, and the murder of lay and clergy involved in the struggle for justice by government agents from the Marcos regime until the leadership of Aquino.

82. Teresa Dagdag, "Emerging Theology in the Philippines Today," in Asedillo, Garibay, and Aviso, *Currents in Philippine Theology*, 70–71.

83. José De Mesa and Lode L. Wostyn, *Doing Christology: The Re-Appropriation of a Tradition* (Quezon City: Claretian Publications, 1993).

84. Dagdag, "Emerging Theology in the Philippines Today."

85. Ibid., 72, 76.

86. Ibid.

87. Ibid.

88. Fabella, "Christology from an Asian Woman's Perspective," 219, 213.

89. Ibid., 217; see also Anthony De Mello, *One Minute Nonsense* (Chicago: Loyola Press, 1992), 132, which includes de Mello's adage, "He [the Master] loved to quote the Eastern saying: 'When the sage points to the moon, all that the idiot sees is the finger.'"

90. Fabella, "Christology from an Asian Woman's Perspective," 221.

91. Lydia L. Lascano, "Women Rising: A Testimony," *Kalinangan* 12, no. 1 (1992): 18.

92. Sharon Rose Joy Ruiz-Duremdes, "Human Rights: A Christian Imperative," *Kalinangan* 17, no. 2 (December 1997): 20, 24.

93. Ellen Ongkiko, ed., "Is Your Gender an Issue?" (Manila: Asian Social Institute Communication Center, 1991), videocassette.

94. Mananzan, "Who Is Jesus Christ?: Responses from the Philippines," 41.

95. Fabella, "Christology from an Asian Woman's Perspective," 214.

96. Ibid., 212.

97. Mananzan, "Who Is Jesus Christ?: Responses from the Philippines," 41.

98. Lascano, "Women Rising," 19.

99. Filipino feminist theologians have written about the issue of sexuality in connection with prostitution and rape. See, e.g., Miclat-Cacayan, "The Little Birds of Prey"; and Elizabeth Dominguez, "Biblical Concept of Human Sexuality," *In God's Image* (March 1989), 31–36. To my knowledge, however, no one has written yet about homophobia in the Philippine church.

100. Mananzan, *Challenges to the Inner Room*, 18.

101. Salvador T. Martinez, "Jesus Christ in Popular Piety in the Philippines," in Sugirtharajah, *Asian Faces of Jesus*, 249.

102. Ibid.

103. Victoria Tauli-Corpus, "Reclaiming Earth-Based Spirituality: Indigenous Women in the Cordillera," in *Women Healing Earth: Third World Women on Ecology, Feminism, and Religion*, ed. Rosemary Radford Ruether (Maryknoll, NY: Orbis Books, 1996).

104. Pieris, *An Asian Theology of Liberation*, 61.

105. Fabella, "Asian Women and Christology," 15.

106. Fabella, "Christology from an Asian Woman's Perspective, 215.

107. Quoted in *Kalinangan* 12, no. 1 (1992): 27.

108. Jane Ella Montenegro, "Women's Ministries: Words and Works of Seven Women Church Workers of the United Church of Christ in the Philippines, 1930–1997" (master's thesis, Institute of Formation and Religious Studies, 2002).

109. Hope Joyce Rambuyon, "Nanay Minda," *Kalinangan* 12, no. 1 (1992): 27.

110. Rebecca Asedillo, "Today Is Mothers' Day. I Say, Let's Celebrate It!" *Kalinangan* 12, no. 1 (1992): 32.

111. Ibid.

112. Ibid.

113. Delia Aguilar, "Ambiguities of Motherhood in the Philippines," *LILA: Asia-Pacific Women's Studies Journal* 6 (1996): 101–2.

114. Patrick Lopez, "Awit ng Isang Ina." Inang Laya performed the song.

115. Arche Ligo and Mary Rosario Battung, "Cosmic Spirituality for the Wholeness of Life," *Asia Pacific Women's Studies Journal* 5 (1995): 53–57.

116. Mary John Mananzan, "Woman and Religion," in *Religion and Society: Towards a Theology of Struggle*, ed. Mary Rosario Battung (Manila: Fides. 1988), 109.

117. Elizabeth S. Tapia, "The Contribution of Philippine Christian Women to Asian Women's Theology" (Ph.D. diss., Claremont Graduate School, 1989), 90–91.

118. Marija Gimbutas, *The Language of the Goddess* (San Francisco: HarperSan Francisco, 1991), 33. Gimbutas also asserts that the breasts, buttocks, and vulvas of the figurines of goddesses in Old European art symbolize the power to give life rather than sexual eroticism. See also Marija Gimbutas, *The Living Goddess* (Berkeley and Los Angeles: Univ. of California Press, 1999).

119. Pieter Jan Raats, *A Structural Study of Bagobo Myths and Rites* (Cebu City: The University of San Carlos, 1969), 30, 31.

120. Agnes Miclat-Cacayan, "Nurturing Goddess and Powerful Priestess: Legacy from Our Indigenous Spirituality," in *From the Womb of Mebuyan*, ed. Belo Caharian (Davao City: Hinabi Women's Circle, 1998), 18–19.

121. Teresita Infante, "Filipino Women as Religious Practitioners," *In God's Image* 12, no. 3 (Autumn 1993): 22–26.

122. Ligo and Battung, "Cosmic Spirituality for the Wholeness of Life," 54.

123. Mananzan, "Woman and Religion," 110.

124. Clement of Alexandria, "The Instructor," in *Fathers of the Second Century: Hermas, Tatian, Athenagoras, Theophilus, and Clement of Alexandria (Entire)*, ed. Cleveland A. Cox (repr. Grand Rapids, MI: Eerdmans, 1979), 3.24.1; and Ambrose of Milan, "St. Ambrose: Select Works and Letters," in *A Select Library of Nicene and Post-Nicene Fathers of the Christian Church*, ed. Philip Schaff and Henry Wace (Grand Rapids, MI: Eerdmans, 1979), 1.5.21–22.

125. Elinor Gadon, *The Once and Future Goddess* (New York: Harper and Row, 1998), 41.

126. J. Massyngbaerde Ford, *Redeemer, Friend and Mother: Salvation in Antiquity and in the Gospel of John* (Minneapolis: Fortress Press, 1997), 134–36.

127. Chung Hyun Kyung, *Struggle to Be the Sun Again* (Maryknoll, NY: Orbis Books, 1990), 65.

128. Anne Jensen, *God's Self-Confident Daughters: Early Christianity and the Liberation of Women* (Louisville, KY: Westminster John Knox Press, 1996), 163.

129. Wendy Kroeker, "Dancing with Miriam," in *Dance amid Struggle.*

5 GAZING AT THE POSTCOLONIAL JESUS: THE MULTIPLE IDENTITY OF CHRIST IN HONG KONG

1. Linda R. Layosa, "Anywhere, Everywhere: The D.H.'s Saga," in *From America to Africa: Voices of Filipino Women Overseas*, ed. Lorna Kalaw-Tirol (Makati: FAI Resource Management Inc., 2000), 149–64; Peter K. H. Lee, "Hong Kong: Living in the Shadow of the Third World," in *Asian Christian Spirituality: Reclaiming Traditions*, ed. Virginia Fabella, Peter K. H. Lee, and David Kwang-sun Suh (Maryknoll, NY: Orbis Books, 1992), 106.

2. Jane C. N. Chui, "A Case: 1997," *In God's Image* (September 1989): 25.

3. Lee, "Hong Kong," 108.

4. Rose Wu, "1997 and the Destiny of the Hong Kong People," *In God's Image* 16, no. 2 (1997): 5.

5. Shum Yun Shan, "1989 . . . China . . . My Reflection," *In God's Image* (September 1989): 33.

6. Chui, "A Case: 1997," 26.

7. Wong Wai-Ching, *"The Poor Woman": A Critical Analysis of Asian Theology and Contemporary Chinese Fiction by Women* (New York: Peter Lang, 2002), 95.

8. World Council of Churches, *Asia: Country Papers* (Geneva: WCC, 1984), 20.

9. Michael Ng, "Rising Poverty on the Agenda for Tung's Address," in *The Standard*, January 10, 2005; Central Intelligence Agency, *The World Factbook 2005.* Both sources are available online.

10. Lui Hon-Kwong, "Poverty and Income Disparity in Hong," *HKCER Letters* 42 (January 1997). Available online.

11. Fok Tin-man, "Elderly Women and Poverty in Hong Kong," paper presented at CEDAW seminar, Hong Kong, November 18, 1998. Available online.

12. Tung Chee-hwa, cited in Ng, "Rising Poverty on the Agenda for Tung's Address."

13. See Marianne Katoppo, "Women That Make Asia Alive," in *New Eyes for Reading: Biblical and Theological Reflections by Women from the Third World*, ed. John S. Pobee and Bärbel Von Wartenberg-Potter (Geneva: WCC, 1986), 99; Walden Bello and Stephanie Rosenfeld, *Dragons in Distress: Asia's Miracle Economy in Crisis* (San Francisco: Institute for Food and Development Policy, 1992), 14, 24.

14. Rose Wu, "Asian Women as the Subject of God's Vision," *In God's Image* 16, no. 2 (1997): 28–29.

15. Ibid.

16. Nicole Constable, *Maid to Order in Hong Kong: Stories of Filipina Workers* (Ithaca, NY: Cornell Univ. Press, 1997).

17. Ibid., vii. Constable relates that a Hong Kong woman told her that Filipinos are "very stupid" because they know very little Chinese, and that they are "dirty and lazy" and morally questionable because they are "willing to leave their children and husbands behind in the Philippines."

18. Ibid., 38, 95–96. In Hong Kong the Chinese term *banmui* has acquired a racial slant and is associated with a "Philippine girl."

19. Arif Dirlik, "The Postcolonial Aura: Third World Criticism in the Age of Global Capitalism," in *Contemporary Postcolonial Theory: A Reader*, ed. Padmini Mongia (London: Arnold, 1996), 296.

20. Edward W. Said, *Orientalism* (New York: Vintage Books, 1977).

21. R. S. Sugirtharajah, *Asian Biblical Hermeneutics and Postcolonialism: Contesting the Interpretations* (Maryknoll, NY: Orbis Books, 1998), 15.

22. Sometimes referred to as meta-narratives or grand narratives, master narratives are stories, myths, legends, and tales that bestow legitimacy upon social institutes. As such, they determine who has the right to speak, what has to be said, how knowledge should be applied, and/or how to represent models of its integration into institutions. See Jean-François Lyotard, *The Postmodern Condition: A Report on Knowledge* (Minneapolis: Univ. of Minnesota Press, 1989), 31–33.

23. Sugirtharajah, *Asian Biblical Hermeneutics and Postcolonialism*, 16.

24. Dirlik, "The Postcolonial Aura," 315–16.

25. Kwok Pui-lan, "Book Review: 'The Poor Woman': A Critical Analysis of Asian Theology and Contemporary Chinese Fiction by Women by Wai-Ching Angela Wong," *Quest* 1, no. 1 (November 2002): 94–104.

26. Kwok Pui-lan, "The Future of Feminist Theology: An Asian Perspective," in *Feminist Theology from the Third World: A Reader*, ed. Ursula King (Maryknoll, NY: Orbis Books, 1994), 65; see also idem, "The Future of Feminist Theology: An Asian Perspective," *Voices from the Third World* 15, no. 1 (June 1992).

27. Kwok Pui-lan, "God Weeps with Our Pain," in Pobee and Von Wartenberg-Potter, *New Eyes for Reading*, 90–95.

28. Ibid., 90–91.

29. Susan Alice Watkins, Marisa Rueda, and Marta Rodriguez, *Introducing Feminism* (Cambridge, UK: Icon Books, 1999), 29.

30. Toni Morrison, *Beloved* (New York: Plume Books, 1988), 200.

31. Kwok, "God Weeps with Our Pain," 92.

32. Ibid., 93–95.

33. Ibid., 92.

34. Kwok Pui-lan, "Chinese Non-Christian Perceptions of Christ," *Concilium 2* (1993): 25–26.

35. The nexus of shame and guilt is prevalent and strong in the Filipino and Japanese psyche and language. In *Women and Jesus in Mark: A Japanese Feminist Perspective* (Maryknoll, NY: Orbis Books, 1994), Hisako Kinukawa explores the theme of shame and guilt in her study of the women and Jesus in the Gospel of Mark.

36. Kwok, "Chinese Non-Christian Perceptions of Christ," 30–31.

37. Kwok, "Book Review: 'The Poor Woman,'" 92.

38. Kwok Pui-lan, *Introducing Asian Feminist Theology* (Cleveland, OH: Pilgrim Press, 2000), 90.

39. Kwok Pui-lan, *Chinese Women and Christianity 1860–1927* (Atlanta, GA: Scholars' Press, 1992), 46.

40. Wong, "*The Poor Woman*," 119.

41. Kwok, *Introducing Asian Feminist Theology*, 90.

42. After Kwok's presentation during the Pacific, Asian, North American-Asian Women in Theology and Ministry (PANAAWTM), in March 27, 1999, at Stony Point, New York, some women expressed their worries to her: "What about the struggle that we have started?"

43. Epifanio San Juan, Jr., *Beyond Postcolonial Theory* (New York: St. Martin's Press, 1998); see also Dirlik, "The Postcolonial Aura."

44. Kwok, "Book Review: 'The Poor Woman,'" 92.

45. Kwok Pui-lan, *Postcolonial Imagination and Feminist Theology* (Louisville, KY: Westminster John Knox Press, 2005), 2–3.

46. Ibid., 170.

47. Linda McDowell and Joanne P. Sharp, eds., *A Feminist Glossary of Human Geography* (London: Arnold, 1999), 131–32.

48. Kwok, *Postcolonial Imagination and Feminist Theology*, 170.

49. Ibid., 171.

50. Ibid.

51. Kwok, *Introducing Asian Feminist Theology*, 89–93.

52. Ibid., 91.

53. Kwok, "Ecology and Christology," *Feminist Theology* 15 (May 1997): 113.

54. Kwok, *Introducing Asian Feminist Theology*, 90–91.

55. Sugirtharajah, *Asian Biblical Hermeneutics and Postcolonialism*, 16. Taking a cue from Edward Said, Sugirtharajah defines hybridity as "the complex web of negotiation and interaction, forced by imaginatively redeploying the local and the imported elements."

56. Sherry Ortner, "Is Female to Male as Nature Is to Culture?" in *Readings in Ecology and Feminist Theology*, ed. Mary Heather McKinnon and Moni McIntyre (Kansas City, MO: Sheed and Ward, 1995), 36–56.

57. Kwok Pui-lan, "Feminist Theology as Intercultural Discourse," in *The Cambridge Companion to Feminist Theology*, ed. Susan Frank Parsons (Cambridge, UK: Cambridge Univ. Press, 2002), 23–39.

58. Kwok, *Introducing Asian Feminist Theology*, 91.

59. Ibid., 93.

60. Ibid.

61. Wong, "*The Poor Woman*," 104–7.

62. Ibid., 63.

63. Wong Wai-Ching, "Negotiating for a Postcolonial Identity," *Journal of Feminist Studies in Religion* 16, no. 2 (Fall 2000): 18–19.

64. Wong, "*The Poor Woman*," 96.

65. Ibid., 50–60.

66. Wong, "Negotiating for a Postcolonial Identity," 21.

67. Wong, "*The Poor Woman*," 101.

68. Ibid.

69. Ibid., 108.

70. Wong, "Negotiating for a Postcolonial Identity," 21.

71. Wong, "*The Poor Woman*," 102.

72. Wong, "Negotiating for a Postcolonial Identity," 22–23.

73. Kang Nam-Soon, "Creating 'Dangerous Memory': Challenges for Asian and Korean Feminist Theology," *Ecumenical Review* 47, no. 1 (1995): 21–31. Kang accuses Korean feminist theologians, and particularly Chung Hyun Kyung, of romanticizing traditional resources. Such idealization, Kang argues, led to Asian women's negligence of the sexism behind such traditions.

74. Wong, "*The Poor Woman*," 4–6, 103.

75. Ibid., 97, 102, 103, 107–8.

76. Ibid., 64.

77. Ibid., 72. Hongkongese is the new identity that Hong Kong locals prefer to that of Chinese.

78. Ibid., 111–12.

79. Ibid., 113–14. For a concise survey of Kristeva's work and post-feminist theory, see Madan Sarup, *An Introductory Guide to Post-Structuralism and Postmodernism*, 2nd ed. (Athens: Univ. of Georgia Press, 1993). In postmodern understanding, the human being as a subject is a construction and a product of signifying activities that are culturally specific and generally unconscious. It is opposite to the Cartesian notion that the subject as an individual is stable, has a fixed identity, and is a free, intellectual agent, as represented by René Descartes's "I think, therefore, I am."

80. Wong, "*The Poor Woman*," 6.

81. Ibid., 126.

82. Ibid., 118.

83. Ibid., 116.

84. Ibid., 119. Other than Kristeva, the writings of the French post-feminists Luce Irigaray and Hélène Cixous also inform Wong's Christology.

85. Kinukawa, *Women and Jesus in Mark*, 49.

86. Wong, "*The Poor Woman*," 118.

87. Dirlik, "The Postcolonial Aura," 294, 303.

88. Martin Luther, "Disputation at Heidelberg: 1518," in *Luther: Early Theological Works*, vol. 16, ed. James Atkinson (Philadelphia: Westminster Press, 1962), 278.

89. San Juan, *Beyond Postcolonial Theory*, 13.

90. Wong, *"The Poor Woman,"* 138.

91. San Juan, *Beyond Postcolonial Theory*, 9.

92. Kwok, "Book Review: 'The Poor Woman,'" 99.

93. Swarnalatha Devi, "The Struggle of Dalit Christian Women in India," in *Feminist Theology from the Third World: A Reader*, ed. Ursula King (Maryknoll, NY: Orbis Books, 1994), 137.

94. The Philippine government's army has bombed villages in Mindanao in the guise of fighting terrorism. With instigation from the US government, this campaign resumed in 2001 after the Twin Tower attack on September 11. See Eric Schmitt, "U.S. Combat Force of 1,700 Is Headed to the Philippines," *New York Times*, February 21, 2003, 1–A16.

95. Constable, *Maid to Order in Hong Kong*, 155–80. Some policies of Hong Kong must be resisted through organized ways, such as the 11 percent cut on domestic helpers' wages and the Immigration Department's infamous "2–week rule," among others.

96. Kwok, "Book Review: 'The Poor Woman,'" 99.

97. Lynn White, Jr., "The Historical Roots of Our Ecological Crisis," *Science* 155, no. 3767 (1967): 1206.

98. Carolyn Merchant, *The Death of Nature: Women, Ecology, and the Scientific Revolution* (San Francisco: HarperSan Francisco, 1989).

99. Kwok Pui-lan, "Ecology and the Recycling of Christianity," in *Ecotheology: Voices from South and North*, ed. David G. Hallman (Geneva: WCC, 1994; Maryknoll, NY: Orbis Books, 1994).

100. Kwok, "Ecology and Christology," 117.

101. Elisabeth Schüssler Fiorenza, *Jesus, Miriam's Child, Sophia's Prophet* (New York: Continuum, 1994).

102. Kwok, *Introducing Asian Feminist Theology*, 92.

103. Kwok, "Chinese Non-Christian Perceptions of Christ," 28–29.

104. Schüssler Fiorenza, *Jesus, Miriam's Child, Sophia's Prophet*, 157.

105. Kwok, *Introducing Asian Feminist Theology*, 92.

106. Grace Ji-Sun Kim, *The Grace of Sophia: A Korean North American Women's Christology* (Cleveland, OH: Pilgrim Press, 2002), 97.

107. Kwok, *Introducing Asian Feminist Theology*, 92.

108. Kim, *The Grace of Sophia*, 91.

109. Ibid., 91–96.

110. Kwok, "Ecology and Christology," 113.

111. Schüssler Fiorenza, *Jesus, Miriam's Child, Sophia's Prophet*, 150–52.

112. Frederick William Danker et al., eds., *A Greek-English Lexicon of the New Testament and Other Early Christian Literature*, 3rd ed. (Chicago: Univ. of Chicago Press, 2000), 934–35.

113. Schüssler Fiorenza, *Jesus, Miriam's Child, Sophia's Prophet*, 151.

114. Elizabeth A. Johnson, *She Who Is: The Mystery of God in Feminist Theological Discourse* (New York: Crossroad, 1994), 169; see also 1 Cor 1:24.

115. Kwok, *Introducing Asian Feminist Theology*, 93.

116. Ibid.

117. John Calvin, *Calvin: Institutes of the Christian Religion*, ed. John T. McNeill, vols. 20–21, Library of Christian Classics (Philadelphia: Westminster Press, 1960), 1.5.1–2, 5.

118. Ibid., 1.5.15.

119. Kwok, "Ecology and Christology," 121–23.

120. Wong Wai-Ching, "For Such a Time as This: Our Moment in God's Time," *CTC Bulletin* 17 (2001): 12–19. Available online.

121. Wong Wai-Ching, "The Wisdom Women in Creation: A Reflection on Proverbs 8," *In God's Image* 17, no. 1 (1998): 25.

122. Wong, "For Such a Time as This."

123. Kwok, "Book Review: 'The Poor Woman,'" 101.

124. Wong Wai-Ching, "Asian Theology in a Changing Asia: Towards an Asian Theological Agenda for the 21st Century," *CTC Bulletin*, Special Supplement 1 (November 1997): 38.

125. Kwok, "Book Review: 'The Poor Woman,'" 101.

126. Alvin Y. So and Yok-shiu F. Lee, eds., *Asia's Environmental Movements: Comparative Perspectives* (New York: M. E. Sharpe, 1999), 55–89.

127. Wu, "Asian Women as Subject of God's Vision," 27.

128. Ibid. See also Hannah Beech, "With Women So Scarce, What Can Men Do? Years of Female Infanticide Help Shatter the Taboo on Incestuous Marriages," *Time*, July 1, 2002, 8.

129. Asian Migrants' Center, "Foreign Domestic Workers in Hong Kong: A Baseline Study," *In God's Image* 14, no. 1 (Spring 1992): 38. Chinese compose 61.8% of the employers in Hong Kong, while the rest are British and other Westerners.

130. Cheung Choi-wan, "Sex Industry in Hong Kong," *In God's Image* (June 1990): 33–34.

131. Rose Wu, "A Hong Kong Feminist's View of Prostitution: Reviewing Sin, Morality and Sexuality," *In God's Image* 20, no. 2 (June 2001): 38.

132. Ibid., 39.

133. Ibid., 40.

134. Ibid., 141–42.

135. Rose Wu, "Women on the Boundary: Prostitution, Contemporary and in the Bible," *Feminist Theology* 28 (2001): 79.

136. Wu, "A Hong Kong Feminist's View of Prostitution," 42–43.

137. Danker et al., *A Greek-English Lexicon of the New Testament*, 389, 95.

138. Iris Marion Young, *Justice and the Politics of Difference* (Princeton, NJ: Princeton Univ. Press, 1990), 239.

139. Audre Lorde, *Sister Outsider* (Freedom, CA: The Crossing Press, 1984), 54, 56.

140. Ibid., 55.

141. Carter Heyward, *Touching Our Strength: The Erotic as Power and the Love of God* (New York: Harper and Row, 1989), 187.

142. Rita Nakashima Brock, *Journeys by Heart: A Christology of Erotic Power* (New York: Crossroad, 1988), 26.

143. Ibid., 25.

144. Wong, "*The Poor Woman*," 119, 120, 121.

145. Luce Irigaray, "This Sex Which Is Not One," in *A Reader in Feminist Knowledge*, ed. Sneja Gunew (New York: Routledge, 1991), 204–11. Irigaray argues that woman finds pleasure almost everywhere, so unlike man, woman's auto-eroticism enables her to write differently from her bodily experience of pleasure and pain. Hélène Cixous, "The Laugh of Medusa," in Gunew, *A Reader in Feminist Knowledge*, 224–32. Cixous contends that a woman's writing is different because she writes with her body. By inscribing herself into her writing, she dismantles everything and "breaks up the truth with laughter." Kinukawa, *Women and Jesus in Mark.*

146. Wong, "*The Poor Woman*," 120.

147. Ibid., 120–21.

148. Irigaray, "This Sex Which Is Not One," 208. See also Cixous, "The Laugh of Medusa," 228.

149. Wong, "*The Poor Woman*," 119–20.

150. Delores S. Williams, *Sisters in the Wilderness: The Challenge of Womanist God-Talk* (Maryknoll, NY: Orbis Books, 1993).

151. Kwok, "The Future of Feminist Theology," 72.

152. Cixous, "The Laugh of Medusa," 229.

153. Kwok, "The Future of Feminist Theology," 73.

154. Ibid., 74. See also McDowell and Sharp, *A Feminist Glossary of Human Geography*, 139. *Jouissance*, a French term without an exact counterpart in English, is used to refer to the Lacanian notion of excess pleasure that is not reducible simply to plain pleasure. In French, it "refers to the enjoyment in the sense of enjoying rights, but also sexual, spiritual, and physical enjoyment."

155. Wong, "*The Poor Woman*," 121.

156. Serene Jones, *Feminist Theory and Christian Theology: Cartographies of Grace* (Minneapolis: Fortress Press, 2000), 36–37.

157. Kwok, "The Future of Feminist Theology," 74–75.

158. *Strategic essentialism* is the phrase used by feminist theorists to describe the position of Luce Irigaray and those who, like her, take the "awkward third option" in the essentialist/constructivist debate. For a simplified overview of the debate from a theological point of view, see Jones, *Feminist Theory and Christian Theology*, 22–48.

159. Kwok, "Book Review: 'The Poor Woman,'" 98.

160. Jones, *Feminist Theory and Christian Theology*, 36–37, 44–45. Constructivists view the self as a "site," "terrain," "territory," or "space" through which cultural constructs navigate. Thus, the self is unstable, constantly attacked, contested, and changed.

EPILOGUE: WHO IS THIS JESUS WHO COMES TO MY HOUSE?

1. Francis Brown, S. R. Driver, and Charles A. Briggs, *The Brown-Driver-Briggs Hebrew and English Lexicon: With an Appendix Containing the Biblical Aramaic* (Peabody, MA: Hendrickson Publishers, 2001), 4187. In the Israelitic tradition, the "anointed" is set apart or consecrated to a particular task by pouring oil over the head.

2. Frederick William Danker et al., eds., *A Greek-English Lexicon of the New Testament and Other Early Christian Literature*, 3rd ed. (Chicago: Univ. of Chicago Press, 2000), 1091.

3. Jon Sobrino, *Jesus the Liberator: A Historical-Theological View* (Maryknoll, NY: Orbis Books, 1993), 50. Sobrino suggests that Christology should empower and liberate rather than encourage "christolatry"; see also Jon Sobrino, "Systematic Christology: Jesus Christ, the Absolute Mediator of the Reign of God," in *Systematic Theology: Perspective from Liberation Theology*, ed. John Sobrino and Ignacio Ellacuría (Maryknoll, NY: Orbis Books, 1993), 124–45.

4. Kwok Pui-lan, "Ecology and Christology," *Feminist Theology* 15 (May 1997): 113–25; see also Gregory J. Riley, *One Jesus, Many Christs: How Jesus Inspired Not One True Christianity But Many* (San Francisco: HarperSan Francisco, 1999). Riley also argues that the early Christians had varied christological models based on this one Jesus, a model they could follow into a "new life of caring community and transcendent hope."

5. Danker et al., *A Greek-English Lexicon of the New Testament and Other Early Christian Literature*, 5–6. The Fourth Gospel uses the verb *agapao*, meaning "to have a warm regard for and interest in another, to have affection or love for, to have concern for the other, to practice, express or to prove one's love."

6. Gail R. O'Day, "John," in *Women's Bible Commentary: Expanded Edition with Apocrypha*, ed. Carol A. Newsom and Sharon H. Ringe (Louisville, KY: Westminster John Knox Press, 1998), 390–91.

7. Ibid.

8. Rita Nakashima Brock, *Journeys by Heart: A Christology of Erotic Power* (New York: Crossroad, 1988), 68–69.

9. Mai Thành, "Aspects of Christianity in Vietnam," *Any Room for Christ in Asia? Concilium* 2 (1993): 108.

10. Kelly Brown Douglas, *The Black Christ* (Maryknoll, NY: Orbis Books, 1994), 77.

11. James H. Cone, *God of the Oppressed,* rev. ed. (Maryknoll, NY: Orbis Books, 1997), 135.

12. Jacquelyn Grant, *White Women's Christ and Black Women's Jesus: Feminist Christology and Womanist Response* (Atlanta, GA: Scholars Press, 1989), 217.

13. Clara Sue Kidwell, Homer Noley, and George E. Tinker, *Native American Theology* (Maryknoll, NY: Orbis Books, 2001), 76–84, 113–25.

14. Mercy Amba Oduyoye, *Introducing African Women's Theology* (Cleveland, OH: Pilgrim Press, 2001), 63.

15. Ivone Gebara, *Out of the Depths: Women's Experience of Evil and Salvation*, trans. Anne Patrick Ware (Minneapolis, MN: Fortress Press, 2002), 118.

16. Mary Rosario Battung, "Indigenous People's Primal Religion and Cosmic Spirituality as Wellsprings of Life," in *Springs of Living Water: Asia, Her Life, Struggles, and Hope*, ed. Marlene Perera and A. Nunuk Murniati (Bangalore: EATWOT, 1997), 118–30.

17. The Filipino primal memory of the Breastfeeding Goddess is found in *Magbabaya* of the Banwaons and Manobos, *Tuglibong* and *Mebuyan* of the Bagobos, *Diwata* of the Tagbanuas, and traces of this are manifest in the myth of *Mariang Makiling* of Laguna and *Alunsina* of Panay Island.

18. Clement of Alexandria, "The Instructor," in *Fathers of the Second Century: Hermas, Tatian, Athenagoras, Theophilus, and Clement of Alexandria (Entire)*, ed. Cleveland A. Cox (repr. Grand Rapids, MI: Eerdmans, 1979), 295–96.

19. Ambrose of Milan, "St. Ambrose: Select Works and Letters," in *A Select Library of Nicene and Post-Nicene Fathers of the Christian Church*, ed. Philip Schaff and Henry Wace (Grand Rapids, MI: Eerdmans, 1979), 266–67, 366.

20. Francis Bacon used this metaphorical phrase to advance the Enlightenment project to explore and gain knowledge about the earth. See parts of his text quoted extensively in Carolyn Merchant, *The Death of Nature: Women, Ecology, and the Scientific Revolution* (San Francisco: HarperSan Francisco, 1989).

21. Muriel Orevillo-Montenegro, "Shall I Cling to the Old Rugged Cross? Interrogating and Re-thinking the Power of the Cross," in *CTC Bulletin* 20, no. 3 (December 2004): 1–13.

Bibliography

Abesamis, Carlos H. "Ano Po Ang Laman Ng Mangkok? How [Not] to Do Theology in Asia Today?" *CTC Bulletin* 15, no. 1 (1998): 7–30.

———. *Backpack of a Jesus-Seeker*, Book One. Quezon City: Claretian Publications/Socio-Pastoral Institute, 2004.

———. *The Mission of Jesus and Good News to the Poor*. Quezon City: Claretian Publications, 1987.

———. *The Third Look at Jesus*. Quezon City: Claretian Publications, 1999.

Abraham, Dulcie. "Jesus the New Creation: Christology in the Malaysian Context." In *Asian Women Dong Theology: Report from Singapore Conference, November 1987*, edited by Dulcie Abraham, 189–94. Hong Kong: AWRC, 1989.

Aguilar, Delia. "Ambiguities of Motherhood in the Philippines." *LILA: Asia-Pacific Women's Studies Journal* 6 (1996): 89–104.

Ahn Byung Mu. "The Body of Jesus-Event Tradition." *East Asia Journal of Theology* 3, no. 2 (1985): 293–309.

———. "Jesus and People (Minjung)." In *The Asian Faces of Jesus*, edited by R. S. Sugirtharajah, 163–72. Maryknoll, NY: Orbis Books, 1993.

———. "Jesus and the Minjung in the Gospel of Mark." In *Voices from the Margin: Interpreting the Bible in the Third World*, edited by R. S. Sugirtharajah. London: SPCK; Maryknoll, NY: Orbis Books, 1995.

———. "The Korean Church's Understanding of Jesus." *Voices from the Third World* 8, no. 1 (1985): 49–59.

Ahn Sang-Nim. "Feminist Theology in the Korean Church." In *We Dare to Dream: Doing Theology as Asian Women*, edited by Virginia Fabella and Sun Ai Lee Park, 127–34 (Hong Kong: AWRC/EATWOT Women's Commission in Asia, 1989; Maryknoll, NY: Orbis Books, 1990).

———. "My Understanding of Feminist Theology." *In God's Image* (April 1984): 16–19.

Aleaz, K. P. "Indigenization." In *Dictionary of Third World Theologies*, edited by Virginia Fabella and R. S. Sugirtharajah, 106–8. Maryknoll, NY: Orbis Books, 2000.

———. *Jesus in Neo-Vedanta: A Meeting of Hinduism and Christianity*. Delhi: Kant Publications, 1995.

Althaus-Reid, Marcella. *Indecent Theology: Theological Perversions in Sex, Gender, and Politics*. London: Routledge, 2000.

Amaladoss, Michael. *Life in Freedom: Liberation Theologies from Asia*. Maryknoll, NY: Orbis Books, 1997.

———. "Nobili, Robert de." In *Biographical Dictionary of Christian Missions*, edited by Gerald H. Anderson, 498–99. Grand Rapids, MI: Eerdmans, 1998.

Ambrose of Milan. "St. Ambrose: Select Works and Letters." In *A Select Library of Nicene and Post-Nicene Fathers of the Christian Church*, edited by Philip Schaff and Henry Wace. Grand Rapids, MI: Eerdmans, 1979.

Amore, Roy C., and Julia Ching. "The Buddhist Tradition." In *World Religions: Eastern Traditions*, edited by Willard G. Oxtoby, 212–345. New York: Oxford Univ. Press, 1996.

Anderson, Gerald H. "Providence and Politics behind Protestant Missionary Beginnings in the Philippines." In *Studies in Philippine Church History*, edited by Gerald H. Anderson, 279–300. Ithaca, NY: Cornell Univ. Press, 1969.

Anderson-Rajkumar, Evangeline. "Asian Feminist Christology," in *In God's Image* 22, no. 4 (December 2003): 2–12.

———. "Dowry: Destroyer of the Human Values." In *Lived Realities: Faith Reflections on Gender Justice*, edited by Elizabeth Joy, 113–19. Bangalore: CISRS/JWP, 1999.

Antone, Hope. "Healed by Her Faith." In Ruiz-Duremdes and Kroeker, *Dance amid Struggle*, 67–72.

Appasamy, Aiyadurai J. *Christianity as Bhakti Marga: A Study of the Johannine Doctrine of Love*. Madras: CLS, 1928.

———. "I and the Father Are One." In Sugirtharajah and Hargreaves, *Readings in Indian Christian Theology*, 195–99.

Asedillo, Rebecca. "Today Is Mothers' Day. I Say, Let's Celebrate It!" *Kalinangan* 12, no. 1 (1992): 30–32.

———. "When Did We See You, Lord?" In *Rice in the Storm: Faith in Struggle in the Philippines*, edited by Rebecca Asedillo and B. David Williams, 135–48. New York: Friendship Press, 1989.

Asian Collective. *Journey through Asia*. Manila: The Asian Collective, 1992.

Asian Migrants' Center. "Foreign Domestic Workers in Hong Kong: A Baseline Study." *In God's Image* 14, no. 1 (Spring 1992): 36–30.

Athyal, Leelamma. "Mariology: A Feminist Perspective." In *Towards a Theology of Humanhood: Women's Perspectives*, edited by Aruna Gnanadason, 49–61. Delhi: ISPCK, 1986.

Azariah, M. "The Church's Healing Ministry to Dalits." In *Towards a Dalit Theology*, edited by M. E. Prabhakar, 113–21. Delhi: ISPCK, 1988.

Balasuriya, Tissa. "Christologies in Dialogue in EATWOT: An Asian Historical Perspective." *Voices from the Third World* 18, no. 2 (December 1995): 46–69.

———. "Humanity's 'Fall' and Jesus the Savior." *Voices from the Third World* 11, no. 2 (December 1988): 41–75.

———. *Mary and the Human Liberation: The Story and the Text.* Harrisburg, PA: Trinity Press International, 1997.

———. *Planetary Theology.* Maryknoll, NY: Orbis Books, 1984.

Baltazar, Stella. "Domestic Violence in Indian Perspective." In *Women Resisting Violence: Spirituality for Life*, edited by Mary John Mananzan, Mercy Amba Oduyoye, Elsa Tamez, J. Shannon Clarkson, May C. Grey, and Letty M. Russell, 56–65. Maryknoll, NY: Orbis Books, 1996.

Barth, Karl. *Church Dogmatics*, edited by Geoffrey W. Bromiley and T. F. Torrance. 14 vols. Edinburgh: T & T Clark, 1956.

Battung, Mary Rosario. "Indigenous People's Primal Religion and Cosmic Spirituality as Wellsprings of Life." In *Springs of Living Water: Asia, Her Life, Struggles, and Hope*, edited by Marlene Perera and A. Nunuk Murniati, 118–30. Bangalore: EATWOT, 1997.

Beech, Hannah. "With Women So Scarce, What Can Men Do?: Years of Female Infanticide Help Shatter the Taboo on Incestuous Marriages." *Time*, July 1. 2002.

Bello, Walden. *The Future in the Balance: Essays on Globalization and Resistance.* London: The Institute for Food and Development Policy/Food First Books, 2001.

Bello, Walden, Shea Cunningham, and Bill Rau. *Dark Victory: The United States, Structural Adjustment and Global Poverty.* London: Pluto Press, 1994.

Bello, Walden, David Kinley, and Elaine Elinson. *Development Debacle: The World Bank in the Philippines.* San Francisco: Food First/Institute for Food and Development Policy, 1982.

Bello, Walden, and Stephanie Rosenfeld. *Dragons in Distress: Asia's Miracle Economy in Crisis.* San Francisco: Institute for Food and Development Policy, 1992.

Brock, Rita Nakashima. *Journeys by Heart: A Christology of Erotic Power.* New York: Crossroad, 1988.

Brock, Rita Nakashima, and Rebecca Ann Parker. *Proverbs of Ashes: Violence, Redemptive Suffering, and the Search for What Saves Us.* Boston: Beacon Press, 2001.

Brown, Francis, S. R. Driver, and Charles A. Briggs. *The Brown-Driver-Briggs Hebrew and English Lexicon: With an Appendix containing the Biblical Aramaic.* Peabody, MA: Hendrickson Publishers, 2001.

Calvin, John. *Calvin: Institutes of the Christian Religion*, edited by John T. McNeill. Vols. 20–21. Library of Christian Classics. Philadelphia: Westminster Press, 1960.

Cariño, Feliciano. "What about the Theology of Struggle?" In *Religion and Society: Towards a Theology of Struggle*, edited by Mary Rosario Battung et al., v–xv. Manila: Forum for Interdisciplinary Endeavors and Studies, 1988.

Central Intelligence Agency. *The World Factbook 2005*. Available on the cia.gov website.

Chakkalakal, Pauline. "Asian Women Reshaping Theology: Challenges and Hopes." *Feminist Theology* 27 (2001): 21–35.

———. "Women's Ordination and Priesthood." In *Lived Realities: Faith Reflections on Gender Justice*, edited by Elizabeth Joy, 134–44. Bangalore: CISRS/JWP, 1999.

Chakkarai, Vengal. "The Historical Jesus and the Christ of Experience." In Sugirtharajah and Hargreaves, *Readings in Indian Christian Theology*.

———. *Jesus the Avatar*. Madras: CLS, 1926.

Chandran, Russell J. "Development of Christian Theology in India: A Critical Survey." In Sugirtharajah and Hargreaves, *Readings in Indian Christian Theology*, 4–13.

Chang Jung-Nim. "You Are the Crucifix of Korea." *In God's Image* 15, no. 2 (Summer 1996): 35–36.

Chenchiah, P. "Where Lies the Uniqueness of Christ? An Indian Christian View." In Sugirtharajah and Hargreaves, *Readings in Indian Christian Theology*, 83–92.

Cheung Choi-wan. "Sex Industry in Hong Kong." *In God's Image* (June 1990): 33–34.

Ching, Julia. "East Asian Religions." In *World Religions: Eastern Traditions*, edited by Willard G. Oxtoby, 346–467. New York: Oxford Univ. Press, 1996.

Choi Man Ja. "Feminine Images of God in Korean Traditional Religion." In *Frontiers in Asian Christian Theology: Emerging Trends*, edited by R. S. Sugirtharajah, 80–89. Maryknoll, NY: Orbis Books, 1994.

———. "Feminist Christology." In *Asian Women Doing Theology: Report from Singapore Conference, November 20–29, 1987*, edited by Dulcie Abraham, 174–80. Hong Kong: AWRC, 1989.

Christ, Carol P. *Diving Deep and Surfacing: Women Writers on Spiritual Quests*. Boston: Beacon Press, 1980.

Chui, Jane C. N. "A Case: 1997." *In God's Image* (September 1989): 25–30.

Chun Kwang-Rye, Yoshiko Isshiki, Hisako Kinukawa, and Satoko Yamaguchi. *Women Moving Mountains: Feminist Theology in Japan*. Translated and edited by Margaret Warren. Malaysia: AWRC, 2000.

Chung Hyun Kyung. "Asian Christologies and People's Religions." *Voices from the Third World* 19, no. 1 (June 1996): 214–27.

———. "Christian Witness amidst Asian Pluralism and the Search for Spirituality from an Asian Feminist Perspective." *Ewha Journal of Feminist Theology* 1 (1996): 27–37.

———. "Come Holy Spirit, Renew the Whole Creation." *In God's Image* 2, no. 3 (1992): 54–61.

———. "Following Naked Dancing and Long Dreaming." In *Inheriting Our Mother's Gardens: Feminist Theology in Third World Perspective*, edited by

Letty Russell, Kwok Pui-lan, Ada María Isasi-Díaz, and Katie Cannon, 54–74. Louisville, KY: Westminster John Knox Press, 1988.

———. *Goddess-spell according to Hyun Kyung*. Seoul: Yolimwon, 2001.

———. "Han-pu-ri: Doing Theology from Korean Women's Perspective." In *Frontiers in Asian Christian Theology: Emerging Trends*, edited by R. S. Sugirtharajah, 52–64. Maryknoll, NY: Orbis Books, 1994.

———. "'Opium or the Seed for Revolution?' Shamanism: Women-Centered Popular Religiosity in Korea." In *Concilium* 199, *Convergences and Differences*, edited by Leonardo Boff and Virgil Elizondo, 96–106. Edinburgh: T & T Clark, 1988.

———. "Re-Imagining God." *The Witness* 77, no. 7 (July 1994): 26–27.

———. *Struggle to Be the Sun Again*. Maryknoll, NY: Orbis Books, 1990.

———. "Wisdom of Mothers Knows No Boundaries." In *Gospel and Cultures Pamphlet 14—Women's Perspectives: Articulating the Liberating Power of the Gospel*, 28–35. Geneva: WCC, 1996.

———. "Your Comfort vs. My Death." In *Women Resisting Violence*, edited by Mary John Mananzan, Mercy Amba Oduyoye, Elsa Tamez, J. Shannon Clarkson, May C. Grey, and Letty Russell, 129–40. Maryknoll, NY: Orbis Books, 1996.

Chung Sook-Ja. "Becoming Christ: A Woman's Vision." In *God's Image* 22, no. 4 (December 2003): 13–18.

Chung Sook-Ja, Chang Soo-Chul, and Kim Hyun-Sook. "All Kinds of Women in One Place: Korean Women Church." *Journal of Women and Religion* 13 (1995): 1–2.

———. "Korean Women Jesus: Drama Worship." *Journal of Women and Religion* 13 (1995): 45–50.

Chupungco, Anscar J. *Liturgical Inculturation: Sacramentals, Religiosity, and Cathechesis*. Collegeville, MN: The Liturgical Press, 1992.

———. *Liturgies of the Future: The Process and Methods of Inculturation*. New York: Paulist Press, 1989.

Cixous, Hélène. "The Laugh of Medusa." In *A Reader in Feminist Knowledge*, edited by Sneja Gunew, 224–32. New York: Routledge, 1991.

Clarke, Sundar. "Dalit Movement—Need for a Theology." In *Towards a Dalit Theology*, edited by M. E. Prabhakar, 30–47. Delhi: ISPCK, 1988.

Clement of Alexandria. "The Instructor." In *Fathers of the Second Century: Hermas, Tatian, Athenagoras, Theophilus, and Clement of Alexandria (Entire)*, edited by Cleveland A. Cox. Repr. Grand Rapids, MI: Eerdmans, 1979.

Cone, James H. *A Black Theology of Liberation*. 20th anniversary edition. Maryknoll, NY: Orbis Books, 1990.

———. *God of the Oppressed*. Rev. ed. Maryknoll, NY: Orbis Books, 1997.

Constable, Nicole. *Maid to Order in Hong Kong: Stories of Filipina Workers*. Ithaca, NY: Cornell Univ. Press, 1997.

Constantino, Renato. *The Philippines: A Past Revisited (Pre-Spanish-1941)*. Quezon City: by the author, 1975.

Constantino, Renato, and Letizia R. Constantino. *The Philippines: The Continuing Past.* Quezon City: The Foundation for Nationalist Studies, 1978.

Conway, Tony. "Christian Signs and Symbols." In *Culture: A Force for Change*, edited by the Socio-Pastoral Institute, 45–55. Manila: Socio-Pastoral Institute, 1988.

Cox, Harvey. *Fire from Heaven: The Rise of Pentecostal Spirituality and the Reshaping of Religion in the Twenty-First Century*. Reading, MA: Perseus Books, 1995.

Curtis, Ken, Beth Jacobson, Diana Severance, Ann T. Snyder, and Dan Snyder. *Glimpses Issue #43: Time for Reorientation.* Part 1 of a 6–part series on the History of the Church in the Orient (Asia). Worcester, PA: Christian History Institute, 2003.

Dagdag, Theresa. "Emerging Theology in the Philippines Today." In *Currents in Philippine Theology*, edited by Rebecca Asedillo, Liliosa Garibay, and Nonie S. Aviso, 67–81. Quezon City: Institute of Religion and Culture, Phils., 1992.

Daly, Mary. *Beyond God the Father*. London: Women's Press, 1975.

Danker, Frederick William, W. F. Arndt, F. W. Gingrich, and Walter Bauer, eds. *A Greek-English Lexicon of the New Testament and Other Early Christian Literature*. 3rd ed. Chicago: Univ. of Chicago Press, 2000.

David, M. D., ed. *Asia and Christianity*. Bombay: Himalaya Publishing House, 1985.

———. "Introduction: The Nature of Western Colonialism." In *Western Colonialism in Asia and Christianity*, edited by M. D. David. Delhi: Himalaya Publishing House, 1988.

De la Torre, Edicio. *Touching Ground, Taking Root: Theological and Political Reflections on the Philippine Struggle.* London: Catholic Institute for International Relations and British Council of Churches, 1986.

De los Reyes, Isabelo. *La religion antigua de los filipinos*. Manila: Imprinta de el Renacimiento, 1909.

———. *La religión del katipunan*. Madrid: Tipolet de J. Corrales, 1900.

De Mello, Anthony. *One Minute Nonsense*. Chicago: Loyola Press, 1992.

De Mesa, José, and Lode L. Wostyn. *Doing Christology: The Re-Appropriation of a Tradition*. Quezon City: Claretian Publications, 1993.

Deats, Richard L. *Nationalism and Christianity in the Philippines*. Dallas: Southern Methodist Univ. Press, 1967.

Demetillo-Abraham, Becky, and Karina Constantino-David. "Inang Laya." Philippines: Dyna Products, 1986. Audiocassette.

de'Souza, T. R. "The Portuguese in Asia and Their Church Patronage." In *Western Colonialism in Asia and Christianity*, edited by M. D. David, 11–29. Bombay: Himalaya Publishing House, 1988.

Devanandan, Paul. *Paul D. Devanandan: A Selection*, edited by Joachim Wietzke. Madras: The Christian Literature Society, 1983.

Devi, Swarnalatha. "The Struggle of Dalit Christian Women in India." In *Feminist Theology from the Third World*, edited by Ursula King, 135–37. Maryknoll, NY: Orbis Books, 1994.

Dietrich, Gabriele. *A New Thing on Earth*. Delhi: ISPCK, 2001.

———. "Sex, Selective Abortions Replacing Female Infanticide: A Feminist Perspective." *In God's Image* 19, no. 1 (2000): 46–49.

Dillenberger, John, ed. *Martin Luther: Selections from His Writings*. New York: Anchor Books, Doubleday, 1962.

Dingayan, Luna. "Towards a Christology of Struggle: A Proposal for Understanding the Christ." *CTC Bulletin* 10, no. 1 (1991): 15–34.

Dirlik, Arif. "The Postcolonial Aura: Third World Criticism in the Age of Global Capitalism." In *Contemporary Postcolonial Theory: A Reader*, edited by Padmini Mongia, 294–321. London: Arnold, 1996.

Dominguez, Elizabeth. "Biblical Concept of Human Sexuality." *In God's Image* (March 1989): 31–36.

Douglas, Kelly Brown. *The Black Christ*. Maryknoll, NY: Orbis Books, 1994.

EATWOT Asian Women's Consultation, ed. *Spirituality for Life: Women Struggling against Violence*. Manila: EATWOT Philippines and Institute of Women's Studies, St. Scholastica's College, 1994.

EATWOT India. "Search for Life Sustaining Spiritualities in the Context of Globalization." *Voices from the Third World* 21, no. 2 (December 1998): 134–51.

Edwards, David L. *Christianity: The First Two Thousand Years*. Maryknoll, NY: Orbis Books, 1998.

Éla, Jean-Marc. *African Cry*. Maryknoll, NY: Orbis Books, 1986.

Esguerra, Christian V. "6,000 Doctors Studying to Be Nurses; DOH Alarmed." *Philippine Daily Inquirer* (August 4, 2005), 1, 4.

Eusebius of Caesarea. *Ecclesiastical History, Complete and Unabridged*. Updated repr. Peabody, MA: Hendrickson Publishers, 1998.

Fabella, Virginia. "Asian Women and Christology." *In God's Image* (September 1987): 14–20.

———. "Christology and Popular Religions." *Voices from the Third World* 18, no. 2 (December 1995): 22–37.

———. "Christology from an Asian Women's Perspective." In *Asian Faces of Jesus*, edited by R. S. Sugirtharajah, 211–22. Maryknoll, NY: Orbis Books, 1993.

———. "A Common Methodology for Diverse Christologies?" In *With Passion and Compassion: Third World Women Doing Theology*, edited by Virginia Fabella and Mercy Amba Oduyoye, 108–17. Maryknoll, NY: Orbis Books, 1988.

———. "Contextualization." In *Dictionary of Third World Theologies*, edited by Virginia Fabella and R. S. Sugirtharajah, 58–59. Maryknoll, NY: Orbis Books, 2000.

———. "Inculturation." In *Dictionary of Third World Theologies*, edited by Virginia Fabella and R. S. Sugirtharajah, 104–6. Maryknoll, NY: Orbis Books, 2000.

———. "Symbols of John's Resurrection Scene." *Voices from the Third World* 10, no. 4 (December 1987): 24–30.

Fabella, Virginia, and Mercy Amba Oduyoye, eds. *With Passion and Compassion: Third World Women Doing Theology*. Maryknoll, NY: Orbis Books, 1996.

Faria, Stella. "A Reflection on the National Consultation: Ecumenicity of Women's Theological Reflections." In *Towards a Theology of Humanhood: Women's Perspectives*, edited by Aruna Gnanadason, 1–4. Delhi: ISPCK, 1986.

Faustina, S. "From Exile to Exodus: Christian Dalit Women and the Role of Religion." In *Frontiers of Dalit Theology*, edited by M. Devasahayam, 92–99. Madras: ISPCK/Gurukul, 1997.

———. "Untouchability: Abuse of the Total Person." In *Lived Realities: Faith Reflections on Gender Justice*, edited by Elizabeth Joy, 31–48. Bangalore: CISRS Publication Trust for Joint Women's Programme, 1999.

Fein, Karen S. *Asia at Crossroads: The Path Ahead.* New York: Asia Society, 1998.

Ferm, Deane William. *Profiles in Liberation: Thirty-six Portraits of Third World Theologians* (Mystic, CT: Twenty-Third Publications, 1988.

Fernandez, Eleazar S. *Toward a Theology of Struggle*. Maryknoll, NY: Orbis Books, 1994.

Fok Tin-man, "Elderly Women and Poverty in Hong Kong," paper presented at CEDAW seminar, Hong Kong, November 18, 1998. Available online.

Ford, J. Massyngbaerde. *Redeemer, Friend and Mother: Salvation in Antiquity and in the Gospel of John*. Minneapolis: Fortress Press, 1997.

Foreman, Charles W. "Upadhyaya, Brahmabandav." In *Biographical Dictionary of Christian Missions*, edited by Gerald H. Anderson, 689. Grand Rapids, MI: Eerdmans, 1998.

Francia, Myrna, Margaret Lacson, and Roy Chiefe. "Asian Women Doing Theology." In *Woman and Religion*, edited by Mary John Mananzan, 55–63. Manila: Institute of Women's Studies, St. Scholastica's College, 1998.

Gadon, Elinor. *The Once and Future Goddess.* New York: Harper and Row, 1998.

Gandhi, Mahatma. *All Men Are Brothers*. New York: Continuum, 2000.

Gaspar, Karl. "Doing Theology (in a Situation) of Struggle." In *Religion and Society: Towards a Theology of Struggle*, edited by Mary Rosario Battung et al., 45–79. Manila: Forum for Interdisciplinary Endeavors and Studies, 1988.

———. *How Long? Prison Reflections from the Philippines*. Quezon City: Claretian Publications, 1984. Repr. Victoria, Australia: Dove Communications; Maryknoll, NY: Orbis Books, 1986.

Gebara, Ivone. *Out of the Depths: Women's Experience of Evil and Salvation.* Minneapolis: Fortress Press, 2002.
Gensichen, Hans-Werner. "Chenciah, Pandipeddi." In *Biographical Dictionary of Christian Missions*, edited by Gerald H. Anderson, 130. Grand Rapids, MI: Eerdmans, 1998.
Gimbutas, Marija. *The Language of the Goddess.* San Francisco: HarperSan Francisco, 1991.
———. *The Living Goddess.* Berkeley and Los Angeles: Univ. of California Press, 1999.
Gnanadason, Aruna. "Christ Came to Us Today!" *In God's Image* 19, no. 1 (2000): 50.
———. "Dalit Women—the Dalit of the Dalit." In Nirmal, *Towards a Common Dalit Theology*, 109–21.
———. "Foreword." In *Towards a Theology of Humanhood: Women's Perspectives*, edited by Aruna Gnanadason, i–ii. Delhi: ISPCK, 1986.
———. "Reclaiming Motherhood: In Search of an Eco-Feminist Vision." In *Sustainability and Globalization*, edited by Julio De Santa Ana, 130–43. Geneva: WCC, 1996.
———. "What Do These Women Speak Of?" *Voices from the Third World* 16, no. 1 (June 1993): 33–47.
———. "Women and Spirituality." In *Feminist Theology from the Third World: A Reader*, edited by Ursula King, 351–60. London: SPCK; Maryknoll, NY: Orbis Books, 1994.
———. "Women, Economy, and Ecology." In *Ecotheology: Voices from South and North*, edited by David G. Hallman, 179–85. Geneva: WCC, 1994.
———. "Women's Oppression: A Sinful Situation." In *With Passion and Compassion: Third World Women Doing Theology*, edited by Virginia Fabella and Mercy Amba Oduyoye, 69–75. Maryknoll, NY: Orbis Books, 1988.
Goizueta, Roberto S. *Caminemos con Jesús: Toward a Hispanic/Latino Theology of Accompaniment.* Maryknoll, NY: Orbis Books, 1995.
Grant, Jacquelyn. *White Women's Christ and Black Women's Jesus: Feminist Christology and Womanist Response.* Atlanta, GA: Scholars Press, 1989.
Grillmeier, Aloys. *Christ in Christian Tradition: From the Apostolic Age to Chalcedon (451).* Rev. ed. 2 vols. Atlanta, GA: John Knox Press, 1975.
Gupta, Lina. "Kali the Savior." In *After Patriarchy: Feminist Transformations of the World Religions*, edited by Paula M. Cooey, William R. Eakin, and Jay B. McDaniel, 15–38. Maryknoll, NY: Orbis Books, 1991.
Gutiérrez, Gustavo. *A Theology of Liberation.* 15th anniversary edition. Maryknoll, NY: Orbis Books, 1988.
———. *Teología de la liberacíon, Pespectivas.* Lima: CEP, 1971.
———. *We Drink from Our Own Wells: The Spiritual Journey of a People.* Maryknoll, NY: Orbis Books; Melbourne: Dove Communications, 1984.

Hackett, Rosalind I. J. "Women in African Religions." In *Religion and Women*, edited by Arvind Sharma, 61–93. Albany: State Univ. of New York, 1994.

Harrison, Beverly Wildung. *Making Connections: Essays in Feminist Social Ethics*, edited by Carol Robb. Boston: Beacon Press, 1985.

Heyward, Carter. *Touching Our Strength: The Erotic as Power and the Love of God*. New York: Harper and Row, 1989.

Hnuni, R. L. "Biblical Basis for Empowerment of Women." In *Transforming Theology for Empowering Women*, edited by R. L. Hnuni, 131–39. Jorhat, Assam: Women's Studies of Eastern Theological College, 1999.

———. "The Role of Women in the Church." In *Transforming Theology for Empowering Women*, edited by R. L. Hnuni, 63–76. Jorhat, Assam: Women's Studies of Eastern Theological College, 1999.

———. "Vision for Women in North East India." In *Transforming Theology for Empowering Women*, edited by R. L. Hnuni, 140–54. Jorhat, Assam: Women's Studies of Eastern Theological College, 1999.

Humbert, Elie. *C. G. Jung: The Fundamentals of Theory and Practice*. Wilmette, IL: Chiron Publications, 1988.

Ibong Malaya. "Ibong Malaya: Songs of Freedom and Struggle from Philippine Prisons." Vol. 1. Singapore: Resource Center for Philippine Concerns, 1982. Audiocassette.

Ileto, Reynaldo C. *Pasyon and Revolution: Popular Movements in the Philippines, 1840–1910*. Quezon City: Ateneo de Manila Univ. Press, 1979.

Infante, Teresita. "Filipino Women as Religious Practitioners." *In God's Image* 12, no. 3 (Autumn 1993): 22–26.

Irigaray, Luce. "This Sex Which Is Not One." In *A Reader in Feminist Knowledge*, edited by Sneja Gunew, 204–11. New York: Routledge, 1991.

Isasi-Díaz, Ada María. *Mujerista Theology*. Maryknoll, NY: Orbis Books, 1996.

Isherwood, Lisa. *Introducing Feminist Christologies*. Cleveland, OH: Pilgrim Press, 2001.

———. *Liberating Christ*. Cleveland, OH: Pilgrim Press, 1999.

Iswary, Nirala. "Violation of Human Rights in Bodo Land." *In God's Image* 19, no. 4 (2000): 15–18.

Jawardena, Kumari. *Feminism and Nationalism in the Third World*. London: Zed Books, 1986.

Jenkins, Philip. *The Next Christendom: The Coming of Global Christianity*. Oxford: Oxford Univ. Press, 2002.

Jensen, Anne. *God's Self-Confident Daughters: Early Christianity and the Liberation of Women*. Louisville, KY: Westminster John Knox Press, 1996.

Johnson, Elizabeth A. *She Who Is: The Mystery of God in Feminist Theological Discourse*. New York: Crossroad, 1994.

Jones, Serene. *Feminist Theory and Christian Theology: Cartographies of Grace*. Minneapolis, MN: Fortress Press, 2000.

Jong Ok-Sun. "Former 'Comfort Woman for the Japanese Army.'" *In God's Image* 15, no. 2 (Summer 1996): 22–23.

Joy, Elizabeth. "Divorce: A Last Resort for Survival." In *Lived Realities: Faith Reflections on Gender Justice*, edited by Elizabeth Joy, 129–33. Bangalore: CISRS/JWP, 1999.

———, ed. *Lived Realities: Faith Reflections on Gender Justice*. Bangalore: CISRS Publications Trust for Joint Women's Programme, 1999.

———. "The Meaning and Origin of Dalit Theology." M.Th. thesis, South Asia Theological Research Institute, 1998.

Justice, Peace, and Creation Team (WCC), *Alternative Globalization Addressing Peoples and Earth (AGAPE): A Background Document*. Geneva: WCC, 2005.

Kähler, Martin. *The So-Called Historical Jesus and the Historic Biblical Christ*. Philadelphia: Fortress Press, 1964.

Kang Nam-Soon. "Creating 'Dangerous Memory': Challenges for Asian and Korean Feminist Theology." *Ecumenical Review* 47, no. 1 (1995): 21–31.

Kappen, Sebastian. *Jesus and Freedom*. Maryknoll, NY: Orbis Books, 1977.

———. "Jesus and Transculturation." In *Asian Faces of Jesus*, edited by R. S. Sugirtharajah, 173–87. Maryknoll, NY: Orbis Books, 1993.

———. "Towards an Indian Theology of Liberation." In Sugirtharajah and Hargreaves, *Readings in Indian Christian Theology*, 24–36.

Katoppo, Marianne. "The Church and Prostitution in Asia." In *Feminist Theology from the Third World: A Reader*, edited by Ursula King, 114–23. Maryknoll, NY: Orbis Books, 1994.

———. *Compassionate and Free: An Asian Women's Theology*. Geneva: WCC, 1979.

———. "Women That Make Asia Alive." In *New Eyes for Reading: Biblical and Theological Reflections by Women from the Third World*, edited by John S. Pobee and Bärbel Von Wartenberg-Potter, 96–100. Geneva: WCC, 1986.

Kidwell, Clara Sue, Homer Noley, and George E. Tinker. *Native American Theology*. Maryknoll, NY: Orbis Books, 2001.

Kim Chi Ha. *The Gold-Crowned Jesus and Other Writings*, edited by Chong Sun Kim and Shelly Killen. Maryknoll, NY: Orbis Books, 1978.

Kim, Grace Ji-Sun. *The Grace of Sophia: A Korean North American Women's Christology*. Cleveland, OH: Pilgrim Press, 2002.

Kim Yong-Bock. "Doing Theology in Asia Today: A Korean Perspective." In *Asian Christian Theology: Emerging Themes*, edited by Douglas Elwood, 315–22. Philadelphia: Westminster Press, 1980.

———. "Jesus Christ among Asian Minjung: A Christological Reflection." *Voices from the Third World* 19, no. 2 (1996): 83–127.

———, ed. *Minjung Theology: People as Subjects of History*. Singapore: The Commission on Theological Concerns, CCA, 1981.

Kinukawa, Hisako. *Women and Jesus in Mark: A Japanese Feminist Perspective*. Maryknoll, NY: Orbis Books, 1994.

Knott, Kim. *Hinduism: A Very Short Introduction*. Oxford: Oxford Univ. Press, 1998.

Ko Chong-hui. "My Neighbor, Mrs. Ku Cha-Myong." *In God's Image*, no. 28 (June 1988).

Koester, Hans. "The Indian Religion of the Goddess Shakti." *The Journal of the Siam Society* 23, no. 1 (1929): 1–18.

Korean Women Theologians. "Declaration of Korean Women Theologians on the Peace and Reunification of the Korean People." *In God's Image* (June 1988): 51–53.

Korten, David C. *When Corporations Rule the World.* West Hartford, CT: Kumarian Press; San Francisco: Berrett-Koehler Publishers, 1995.

Kostyal, K. M., ed. *National Geographic: Peoples of the World.* Washington, DC: National Geographic Society, 2001.

Kraemer, Hendrik. *The Christian Message in a Non-Christian World.* New York: Harper and Brothers, 1938. Repr. Grand Rapids, MI: Kregel Publications, 1977.

Kroeker, Wendy. "Dancing with Miriam." In Ruiz-Duremdes and Kroeker, *Dance amid Struggle*, 13–20.

Kumari, Prema Shantha. "The Christian Dalit Women Today." In *Towards a Dalit Theology*, edited by M. E. Prabhakar, 164–65. Delhi: ISPCK, 1988.

Kuribayashi, Teruo. "*Burakumin* Liberation Theology." In *Dictionary of Third World Theologies*, edited by Virginia Fabella and R. S. Sugirtharajah, 33. Maryknoll, NY: Orbis Books, 2000.

Kwok Pui-lan. "Book Review: 'The Poor Woman': A Critical Analysis of Asian Theology and Contemporary Chinese Fiction by Women by Wai-Ching Angela Wong." *Quest* 1, no. 1 (November 2002): 94–104.

———. "Chinese Non-Christian Perceptions of Christ." *Concilium* 2 (1993): 24–32.

———. "A Chinese Perspective." In *Theology by the People*, edited by Samuel Amirtham and John S. Pobee, 78–83. Geneva: WCC, 1986.

———. *Chinese Women and Christianity 1860–1927*. Atlanta, GA: Scholars' Press, 1992.

———. *Discovering the Bible in the Non-Biblical World.* Maryknoll, NY: Orbis Books, 1995.

———. "Ecology and Christology." *Feminist Theology* 15 (May 1997): 113–25.

———. "Feminist Theology as Intercultural Discourse." In *The Cambridge Companion to Feminist Theology*, edited by Susan Frank Parsons, 23–39. Cambridge, UK: Cambridge Univ. Press, 2002.

———. "The Future of Feminist Theology: An Asian Perspective." In *Feminist Theology from the Third World: A Reader*, edited by Ursula King, 63–76. Maryknoll, NY: Orbis Books, 1994.

———. "God Weeps with Our Pain." In *New Eyes for Reading*, edited by John S. Pobee and Bärbel Von Wartenberg-Potter, 90–95. Geneva: WCC, 1986.

———. *Introducing Asian Feminist Theology*. Cleveland, OH: Pilgrim Press, 2000.
———. "Jesus/the Native: Biblical Studies from a Postcolonial Perspective." In *Teaching the Bible: Discourses and Politics of Biblical Pedagogy*, edited by Fernando Segovia and Mary Ann Tolbert, 69–85. Maryknoll, NY: Orbis Books, 1998.
———. "On Color-Coding Jesus: An Interview with Kwok Pui Lan." In *The Postcolonial Bible*, edited by R. S. Sugirtharajah, 176–88. Sheffield: Sheffield Academic Press, 1998.
———. *Postcolonial Imagination and Feminist Theology*. Louisville, KY: Westminster John Knox Press, 2005.
Labayen, Julio X. "Cry of the People—Challenge to the Churches." *Voices from the Third World* 10, no. 1 (1987): 3–10.
Lascano, Lydia L. "Signs of New Life." *In God's Image* (March 1989): 5–8.
———. "Women and the Christ Event." Paper presented at the EATWOT meeting, Manila, 1985.
———. "Women Rising: A Testimony." *Kalinangan* 12, no. 1 (1992): 17–19.
Layosa, Linda R. "Anywhere, Everywhere: The D.H.'S Saga." In *From America to Africa: Voices of Filipino Women Overseas*, edited by Lorna Kalaw-Tirol, 149–64. Makati, Philippines: FAI Resource Management, 2000.
Lee Hya-Jae. "Celebrating International Women's Day: Korean Women's Perspective." *In God's Image* (April 1986): 22.
Lee Mi Kung. "U.S. Troops in South Korea and Prostitution." *In God's Image* (March 1990): 9–11.
Lee Oo Chung. *In Search for Our Foremothers' Spirituality*. Seoul: AWRC, 1994.
———. "Korean Culture and Feminist Theology." *In God's Image* (September 1987): 36–38.
———, ed. *Women of Courage: Asian Women Reading the Bible*. Seoul: AWRC, 1992.
Lee, Peter K. H. "Hong Kong: Living in the Shadow of the Third World." In *Asian Christian Spirituality: Reclaiming Traditions*, edited by Virginia Fabella, Peter K. H. Lee, and David Kwang-sun Suh, 106–20. Maryknoll, NY: Orbis Books, 1992.
Ligo, Arche, and Mary Rosario Battung. "Cosmic Spirituality for the Wholeness of Life." *Asia Pacific Women's Studies Journal* 5 (1995): 53–57.
Longkumer, N. Limatula. "Christianity and Naga Women." In *Transforming Theology for Empowering Women*, edited by R. L. Hnuni, 53–62. Jorhat, Assam: Women's Studies of Eastern Theological College, 1999.
Lorde, Audre. *Sister Outsider*. Freedom, CA: The Crossing Press, 1984.
Lui Hon-Kwong. "Poverty and Income Disparity in Hong Kong." *HKCER Letters* 42 (January 1997). Available online.
Lung Ngan Ling. "An Overview of Women's Situation in Asia." *In God's Image* 17, no. 4 (1998): 2–8.

Luther, Martin. "Disputation at Heidelberg, 1518." In *Luther: Early Theological Works*, vol. 16, edited by James Atkinson, 274–307. Philadelphia: Westminster Press, 1962.

Lyotard, Jean-François. *The Postmodern Condition: A Report on Knowledge*. Minneapolis: Univ. of Minnesota Press, 1989.

Magtolis-Briones, Leonor. "Foreword," in *Social Watch Philippines 2005 Report: Race for Survival.* Quezon City: Social Watch Philippines, 2005.

Manalo, Ma. Corazon. "Dance: A Woman's Way to Peace." *Religious Studies De La Salle Journal* 19, no. 2 (December 1996): 77–86.

Mananzan, Mary John. *Challenges to the Inner Room: Selected Essays and Speeches on Women*. Manila: Institute of Women's Studies, St. Scholastica's College, 1998.

———. "Emerging Alternatives to Globalization and Transformative Action." *Voices from the Third World* 21, no. 1 (June 1998): 119–33.

———, ed. *Essays on Women.* Rev. ed. Manila: St. Scholastica's College, 1991.

———. "Paschal Mystery from a Philippine Perspective." In *Concilium 2: Any Room for Christ in Asia?*, 86–94. London: T & T Clark, 1993.

———. "Theological Perspective of a Religious Woman Today." In *The Future of Liberation Theology: Essays in Honor of Gustavo Gutiérrez*, edited by Marc H. Ellis and Otto Maduro, 420–31. Maryknoll, NY: Orbis Books, 1989.

———. "Who Is Jesus Christ?: Reflection from the Philippines." *Voices from the Third World* 11, no. 2 (December 1988): 1–16.

———. "Who Is Jesus Christ?: Responses from the Philippines." *In God's Image* 12, no. 3 (Autumn 1993): 39–41.

———. "Woman and Religion." In *Religion and Society: Towards a Theology of Struggle*, edited by Mary Rosario Battung, 107–20. Manila: Fides, 1988.

Mangahas, Fe. "Are Babaylans Extinct? How the Spanish Colonialist Banished the Native Priestess in the Philippines." *In God's Image* 12, no. 3 (Autumn 1993): 27–33.

Martinez, Salvador T. "Jesus Christ in Popular Piety in the Philippines." In *Asian Faces of Jesus*, edited by R. S. Sugirtharajah, 247–57. Maryknoll, NY: Orbis Books, 1993.

Marx, Karl, and Friedrich Engels. *On Religion*. Repr. Atlanta, GA: Scholars Press, 1982.

Massey, James. "Ingredients for a Dalit Theology." In *Towards a Dalit Theology*, edited by M. E. Prabhakar, 57–63. Delhi: ISPCK, 1988.

———. *Roots of Dalit History, Christianity, Theology, and Spirituality*. Delhi: ISPCK, 1996.

Mataji, Vandana. *Jesus the Christ: Who Is He? What Was His Message?* Anand, India: Gujarat Sahitya Prakash, 1987.

———. "Water Symbolism in the Gospel of St. John in the Light of Indian Spirituality." In Sugirtharajah and Hargreaves, *Readings in Indian Christian Theology*, 200–213.

Mathews, Omana. "Rape: A Trauma until Death." In *Lived Realities: Faith Reflections on Gender Justice*, edited by Elizabeth Joy, 58–64. Bangalore: CISRS Publications Trust for Joint Women's Programme, 1999.

McDowell, Linda. "Enlightenment/Enlightenment Theory." In *A Feminist Glossary of Human Geography*, edited by Linda McDowell and Joanne P. Sharp, 71. New York: Arnold, 1999.

McDowell, Linda, and Joanne P. Sharp, eds. *A Feminist Glossary of Human Geography*. London: Arnold, 1999.

Melanchton, Monica. "Christology and Women." In *We Dare to Dream: Doing Theology as Asian Women*, edited by Virginia Fabella and Sun Ai Lee Park, 15–23. Hong Kong: AWRC/EATWOT Women's Commission in Asia, 1989.

———. "Jesus as Wisdom." In *Envisioning a New Heaven and a New Earth*, edited by Lalrinawmi Ralte, 238–44. Delhi: National Council of Churches of India/ISPCK, 1998.

Mendoza, Everett. *Radical and Evangelical: Portrait of a Filipino Christian*. Quezon City: New Day Publishers, 1999.

Merchant, Carolyn. *The Death of Nature: Women, Ecology, and the Scientific Revolution*. San Francisco: HarperSan Francisco, 1989.

Messer, Donald. "The Asian Face of the Global HIV/AIDS Scenario." In *Health, Healing, and Wholeness: Asian Theological Perspectives on HIV/AIDS*, edited by A. Wati Longchar, 1–14. Jorhat, Assam: ETE-WCC/CCA, 2005.

Miclat-Cacayan, Agnes. "The Little Birds of Prey: Two Faces of the Prostituted Girl Child in the Philippines." *In God's Image* 17, no. 2 (1998): 16–26.

———. "Nurturing Goddess and Powerful Priestess: Legacy from Our Indigenous Spirituality." In *From the Womb of Mebuyan*, edited by Belo Caharian, 10–35. Davao City, Philippines: Hinabi Women's Circle, 1998.

Migrante International. *The Progressive Movement of Overseas Compatriots*. Quezon City: Migrante International, 1999.

Moffet, Samuel Hugh. *A History of Christianity in Asia*. Vol. 1. Maryknoll, NY: Orbis Books, 1998.

Moltmann, Jürgen. *The Crucified God*. Minneapolis: Fortress Press, 1993.

Montenegro, Jane Ella. "Women's Ministries: Words and Works of Seven Women Church Workers of the United Church of Christ in the Philippines, 1930–1997." Master's thesis, Institute of Formation and Religious Studies, 2002.

Mookerjee, Ajit. *Kali the Feminine Force*. Bennington, VT: Destiny Books, 1988.

Morin, Karen. "Autobiography." In *A Feminist Glossary of Human Geography*, edited by Linda McDowell and Joanne P. Sharp, 10. New York: Arnold, 1999.

Morley, Janet. *All Desires Known*. Wilton, CT: Morehouse-Barlow, 1988.

Morrison, Toni. *Beloved*. New York: Plume Books, 1988.

Mveng, Engelbert. "Third World Theology—What Theology? What Third World?" In *Irruption of the Third World*, edited by Virginia Fabella and Sergio Torres, 217–21. Maryknoll, NY: Orbis Books, 1983.

Naranayan, Vasudha. "The Hindu Tradition." In *World Religions: Eastern Traditions*, edited by Willard G. Oxtoby, 13–133. New York: Oxford Univ. Press, 1996.

Narciso-Apuan, Victoria. "In Search of Authentic Discipleship." In *And She Said No!*, edited by Liberato C. Bautista and Elizabeth Rifareal, 113–18. Quezon City: National Council of Churches in the Philippines, 1990.

Ng, Michael. "Rising Poverty on the Agenda for Tung's Address." In *The Standard*, January 10, 2005. Available online.

Nirmal, Arvind P. "Towards a Christian Dalit Theology." In *A Reader in Dalit Theology*, edited by Arvind P. Nirmal, 53–70. Madras: Gurukul Lutheran Theological College and Research Institute.

———, ed. *Towards a Common Dalit Ideology*. Madras: Gurukul Lutheran Theological College and Research Institute, 1989.

O'Brian, Niall. *Island of Tears, Island of Hope: Living the Gospel in a Revolutionary Situation*. Maryknoll, NY: Orbis Books, 1993.

Obusan, Teresita B. "Foreword." In *Roots of Filipino Spirituality*, edited by Teresita B. Obusan. Philippines: Mamamathala, 1998.

O'Day, Gail R. "John." In *Women's Bible Commentary: Expanded Edition with Apocrypha*, edited by Carol A. Newsom and Sharon H. Ringe, 381–93. Louisville, KY: Westminster John Knox Press, 1998.

Oduyoye, Mercy Amba. *Daughters of Anowa: African Women and Patriarchy*. Maryknoll, NY: Orbis Books, 1995.

———. *Hearing and Knowing: Theological Reflections on Christianity in Africa*. Maryknoll, NY: Orbis Books, 1991.

———. *Introducing African Women's Theology*. Cleveland, OH: Pilgrim Press, 2001.

Ongkiko, Ellen. "Is Your Gender an Issue?" edited by Ellen Ongkiko. Manila: Asian Social Institute Communication Center, 1991. Videocassette.

Oracion, Levi. *God with Us: Reflections on the Theology of Struggle in the Philippines*. Dumaguete City: Silliman Univ. Divinity School, 2001.

Orevillo-Montenegro, Muriel. "Shall I Cling to the Old Rugged Cross? Interrogating and Re-thinking the Power of the Cross." *CTC Bulletin* 20, no. 3 (December 2004): 1–13.

Ortner, Sherry. "Is Female to Male as Nature Is to Culture?" In *Readings in Ecology and Feminist Theology*, edited by Mary Heather McKinnon and Moni McIntyre. Kansas City, MO: Sheed and Ward, 1995.

Oxtoby, Willard G. "The Nature of Religion." In *World Religions: Eastern Traditions*, edited by Willard G. Oxtoby, 486–506. New York: Oxford Univ. Press, 1996.

Padillo-Olesen, Elizabeth Soriso. "Easter Morning." *In God's Image* 20, no. 1 (March 2000): 49.

———. "Holy Friday." *In God's Image* 20, no. 1 (March 2001): 48.

Pangilinan-Gran, Vizminda. *Kalinangan* 12, no. 1 (1992): 27.

Panikkar, K. M. *Asia and Western Dominance: A Survey of the Vasco Da Gama Epoch of Asian History 1498–1945*. London: George Allen and Unwin Ltd., 1959.

Panikkar, Raimundo. "The Jordan, the Tiber, and the Ganges: Three Kairological Moments of Christic Self-Consciousness." In *The Myth of Christian Uniqueness*, edited by John Hick and Paul Knitter, 89–116. Maryknoll, NY: Orbis Books, 1987.

———. *The Unknown Christ of Hinduism: Towards an Ecumenical Christophany*. Maryknoll, NY: Orbis Books, 1981.

Park Soon Kyung. "Unification of Korea and the Task of Feminist Theology." *In God's Image* (June 1988): 17–23.

Park Sun Ai Lee. "Asian Women's Theological Reflection." *East Asia Journal of Theology* 3, no. 2 (1985): 182.

———. "Behold I Make All Things New." *In God's Image* (December 1987–March 1988): 6.

———. "Confucianism and Women." *In God's Image* (June 1989): 27–29.

———. "Korean Women as the Lamb Bearing the Sins of the World." *In God's Image* (June 1988): 30–32.

———. "Reflections." *In God's Image* (September 1987).

———. "Religion and Menstruation." *In God's Image* (December 1982): 4–7, 10.

———. "A Theological Reflection." In *We Dare to Dream*, edited by Virginia Fabella and Park Sun Ai Lee, 72–82. Maryknoll, NY: Orbis Books, 1989.

Park Young-sook. "Justice, Peace, and the Integrity of Creation: Justice and Peace (Life) Movement and Korean Women." *In God's Image* 10, no. 1 (1991): 41–49.

Paul, Rose. "Educated Women in the Marriage Market." In *Dalit and Women: Quest for Humanity*, edited by V. Devasahayam, 168–78. Madras: Gurukul Lutheran Theological College and Research Institute, 1992.

PCPR (Promotion of Church People's Rights). *That We May Remember*. Quezon City: Promotion of Church People's Rights, 1989.

PCPR and Kasimbayan. "Lakbayan Ng Mamamayan Laban Sa Kahirapan." *Kalinangan* 7, no. 2 (December 1997).

Philippine Delegates to Asian Theological Conference I. "Philippine Group Reflection." *Voices from the Third World* 2, no. 1 (June 1979): 19–20.

Philippine Delegates to Asian Theological Conference III. "Philippine Search for a Liberation Spirituality." In *Currents in Philippine Theology*, edited by Rebecca Asedillo, Liliosa Garibay, and Nonie S. Aviso, 39–52. Quezon City: Institute of Religion and Culture, Phils., 1992.

Pieris, Aloysius. *An Asian Theology of Liberation*. Maryknoll, NY: Orbis Books, 1988.

———. "The Buddha and the Christ: Mediators of Liberation." In *Asian Faces of Jesus*, edited by R. S. Sugirtharajah, 46–61. Maryknoll, NY: Orbis Books, 1993.

———. "Christology in Asia." *Voices from the Third World* 11, no. 2 (1988): 155–72.

———. "The Dynamics of A.T.C.: A Reply to the Editor of Satyodaya." *Voices from the Third World* 2, no. 1 (June 1979): 23–28.

———. *Fire and Water: Basic Issues in Asian Buddhism and Christianity*. Maryknoll, NY: Orbis Books, 1996.

———. "Ideology and Religion: Some Debatable Points." *Voices from the Third World* 8, no. 4 (December 1985): 74–83.

———. "Inter-Religious Dialogue and Theology of Religions." *Voices from the Third World* 15, no. 2 (December 1992): 177–88.

———. *Love Meets Wisdom: A Christian Experience of Buddhism*. Maryknoll, NY: Orbis Books, 1988.

———. "Towards an Asian Theology of Liberation: Some Religio-Cultural Guidelines." In *Asia's Struggle for Full Humanity: Toward a Relevant Theology*, edited by Virginia Fabella, 75–95. Maryknoll, NY: Orbis Books, 1988.

———. "Two Encounters in My Theological Journey." In *Frontiers in Asian Christian Theology: Emerging Trends*, edited by R. S. Sugirtharajah, 141–46. Maryknoll, NY: Orbis Books, 1994.

Pomaika'i-McGregor, Davianna. "1989–1998: Rethinking the US in Paradise." *Rethinking the US in Paradise Newsletter* 1, no. 1 (July 1998): 1–3.

Prabhakar, M. E. "The Search for a Dalit Theology." In *A Reader in Dalit Theology*, edited by Arvind P. Nirmal, 41–52. Madras: Gurukul Lutheran College and Research Institute, 1990.

Prasuna, N. G. "The Dalit Woman." In *Frontiers of Dalit Theology*, edited by V. Devasahayam, 100–116. Madras: ISPCK/Gurukul, 1997.

Raats, Pieter Jan. *A Structural Study of Bagobo Myths and Rites*. Cebu City, Philippines: The Univ. of San Carlos, 1969.

Rahner, Karl. "What Is a Christian?" In *Readings in Christian Thought*, edited by Hugh T. Kerr, 364–68. Nashville. TN: Abingdon Press, 1966.

Raj, Anthony. "Disobedience: A Legitimate Act for Dalit Liberation." In Nirmal, *Towards a Common Dalit Theology*, 39–51.

Rajaratnam, K. "Woman through the Ages: A Brief Survey." In *Feminist Theology: Perspectives and Praxis*, edited by Prasana Kumari, 1–23. Chennai: Gurukul Lutheran Theological College and Research Institute, 1999.

Rajashekar, Esther. "Devadasi System: Sexual Abuse in the Name of God." In *Lived Realities: Faith Reflections on Gender Justice*, edited by Elizabeth Joy, 49–57. Bangalore: CISRS Publications Trust, 1999.

Ralte, Lalrinawmi. "Doing Tribal Women's Theology." *In God's Image* 19, no. 4 (2000): 2–4.

———. "A Silent Cry." *In God's Image* 19, no. 4 (2000): 12–14.

Rambuyon, Hope Joyce. "Nanay Minda." *Kalinangan* 12, no. 1 (1992): 27.

Riley, Gregory J. *One Jesus, Many Christs: How Jesus Inspired Not One True Christianity but Many*. San Francisco: HarperSan Francisco, 1999.

Rizál, José. *Noli Me Tangere*. Honululu: Univ. of Hawaii Press, 1997.

Robinson, Gnana. "Purity and Pollution: A Theological Perspective." In *Feminist Theology: Perspective and Praxis*, edited by Prasanna Kumari, 316–30. Chennai: Gurukul Lutheran Theological College and Research Institute, 1999.

Rose, Renate. "Messianic Economics and Cultures of Hospitality." Honolulu, HI: n.p., August 1998.

Ruether, Rosemary Radford. *Sexism and God-Talk*. Boston: Beacon Press, 1983.

Ruiz-Duremdes, Sharon Rose Joy. "Human Rights: A Christian Imperative." *Kalinangan* 17, no. 2 (December 1997): 21–24.

———. "Peopling Theology." *In God's Image* 19, no. 1 (2000): 15–21.

———. "Solidarity and Spirituality: A Theology of Life." In Ruiz-Duremdes and Kroeker, *Dance amid Struggle*, 5–11.

Ruiz-Duremdes, Sharon Rose Joy, and Wendy Kroeker, eds. *Dance amid Struggle: Stories and Songs of Hope*. Quezon City: AWIT Publications, 1998.

Said, Edward W. *Orientalism*. New York: Vintage Books, 1977.

Samartha, Stanley J. "The Cross and the Rainbow." In *The Myth of Christian Uniqueness*, edited by John Hick and Paul Knitter, 69–88. Maryknoll, NY: Orbis Books, 1987.

———. *The Hindu Response to the Unbound Christ*. Madras: The Christian Literature Society, 1974.

———. *One Christ—Many Religions: Toward a Revised Christology*. Maryknoll, NY: Orbis Books, 1991.

———. *The Search for New Hermeneutics in Asian Christian Theology*. Bangalore: Board of Theological Education of the Senate of Serampore College, 1987.

———. "The Unbound Christ: Toward a Christology in India Today." In *Asian Christian Theology: Emerging Themes*, edited by Douglas Elwood, 135–45. Philadelphia: The Westminster Press, 1980.

Samuel, Prasanna K. "Church and Women." In *Dalits and Women: Quest for Humanity*, edited by V. Devasahayam, 190–94. Madras: Gurukul Lutheran Theological College and Research Institute, 1992.

San Juan, Epifanio, Jr.. *Beyond Postcolonial Theory*. New York: St. Martin's Press, 1998.

Saraswathy, Govindarajan. "Caste, Women and Violence." In *Dalits and Women: Quest for Humanity*, edited by M. Devasahayam, 149–57. Madras: Gurukul Lutheran Theological College and Research Institute, 1992.

Sarup, Madan. *An Introductory Guide to Post-Structuralism and Postmodernism*. 2nd ed. Athens: Univ. of Georgia Press, 1993.

Scherer, James A. "International Missionary Council." In *The Encyclopedia of Christianity*, edited by Geoffrey W. Bromiley, 726–28. Grand Rapids, MI: Eerdmans; Leiden: Brill, 2001.

Schmitt, Eric. "U.S. Combat Force of 1,700 Is Headed to the Philippines." *The New York Times*, February 21, 2003, 1–A16.

Schüssler Fiorenza, Elisabeth. *Jesus, Miriam's Child, Sophia's Prophet*. New York: Continuum, 1994.

———. *Jesus and the Politics of Interpretation*. New York: Continuum, 2000.

Schweitzer, Albert. *The Quest of the Historical Jesus: A Critical Study of Its Progress from Reimarus to Wrede*. New York: Macmillan, 1968.

Scofield, David. "Sex and Denial in South Korea." *Asia Times Online*.

Selvi, Kamal Raja. "The Dalit Woman—Fourth Class Citizen." In *Frontiers of Dalit Theology*, edited by M. Devasahayam, 117–29. Madras: ISPCK/ Gurukul, 1997.

Shanti, Margaret. "Hinduism: Caste, Gender and Violence." *LILA: Asia-Pacific Women's Studies Journal* 5, (1995): 17–22.

Shiva, Vandana. *Staying Alive: Women, Ecology, and Development*. London: Zed Books, 1989.

Shum Yun Shan. "1989 . . . China . . . My Reflection." *In God's Image* (September 1989): 31–33.

Sionil Jose, F. *Three Filipino Women*. Manila: Solidaridad Publishing House, 1999.

Smith, Andy. "For All Those Who Were Indian in a Former Life." In *Ecofeminism and the Sacred*, edited by Carol Adams, 168–71. New York: Continuum, 1992.

Snyder, Mary Hembrow. *The Christology of Rosemary Radford Ruether: A Critical Introduction*. Mystic, CT: Twenty-Third Publications, 1988.

So, Alvin Y., and Yok-shiu F. Lee, eds. *Asia's Environmental Movements: Comparative Perspectives*. New York: M. E. Sharpe, 1999.

Sobrino, Jon. "The Crucified Peoples: Yahweh's Suffering Servant Today." *Voices from the Third World* 16, no. 1 (1993): 85–98.

———. *Jesus the Liberator: A Historical-Theological View*. Maryknoll, NY: Orbis Books, 1993.

———. "Preface." In *Systematic Theology: Perspective from Liberation Theology*, edited by Jon Sobrino and Ignacio Ellacuría, vii–xi. Maryknoll, NY: Orbis Books, 1993.

———. "Systematic Christology: Jesus Christ, the Absolute Mediator of the Reign of God." In *Systematic Theology: Perspective from Liberation Theology*, edited by Jon Sobrino and Ignacio Ellacuría, 124–45. Maryknoll, NY: Orbis Books, 1993.

Social Watch Philippines 2005 Report: Race for Survival. Quezon City: Social Watch Philippines, 2005.

Somebang-Ocampo, Laura. "A Response to the Paper [Christology in a Changing Church and Society by Melanio Aoanan]." *CTC Bulletin* 8–9, no. 3–4 (October 1995): 42–45.

Song, Choan-Seng. "Christ behind the Mask Dance—Christology of People and Their Cultures." *CTC Bulletin* 3, no. 3 (December 1982): 29–43.

———. *The Compassionate God*. Maryknoll, NY: Orbis Books, 1982.

———. *Jesus, the Crucified People*. Minneapolis: Fortress Press, 1996.

———. "Oh, Jesus, Here with Us!" In *Asian Faces of Jesus*, edited by R. S. Sugirtharajah, 131–48. Maryknoll, NY: Orbis Books, 1993.

———. *The Tears of Lady Meng: A Parable of People's Political Theology*. Maryknoll, NY: Orbis Books, 1982.

———. *Theology from the Womb of Asia*. Maryknoll, NY: Orbis Books, 1986.

Stiglitz, Joseph E. *Globalization and Its Discontents*. New York: W. W. Norton, 2001.

Suarez, Oscar S. *Protestantism and Authoritarian Politics: The Politics of Repression and the Future of Ecumenical Witness in the Philippines.* Quezon City: New Day Publishers, 1999.

Sugirtharajah, R. S. *Asian Biblical Hermeneutics and Postcolonialism: Contesting the Interpretations*. Maryknoll, NY: Orbis Books, 1998.

———. "Prologue and Perspective." In *Asian Faces of Jesus,* edited by R. S. Sugirtharajah. Maryknoll, NY: Orbis Books, 1993.

Sugirtharajah, R. S., and Cecil Hargreaves, eds. *Readings in Indian Christian Theology*. London: SPCK, 1993.

Suh David Kwang-sun. "Asian Theology in a Changing Asia: Towards an Asian Theological Agenda for the 21st Century." *CTC Bulletin,* Special Supplement 1 (November 1997).

———. "Jesus and Messianic Theology." *Voices from the Third World* 8, no. 1 (March, 1985): 86–87.

———. *Korean Minjung in Christ*. Hong Kong: Christian Conference of Asia, 1991.

———. "Theology of Story Telling: A Theology by Minjung." *Voices from the Third World* 9, no. 2 (1986): 43–49.

Suh Nam-Dong. "Towards a Theology of Han." In *Minjung Theology: People as the Subjects of History*, edited by the Commission on Theological Concerns of CCA, 55–69. London: Zed; Maryknoll, NY: Orbis Books; Singapore: CCA, 1981.

Sun Soon-Hwa. "Women Ministers and the Oppressed in Korea." *In God's Image* 2, no. 2 (Summer 1992): 48–57.

Swidler, Leonard. "Jesus Was a Feminist," *Catholic World* 212 (January 1971): 177–83. Available online.

Tamez, Elsa, ed. *Through Her Eyes: Women's Theology from Latin America.* Maryknoll, NY: Orbis Books, 1989.

Tapia, Elizabeth S. "Asian Women Doing Theology: The Challenge of Feminism for Theologizing." In Ruiz-Duremdes and Kroeker, *Dance amid Struggle*.

———. "The Contribution of Philippine Christian Women to Asian Women's Theology." Ph.D. diss., Claremont Graduate School, 1989.

———. "Women Leaders Are Wounded Healers." *In God's Image* 21, no. 1 (March 2002): 3–5.

Tauli-Corpus, Victoria. "Reclaiming Earth-Based Spirituality: Indigenous Women in the Cordillera." In *Women Healing Earth*, edited by Rosemary Radford Ruether, 99–106. Maryknoll, NY: Orbis Books, 1996.

Terrell, JoAnne Marie. *Power in the Blood? The Cross in the African-American Experience*. Maryknoll, NY: Orbis Books, 1998.

Thành, Mai. "Aspects of Christianity in Vietnam." In *Any Room for Christ in Asia? Concilium* 2 (1993): 95–109.

Thomas, M. M. *The Acknowledged Christ of the Indian Renaissance.* London: SCM Press, 1969.

———. *Religion and the Revolt of the Oppressed*. Delhi: ISPCK, 1981.

———. *Risking Christ for Christ's Sake: Towards an Ecumenical Theology of Pluralism*. Geneva: WCC, 1987.

———. "Secular Ideologies of India and the Secular Meaning of Christ." In Sugirtharajah and Hargreaves, *Readings in Indian Christian Theology*, 93–101.

———. *Some Theological Dialogues.* Madras: The Christian Literature Society, 1977.

Tillich, Paul. *Systematic Theology.* 3 vols. Chicago: Univ. of Chicago Press, 1957.

Tinker, George E. *Missionary Conquest: The Gospel and Native American Cultural Genocide*. Minneapolis: Augsburg Fortress, 1993.

Truth, Sojourner. "Sojourner Truth." In *Black Women in Nineteenth-Century American Life: Their Words, Their Thoughts, Their Feelings*, edited by Bert James Loewenberg and Ruth Bogin, 234–42. University Park: Pennsylvania State Univ., 1976.

Twain, Mark. *Mark Twain's Weapons of Satire: Anti-Imperialist Writings on the Philippine-American War*, edited by Jim Zwick. Syracuse, NY: Syracuse Univ. Press, 1992.

Ulanov, Ann and Barry. *Religion and the Unconscious*. Philadelphia: The Westminster Press, 1975.

United States Information Service. "The American Contribution to Philippine Education: 1898–1998." Manila: United States Information Service, 1998.

Veale, Jennifer. "It's Tough to Be a Working Woman . . . But the Web Is a Bright Spot," *Business Week Online* (2000).

Villalba, May-an. "Migrant Workers Challenge Globalization." *In God's Image* 19, no. 1 (2000): 30–34.

Villegas, Emelina. "Out of Struggles Comes Hope." *In God's Image* 21, no. 2 (June 2002): 17–21.

———. "Towards a Culture of Struggle." In *Culture: A Force for Change*, edited by Socio-Pastoral Institute, 1–8. Manila: Socio-Pastoral Institute, 1988.

Ware, Timothy. *The Orthodox Church*. New ed. London: Penguin Books, 1963.

Watkins, Susan Alice, Marisa Rueda, and Marta Rodriguez. *Introducing Feminism*. Cambridge, UK: Icon Books, 1999.

Weiser, Stanley, and Oliver Stone. *Wall Street*. Directed by Oliver Stone. Los Angeles: Twentieth Century Fox, 1987. Videocassette.

West, Charles C. "Thomas, M(adathilparpampil) M(amen)." In *Biographical Dictionary of Christian Missions*, edited by Gerald H. Anderson, 666–67. Grand Rapids, MI: Eerdmans, 1998.

White, Lynn Jr. "The Historical Roots of Our Ecological Crisis." *Science* 155, no. 3767 (1967): 1203–7.

Witek, John W. "Ricci, Matteo." In *Biographical Dictionary of Christian Missions*, edited by Gerald H. Anderson, 566–67. Grand Rapids, MI: Eerdmans, 1998.

Williams, Delores S. *Sisters in the Wilderness: The Challenge of Womanist God-Talk*. Maryknoll, NY: Orbis Books, 1993.

Wong Wai-Ching. "Asian Theology in a Changing Asia: Towards an Asian Theological Agenda for the 21st Century." *CTC Bulletin* Special Supplement, no. 1 (November 1997): 30–39.

———. "For Such a Time as This: Our Moment in God's Time," *CTC Bulletin* 17 (2001): 12–19. Available online.

———. "Negotiating for a Post Colonial Identity." *Journal of Feminist Studies in Religion* 16, no. 2 (Fall 2000): 5–23.

———. *"The Poor Woman:" A Critical Analysis of Asian Theology and Contemporary Chinese Fiction by Women*. Vol. 42 in *Asian Thought and Culture*, edited by Sandra A. Wawrytko. New York: Peter Lang, 2002.

———. "The Wisdom Women in Creation: A Reflection on Proverbs 8." *In God's Image* 17, no. 1 (1998): 25–27.

World Council of Churches (WCC). *Asia: Country Papers*. Geneva: WCC, 1984.

———. *Lead Us Not into Temptation . . . Churches' Response to the Policies of International Financial Institutions*. Geneva: WCC, 2001.

Wu, Rose. "1997 and the Destiny of the Hong Kong People." *In God's Image* 16, no. 2 (1997): 3–11.

———. "Asian Women as the Subject of God's Vision." *In God's Image* 16, no. 2 (1997): 27–31.

———. "A Hong Kong Feminist's View of Prostitution: Reviewing Sin, Morality and Sexuality." *In God's Image* 20, no. 2 (June 2001): 38–43.

———. "Women on the Boundary: Prostitution, Contemporary and in the Bible." *Feminist Theology* 28 (2001): 69–81.

Yamashita, Akiko. "A Review of Asian Women's Theology: From the Perspective of Women's Life Dialogue in Asia." *In God's Image* 18, no. 1 (1999): 2–12.

Yayori, Matsui. *Women's Asia*. London: Zed Books, 1989.

Young, Iris Marion. *Justice and the Politics of Difference*. Princeton, NJ: Princeton Univ. Press, 1990.

Young, Katherine K. "Introduction." In *Religion and Women*, edited by Arvind Sharma, 1–38. Albany: State Univ. of New York, 1994.

Yusa, Michiko. "Women in Shinto: Images Remembered." In *Religion and Women*, edited by Arvind Sharma, 93–138. Albany: State Univ. of New York, 1994.

Zaide, Gregorio F. *Political and Cultural History of the Philippines*. 2 vols. Manila: Garcia Book Store, 1957.

Index

Other Books in the "Women from the Margins" Series

Choi Hee An

Korean Women and God

Experiencing God in a Multi-religious Colonial Context

ISBN 1-57075-622-8

"A significant contribution to Asian feminist theology! Combining story telling with critical scholarship . . . the book advances the discourse on cross-cultural theology and ministry."

–*Kwok Pui-lan, Episcopal Divinity School, Cambridge, Massachusetts*

"An extraordinary book on the mutual penetration of self-image and the image of God!"

—*Andrew Sung Park, United Theological Seminary, Dayton, Ohio*

Mary Judith Ress

Ecofeminism in Latin America

ISBN 1-57075-636-8

"Explores new territory in liberation theology and ecofeminism."–*Letty Russell*

"Judith Ress . . . helps us build bridges across different traditions of wisdom and theology to connect with our own selves, with others, and with the living and breathing mystery of the cosmos."–*Ivone Gebara*

Thank you for reading *The Jesus of Asian Women*.
We hope you profited from it.

Of Related Interest

Chung Hyun Kyung

Struggle to Be the Sun Again

Introducing Asian Women's Theology

ISBN 0-99344-684-7

What are the distinctive challenges of Asian women to theology and the church? *Struggle to Be the Sun Again* offers answers to this crucial question as it articulates the specific contribution of emerging Asian women's theology to the meaning of the gospel.

"A truly artful presentation of many voices. . . ."

—*Beverly Harrison*

Isabel Apawo Phiti and Sarojini Nadar, editors

African Women, Religion, and Health

Essays in Honor of Mercy Amba Ewudziwa Oduyoye

Also in the "Women from the Margins" Series.

ISBN 0-88344-635-X

"A significant and critically important work [which] clearly reveals why Oduyoye is seen as the mother of an African women's theology that is communal, ecumenical, and culturally grounded . . . while at the same time remaining authentically African."

–*Diana L. Hayes, Georgetown University*

Please support your local bookstore, or call 1-800-258-5838.
For a free catalogue, please write us at

Orbis Books, Box 308
Maryknoll NY 10545-0308

or visit our website at www.orbisbooks.com

Thank you for reading *The Jesus of Asian Women*.
We hope you profited from it.